Electing the President, 2012

Electing the President, 2012

The Insiders' View

EDITED BY
KATHLEEN HALL JAMIESON

PENN

University of Pennsylvania Press

Philadelphia

Published by
University of Pennsylvania Press
Philadelphia, Pennsylvania 19104-4112
www.upenn.edu/pennpress

Printed in the United States of America on acid-free paper
10 9 8 7 6 5 4 3 2 1

Library of Congress Cataloging-in-Publication Data

Electing the president, 2012 : the insiders' view / edited by Kathleen Hall Jamieson.—1st ed.
    p.   cm.
    Digest of a daylong discussion among top strategists from the Romney and Obama campaigns that took place at the Annenberg Public Policy Center in Philadelphia on December 6, 2012.
    Includes bibliographical references and index.
    ISBN 978-0-8122-2290-6 (hardcover : alk. paper)
    1. Presidents—United States—Elections—2012—Congresses   2. Political campaigns—United States—Case studies—Congresses.   I. Jamieson, Kathleen Hall.
II. Annenberg Public Policy Center.
JK5262012.E54   2013
324.973′0932—dc23   2013020963

Contents

Introduction

President Barack Obama's 2012 victory over former Massachusetts governor Mitt Romney was not a foregone conclusion. No incumbent since FDR in 1936 had retained the Oval Office with an unemployment rate as high as the one that dogged the Obama presidency. But with housing starts and the stock market up and a 7.8 percent unemployment rate undercutting the challenger's earlier refrain that the country had experienced "43 straight months with unemployment above 8 percent," the country's first African American to be elected president became the second Democrat since FDR to claim a second term. When the dust settled, the incumbent had 332 electoral votes to the challenger's 206. Obama's 51.1 percent of the popular vote made him the second president since Ike to top 50 percent in the popular vote in two presidential elections, a standard President Ronald Reagan also met.

The demographic divide separating Obama and Romney voters was wide and clear. As the exit polls confirmed, the 2012 Obama-Biden ticket had once again assembled the coalition of women, young people, Hispanics, blacks, and Asians that had cemented its 2008 victory. By so doing, the Democratic campaign defied the presumed "enthusiasm gap" that favored Romney's election.[1]

Among the many reasons that Romney's 47.2 percent of the popular vote was remarkable was its composition. As Juan Williams noted in the *Wall Street Journal*,[2] "Mitt Romney won the white vote 59 to 39 percent, the biggest share for a Republican since 1988—and it was still not enough to put him in the White House." These figures prompted the *Huffington Post*'s Howard Fineman to observe that President Barack Obama's victory "signaled the irreversible triumph of a new, 21st-century America: multiracial, multi-ethnic, global in outlook and moving beyond centuries of racial, sexual, marital and religious tradition."[3]

One of the secrets of the Democratic campaign's success was its skillful use of social media to energize potential supporters and donors. Where the microtargeting done by the 2008 Obama operation was groundbreaking, its use by the 2012 team all but redefined the term. As *Time* noted, the path to the Democratic win was paved by "a massive data effort that helped Obama raise $1 billion, remade the process of targeting TV ads and created detailed models of swing-state voters that could be used to increase the effectiveness of everything from phone calls and door knocks to direct mailings and social media."[4]

Microtargeting was not the only practice the Democratic campaign mastered. Like his two immediate predecessors, President Obama not only translated the powers of the office into campaign capital but his campaign concentrated its overwhelmingly negative paid media on eroding Romney's credentials as a businessman and governor. Uses of presidential power included a rescue plan for the auto industry, an executive order protecting young immigrants from deportation, and federal resources dispatched to the coastal regions devastated by Hurricane Sandy in the final week of the campaign. In the hands of the Obama campaign team, these actions became resonant messages delivered to those most likely to find them persuasive and were used to define the challenger as unfit for the presidency. Where Obama rescued the auto industry and its jobs in Michigan and Ohio, Romney, said this narrative, had opposed the bailout. Where Obama had given the young immigrants known as "Dreamers" the opportunity to come out of the shadows, Romney championed "self-deportation." Where Obama believed in federal response to natural disasters such as Hurricane Sandy, Romney supported cutting the budget for federal emergency relief management and shifting responsibility to the states.

In response to Romney's efforts to cast the election as a referendum on the disappointments of the Obama first term, the Democratic campaign mimicked the model deployed successfully by incumbent George W. Bush against Democratic challenger John Kerry in 2004 to frame the contest as a choice. In the Democratic narrative, one could cast a vote for an incumbent who had done the best anyone (including Bill Clinton) could have to clean up the mess left by his predecessor or one could cast a ballot for a challenger whose plans were indistinguishable from the ones that got the country into trouble in the first place. Where Romney's policies benefited the rich, said this storyline, Obama's helped the middle class. The success of the Obama strategy was reflected in the exit poll finding that nearly half the voters surveyed blamed President George W. Bush more than President Barack Obama for the country's economic problems.

Electing the President, 2012: The Insiders' View digests a unique daylong discussion in which top strategists from the Romney and Obama campaigns explained how all this came about and in the process justified their decisions, questioned those on the other side about their strategic choices, and wondered aloud about what might have been. We are grateful to the talented professionals who, election cycle after cycle, have participated in debriefings designed to help the scholarly community better understand their take on what happened. David Axelrod, Joel Benenson, Jim Margolis, and Anita Dunn were the Obama staffers featured at both the 2008 and 2012 debriefings. Stephanie Cutter rounded out the roster of Obama presenters in 2012. From the Romney team, we heard from Stuart Stevens, Beth Myers, Neil Newhouse, Eric Fehrnstrom, and Kevin Madden.

In this volume you will hear our guests' answers to such questions as: What accounted for President Obama's lethargic performance in the first debate and Governor Romney's commanding one? What led the Republicans to believe that victory was within their reach? How did the Obama 2012 strategy build on the 2008 one and in what ways did it represent a sea change? What was the rationale behind the Ryan pick? How did the ad and media strategies of the two teams differ and how were they the same? How have social media changed campaign tactics and content? Was the fact checking done by the major national organizations (including our own) fair? And whether fair or foul, was it a futile enterprise?

Annenberg debriefings of this sort have been around for a while. From 1992 through 2012, the Annenberg School for Communication (1992–2000) and its Annenberg Public Policy Center (2004–2012) have hosted this sort of presidential election debriefing. First on tape and from 2000 on in book form as well, we have shared this event with the scholarly community. As in the past we asked the consultants on each side to make formal presentations followed by questions from those representing the opposing campaign. Unlike some past years, we were unable to include representatives from the third-party groups because we could not work out a schedule that would make it possible for the full range to attend on a single day. In 2016, we will work even harder than we did in 2012 to fill in that important piece of the election puzzle.

This volume opens with a timeline of election year events followed by the edited transcripts of the all-day event that took place at the Annenberg Public Policy Center in Philadelphia on December 6. The transcripts have been edited to remove some of the peculiarities of oral speech, add punctuation, and bracket information for context. The edited versions were sent to the participants for clarifications, corrections, and clean-up of transcription errors as well.

The logistics of the debriefing were handled by Alexandria Kierst, Karen Riley, and Deborah Stinnett, the timeline constructed by Ms. Stinnett and Dr. Ken Winneg and verified by Robyn Chan, Alex Luzi, and Melissa Parratto, the photos taken by Kyle Cassidy, the editing finalized by Ms. Riley and Ms. Stinnett, and the sessions included at the back of the volume taped by Denis O'Keefe with touch-up editing by Jeremy Quattlebaum. My thanks to all. The audience for the debriefing included faculty from the Annenberg School and Penn's Political Science Department, Annenberg undergraduate and graduate students, and the staff of two signature APPC projects, FactCheck.org and Flack-Check.org.

Notes

1. http://www.usnews.com/opinion/blogs/peter-roff/2012/08/13/enthusiasm-gap-means-mitt-romney-could-blow-out-president-obama.
2. November 7, 2012, http://online.wsj.com/article/SB10001424127887324439804578105072331776096.html.
3. http://www.huffingtonpost.com/2012/11/06/barack-obama-reelection_n_2085819.html.
4. Read more: http://swampland.time.com/2012/11/07/inside-the-secret-world-of-quants-and-data-crunchers-who-helped-obama-win/.

2012 Presidential Campaign Timeline

Date	Event	Detail
5/5/2011	GOP Primary Debate	**Location:** Peace Center in Greenville, S.C. **Sponsors:** Fox News and South Carolina Republican Party **Participants**: Johnson, Paul, Cain, Pawlenty, Santorum
5/11/2011	Gingrich declares	Former Republican Representative from Georgia and House Speaker Newt Gingrich officially declares his candidacy for president on Fox News
5/13/2011	Paul declares	Republican Representative Ron Paul from Texas declares his candidacy for president
5/21/2011	Cain declares	Republican businessman from Georgia Herman Cain declares his candidacy for president
5/23/2011	Pawlenty declares	Former Republican Governor of Minnesota Tim Pawlenty declares his candidacy for president
6/2/2011	Romney declares	Former Republican Governor of Massachusetts Mitt Romney declares his candidacy for president
6/6/2011	Santorum declares	Former Republican Senator from Pennsylvania Rick Santorum declares his candidacy for president

6/13/2011	GOP Primary Debate	**Location:** Saint Anselm College in Manchester, N.H. **Sponsors:** CNN, WMUR-TV, and *New Hampshire Union Leader* **Participants:** Bachmann, Cain, Gingrich, Paul, Pawlenty, Romney, Santorum
6/21/2011	Roemer declares	Former Republican Governor of Louisiana Buddy Roemer declares his candidacy for president
6/21/2011	Huntsman declares	Former Republican Governor of Utah Jon Huntsman, Jr., declares his candidacy for president
6/27/2011	Bachmann declares	Republican Representative Michele Bachmann of Minnesota declares her candidacy for president
8/11/2011	GOP Primary Debate	**Location:** Iowa State University in Ames **Sponsors:** Fox News, *Washington Examiner,* and Republican Party of Iowa **Participants:** Bachmann, Romney, Pawlenty, Paul, Cain, Huntsman, Santorum, Gingrich
8/13/2011	Perry declares	Republican Governor of Texas Rick Perry declares his candidacy for president
9/5/2011	GOP Primary Debate: Palmetto Freedom Forum	**Location:** Columbia, S.C. **Sponsors:** Senator Jim DeMint and the American Principles Project **Participants:** Romney, Gingrich, Bachmann, Cain, Paul
9/7/2011	GOP Primary Debate	**Location:** Reagan Library in Simi Valley, Calif.

		Sponsors: Reagan Library, NBC News and Politico **Participants:** Perry, Paul, Huntsman, Romney, Santorum, Gingrich, Bachmann, Cain
9/12/2011	GOP Primary Debate	**Location:** Florida State Fair Grounds in Tampa **Sponsors:** CNN and Tea Party Express **Participants:** Perry, Bachmann, Romney, Paul, Gingrich, Cain, Santorum, Huntsman
9/22/2011	GOP Primary Debate	**Location:** Orange County Convention Center in Orlando, Fl. **Sponsors:** Fox News, Google, and Republican Party of Florida **Participants:** Perry, Bachmann, Romney, Paul, Gingrich, Cain, Santorum, Huntsman, Johnson
10/11/2011	GOP Primary Debate	**Location:** Dartmouth College in Hanover, N.H. **Sponsors:** Bloomberg, *Washington Post*, and WBIN-TV **Participants:** Bachmann, Cain, Gingrich, Huntsman, Paul, Perry, Romney, Santorum
10/18/2011	GOP Primary Debate	**Location:** Sands Expo Convention Center in Las Vegas, Nev. **Sponsors:** CNN and Western Republican Leadership Conference **Participants:** Bachmann, Cain, Gingrich, Paul, Perry, Romney, Santorum

10/20/2011	Death of Gaddafi	Muammar Gaddafi is captured and killed.
11/5/2011	GOP Primary Debate: The Cain/Gingrich Lincoln-Douglas Debate	**Location:** Woodlands Resort & Conference Center in Houston, Tex. **Sponsor:** Texas Tea Party Patriots PAC **Participants**: Cain, Gingrich
11/9/2011	GOP Primary Debate	**Location**: Oakland University in Rochester, Mich. **Sponsors**: CNBC, the Michigan Republican Party, and Oakland University **Participants**: Bachmann, Cain, Gingrich, Huntsman, Paul, Perry, Romney, Santorum
11/12/2011	GOP Primary Debate	**Location:** Wofford College in Spartanburg, S.C. **Sponsors:** CBS News, *National Journal,* and South Carolina Republican Party **Participants**: Bachmann, Cain, Gingrich, Huntsman, Paul, Perry, Romney, Santorum
11/19/2011	GOP Primary Debate: Thanksgiving Family Forum	**Location:** First Federated Church in Des Moines, Iowa **Sponsor:** *Family Leader* **Participants**: Bachmann, Cain, Gingrich, Paul, Perry, Santorum
11/22/2011	GOP Primary Debate	**Location:** DAR Constitution Hall in Washington, D.C. **Sponsors**: CNN, Heritage Foundation, and American Enterprise Institute **Participants**: Bachmann, Cain, Gingrich, Huntsman, Paul, Perry, Romney, Santorum

12/3/2011	Cain withdraws	Herman Cain ends his presidential campaign following accusations of sexual misconduct
12/3/2011	GOP Primary Debate: Mike Huckabee Presidential Forum	**Location:** Fox News Headquarters in New York City **Sponsors:** Former Arkansas Governor Mike Huckabee and Fox News **Participants**: Romney, Perry, Bachmann, Gingrich, Santorum, Paul
12/10/2011	GOP Primary Debate	**Location:** Drake University in Des Moines, Iowa **Sponsors:** ABC News, ABC5/WOI-DT, *Des Moines Register,* and Republican Party of Iowa **Participants:** Romney, Perry, Bachmann, Gingrich, Santorum, Paul
12/12/2011	GOP Primary Debate: Gingrich/Huntsman Lincoln-Douglas Debate	**Location:** Saint Anselm College in Manchester, N.H. **Sponsor:** Saint Anselm College **Participants:** Gingrich, Huntsman
12/15/2011	GOP Primary Debate	**Location:** Sioux City Convention Center in Sioux City, Iowa **Sponsors:** Fox News and Republican Party of Iowa **Participants**: Bachmann, Gingrich, Huntsman, Paul, Perry, Romney, Santorum
1/1/2012	Unemployment rate: 8.3%	
1/3/2012	GOP Iowa Caucuses	Rick Santorum wins the Iowa Caucuses by 34 votes over Mitt Romney
1/4/2012	Bachmann withdraws	Representative Michele Bachmann of Minnesota

		withdraws her candidacy after a 6th place showing in Iowa Caucuses
1/4/2012	Perry thinks about suspending campaign	After initially announcing he would semi-suspend his campaign to reevaluate after his 5th place Iowa finish, Perry tweets, "And the next leg of the marathon is the Palmetto State . . . Here we come South Carolina!!!" along with a picture of a thumbs-up candidate.
1/7/2012	GOP Primary Debate	**Location**: Saint Anselm College in Manchester, N.H. **Sponsors:** ABC News and WMUR **Participants:** Santorum, Romney, Paul, Perry, Gingrich, Huntsman
1/8/2012	GOP Primary Debate	**Location:** Chubb Theatre at the Capitol Center for the Arts in Concord, N.H. **Sponsors:** NBC News, Facebook, and *Union Leader* **Participants**: Santorum, Romney, Paul, Perry, Gingrich, Huntsman
1/10/2012	New Hampshire Primary	Winner: Romney
1/14/2012	GOP Primary Debate: Huckabee Forum II	**Location:** Sottile Theatre College of Charleston, S.C. **Sponsors:** Former Arkansas Governor Mike Huckabee, Representative. Tim Scott (R-S.C.), and Fox News **Participants**: Romney, Perry, Gingrich, Santorum, Huntsman
1/15/2012	Huntsman withdraws	Former Republican Governor of Utah Jon Huntsman, Jr., ends bid for the GOP nomination; endorses Romney

1/16/2012	GOP Primary Debate	**Location:** Myrtle Beach Convention Center in Myrtle Beach, S.C. **Sponsors:** Fox News, *Wall Street Journal*, and South Carolina Republican Party **Participants:** Romney, Perry, Gingrich, Santorum, Paul
1/19/2012	Perry withdraws	Republican Governor of Texas Rick Perry ends campaign and endorses Newt Gingrich
1/19/2012	GOP Primary Debate	**Location:** Charleston, S.C. **Sponsors:** CNN and Southern Republican Leadership Conference **Participants:** Romney, Gingrich, Santorum, Paul
1/21/2012	South Carolina Primary	Winner: Gingrich
1/23/2012	GOP Primary Debate	**Location:** University of South Florida in Tampa **Sponsors:** *Tampa Bay Times*, NBC News, *National Journal*, and Florida Council of 100 **Participants:** Romney, Gingrich, Santorum, Paul
1/24/2012	State of the Union Address	President Obama concentrates on economic issues
1/26/2012	GOP Primary Debate	**Location:** University of North Florida in Jacksonville **Sponsors:** CNN, CNN en Español, Hispanic Leadership Network, and Republican Party of Florida **Participants:** Romney, Gingrich, Santorum, Paul
1/31/2012	Florida Primary	Winner: Romney
2/1/2012	Unemployment rate: 8.3%	
2/4/2012	Nevada Caucuses	Winner: Romney
2/7/2012	Colorado Caucuses	Winner: Santorum
2/7/2012	Minnesota Caucuses	Winner: Santorum

2/11/2012	Maine Caucuses	Winner: Romney
2/21/2012	Dow hits 13,000	Dow Jones Industrial Average goes above 13,000 for first time since May 2008
2/22/2012	GOP Primary Debate	**Location:** Mesa Arts Center in Mesa, Ariz. **Sponsors:** CNN and Republican Party of Arizona **Participants:** Romney, Santorum, Paul, Gingrich
2/28/2012	Arizona Primary	Winner: Romney
2/28/2012	Michigan Primary	Winner: Romney
3/1/2012	Unemployment rate: 8.2%	
3/3/2012	Washington Caucuses	Winner: Romney
3/3/2012	GOP Primary Debate: Huckabee Forum 3: Jobs	**Location:** Wilmington Air Park in Wilmington, Ohio **Sponsors:** Former Arkansas Governor Mike Huckabee and Fox News **Participants**: Romney, Gingrich, Santorum
3/6/2012	Alaska Caucuses	Winner: Romney
3/6/2012	Georgia Primary	Winner: Gingrich
3/6/2012	Idaho Caucuses	Winner: Romney
3/6/2012	Massachusetts Primary	Winner: Romney
3/6/2012	North Dakota Caucuses	Winner: Santorum
3/6/2012	Ohio Primary	Winner: Romney
3/6/2012	Oklahoma Primary	Winner: Santorum
3/6/2012	Tennessee Primary	Winner: Santorum
3/6/2012	Vermont Primary	Winner: Romney
3/6/2012	Virginia Primary	Winner: Romney
3/6/2012	GOP Super Tuesday	Winner: Romney (6 states), Santorum (3 states), Gingrich (1 state)
3/10/2012	Kansas Caucuses	Winner: Santorum
3/10/2012	Wyoming Caucuses	Winner: Romney
3/13/2012	Hawaii Caucuses	Winner: Romney
3/13/2012	Alabama Primary	Winner: Santorum
3/13/2012	Mississippi Primary	Winner: Santorum
3/17/2012	Missouri Primary	Winner: Santorum
3/20/2012	Illinois Primary	Winner: Romney

3/24/2012	Louisiana Primary	Winner: Santorum
4/1/2012	Unemployment rate: 8.1%	
4/3/2012	D.C. Primary	Winner: Romney
4/3/2012	Wisconsin Primary	Winner: Romney
4/3/2012	Maryland Primary	Winner: Romney
4/10/2012	Santorum withdraws	Former Republican Senator from Pennsylvania Rick Santorum withdraws his candidacy
4/24/2012	Connecticut Primary	Winner: Romney
4/24/2012	Delaware Primary	Winner: Romney
4/24/2012	New York Primary	Winner: Romney
4/24/2012	Pennsylvania Primary	Winner: Romney
4/24/2012	Rhode Island Primary	Winner: Romney
4/25/2012	Romney presumptive nominee	RNC officially declares Mitt Romney the presumptive party nominee after he wins 5 Northern state primaries the day before
5/1/2012	Unemployment rate: 8.2%	
5/2/2012	Gingrich withdraws	Former Republican Representative from Georgia and House Speaker Newt Gingrich withdraws his candidacy
5/8/2012	Indiana Primary	Winner: Romney
5/8/2012	North Carolina Primary	Winner: Romney
5/8/2012	West Virginia Primary	Winner: Romney
5/9/2012	Obama for gay marriage	Barack Obama announces support for same-sex marriage in an ABC News interview
5/15/2012	Nebraska Primary	Winner: Romney
5/15/2012	Oregon Primary	Winner: Romney
5/22/2012	Arkansas Primary	Winner: Romney
5/22/2012	Kentucky Primary	Winner: Romney
5/29/2012	Texas Primary	Winner: Romney
5/29/2012	Romney surpasses 1,144 delegates	Mitt Romney officially surpasses 1,144 delegates,

		the minimum necessary to capture GOP presidential nomination
6/1/2012	Unemployment rate: 8.2%	
6/5/2012	California Primary	Winner: Romney
6/5/2012	Montana Primary	Winner: Romney
6/5/2012	New Jersey Primary	Winner: Romney
6/5/2012	New Mexico Primary	Winner: Romney
6/5/2012	South Dakota Primary	Winner: Romney
6/5/2012	Walker wins Wisconsin recall	Wisconsin Governor Scott Walker wins recall election; Wisconsin becomes swing state
6/15/2012	Obama halts deportation	Barack Obama announces the end of deportation of some illegal immigrants who came to the United States as children
6/26/2012	Utah Primary	Winner: Romney; Primary season ends officially
6/28/2012	Holder held in contempt	U.S. Attorney General Eric Holder held in contempt of Congress
6/28/2012	Affordable Care Act upheld	Supreme Court upholds constitutionality of Patient Protection and Affordable Care Act by 5-4 decision
7/1/2012	Unemployment rate: 8.2%	
7/11/2012	Romney booed	Mitt Romney is booed during speech to the NAACP in which he said he would repeal Obamacare
7/13/2012	"You didn't build that"	Barack Obama makes his "you didn't build that" comment
7/19/2012	Presidential Campaign Funding hits $1 billion	2012 Presidential election reaches record $1 billion funding milestone
7/20/2012	Aurora shooting	Movie theater shooting in Aurora, Colo.; Obama and

		Romney both suspend negative campaigning that day
7/25–31/ 2012	Romney Overseas Trip	Romney visits the UK, Israel, and Poland
7/31/2012	Reid accuses Romney of not paying taxes for past 10 years	Senate Majority Leader Harry Reid claims Romney hasn't paid taxes in 10 years (fact checkers rate the claim false)
8/1/2012	Unemployment rate 8.2%	
8/1/2012	Extension of government funding	Senator Reid and Speaker Boehner agree to a six-month extension on government funding, postponing any action until after the election
8/2/2012	Reid doesn't back down	Reid repeats attack on Romney for not paying taxes on the Senate floor
8/5/2012	Romney July fundraising	Romney raised $101.3 million in the month of July
8/5/2012	Sikh Temple Shooting	Sikh Temple shooting in Oak Creek, Wisconsin
8/11/2012	Ryan chosen GOP VP nominee	Mitt Romney chooses Representative Paul Ryan to be the Vice Presidential nominee
8/13/2012	Ryan will release some tax returns	Paul Ryan announces that he will release only two years of tax returns
8/14/2012	VP Biden uses controversial language addressing a largely black audience	VP Biden tells a largely black audience in southern Virginia that as a result of Romney/Ryan's deregulation of the financial industry, "They're going to put y'all back in chains." The Romney campaign accuses Obama of running a "campaign of hate." Biden

		later clarifies that he meant to say "unshackled" rather than "unchained."
8/19/2012	Rep. Todd Akin makes controversial comments about rape	GOP nominee for Missouri Senate seat Rep. Todd Akin says in an interview that in the event of a "legitimate rape," a woman rarely gets pregnant
8/27–30/ 2012	Republican Convention	Held in Tampa, Florida. Schedule shortened because of Hurricane Isaac
8/28/2012	Ann Romney and Chris Christie Speak	Tuesday night's speakers include Mitt Romney's spouse, Ann Romney, and keynote speaker New Jersey Governor Chris Christie
8/29/2012	Paul Ryan Accepts VP Nomination	Rep. Paul Ryan formally accepts the GOP nomination for vice president and speaks to the delegates
8/30/2012	Romney Accepts Nomination; Rubio and Eastwood speak	Mitt Romney formally accepts the GOP nomination for president. Florida Sen. Marco Rubio addresses the delegates, as does actor Clint Eastwood (speaking to an empty chair representing Obama)
9/1/2012	Unemployment rate: 7.8%	Announcement that September unemployment rate dropped below 8% for first time in 43 months
9/4–9/6/ 2012	Democratic Convention	Held in Charlotte, N.C.
9/4/2012	Julian Castro and Michelle Obama speak to convention	San Antonio Mayor Julian Castro gives the keynote address, followed by First Lady Michelle Obama
9/5/2012	DNC Platform changes amid protests	Following criticism, DNC platform is changed to include God and affirm

		Jerusalem as the capital of Israel
9/5/2012	Bill Clinton speaks to convention	Former President Bill Clinton addresses the delegates
9/6/2012	Obama and Biden formally accept the Democratic nomination for president and vice president	Barack Obama and Joe Biden accept the Democratic nomination for president and vice president. Both address the delegates
9/11/2012	U.S. ambassador killed	The U.S. Embassy in Cairo, Egypt, and Consulate in Benghazi, Libya, are attacked and the U.S. ambassador to Libya killed
9/17/2012	Change in Romney campaign strategy	Chief Romney strategist Stuart Stevens announces that the campaign will take a strategic pivot, reframing the campaign as "status quo vs. change" as opposed to merely a referendum on the Obama years.
9/17/2012	47% tape released	Mother Jones releases video of Mitt Romney discussing 47% "entitled" at private Republican fundraiser
9/21/2012	Romney Tax Returns	Romney's campaign releases his 2011 tax returns
9/27/2012	Priorities USA Action surpasses Restore Our Future in fundraising	George Soros agrees to contribute $1 million to Priorities USA Action, Obama Super PAC. Priorities reports $10.1 million in August fundraising, surpassing for the first time Romney's Restore Our Future
10/2/2012	American Crossroads one-week $16 million ad blitz	American Crossroads releases a $16 million one-week ad buy in Senate and presidential contests in

		Colo., Fl., Ia., N.C., N.H., Nev., Oh., and Va.
10/3/2012	First Presidential Debate	**Location:** University of Denver, Denver, Colo. **Moderator:** Jim Lehrer, PBS NewsHour
10/5/2012	Unemployment rate: 7.9%	
10/6/2012	Obama September Fundraising	Obama campaign raises $181 million in September
10/11/2012	VP Debate	**Location:** Centre College, Danville, Ky. **Moderator:** Martha Raddatz, ABC News
10/16/2012	Second Presidential Debate	**Location:** Hofstra University, Long Island, N.Y. **Moderator:** Candy Crowley, CNN; Town Meeting format
10/22/2012	Third Presidential Debate	**Location:** Lynn University, Boca Raton, Fl. **Moderator:** Bob Schieffer, CBS
10/23/2012	Republican Senate candidate in Indiana makes a controversial remark about rape	Indiana Senate candidate Richard Mourdock, when asked about abortion in the case of rape or incest, says: "I think even when life begins in that horrible situation of rape, that's something God intended to happen."
10/28/2012	Superstorm Sandy	Superstorm Sandy hits the Eastern seaboard
11/1/2012	Pres. Campaign Spending hits $2 billion	2012 Presidential election reaches record $2 billion funding milestone
11/1/2012	Unemployment rate 7.9%	Final unemployment rate before general election remains under 8%
11/6/2012	Presidential Election	Barack Obama reelected President of the United States

Chapter 1
Election Overview

David Axelrod

David Axelrod *is one of the preeminent political media consultants in the United States, having produced winning media and messages for over 150 campaigns at the local, state, and national levels. Most recently, Axelrod served as media advisor to President Barack Obama's campaign for the White House. In 2006, he oversaw the Democratic Congressional Campaign Committee's independent expenditure media program, helping Democrats regain the House majority for the first time since 1994. He has worked for leading Democrats across the country, including Senator Hillary Clinton in New York, Governor Tom Vilsack in Iowa, and Representative Rahm Emanuel in Illinois. A specialist in urban politics, Axelrod has produced victories for mayoral candidates in Chicago, Houston, Philadelphia, Cleveland, Detroit, and Washington, D.C. Axelrod is currently Director of the University of Chicago's Institute of Politics.*

Our first assumption when we were thinking through this campaign was that presidential elections are not a referendum. They're a choice. They're always a choice. More than any other race, people measure not just the views but the qualities of two candidates and make very sophisticated judgments about who they want to lead them. We'll have a discussion later about this. One of the central struggles of the campaign was "Is it a referendum or is it a choice?" We knew that it would be a choice. We wanted to drive it that way as well. Obviously we weren't running in the most optimal of circumstances. If you narrowly define the race, you could see where we would be in maximum peril. But we believed that we would prosper from putting it in the context of a choice.

I'm very dubious about historical analogies in presidential races because I think we live in a dynamic country and history is a dynamic process. Every race is different. Every race is unique. [But] there are things that you can draw from previous campaigns. We obviously looked at the last reelection, in 2004. While there were fundamental differences, there was one large similarity: a president in a difficult situation ultimately won a race that many thought at the beginning that he might

David Axelrod

lose because the race was put in a context of a choice. When people were faced with that choice, they resolved [it] in favor of President Bush in 2004. There were some lessons to be gleaned from that.

I think one thing that we all agree on is that the economy was the overarching issue in this campaign. It's the issue of our day. The question is, how did you define that economic debate? You could define it narrowly [in terms of] how much progress have we made from the time the president took office at the depths of the worst economic crisis since the Great Depression to the moment of the election. I think that's how our opponents sought to define the test. But when we talked to voters, what was clear to us was that they were looking at the economy in a much broader way [and not simply focusing on] unemployment rates gauged from the time of the crisis. [Instead] they were looking at the long-term struggle of the middle class in this country, the long-term struggle of maintaining economic security in a time when so many forces were conspiring against that for so many Americans.

We live in a time of really revolutionary change, change in technology, change in communications, all of which, along with some public policies, have conspired against the economic security of so many Americans. This issue informed Obama's politics from the very beginning.

And I've known him for a long time. The notion of creating opportunity, the notion of making sure that people get a fair shot, was central to our theme in 2008 when he talked about the erosion of the American dream. It was central to many of the decisions he's made as president. And we knew that it had to be central to this debate. So when we defined the economic debate it was in terms of the middle class. If you accept the first definition, Governor Romney was a very strong candidate. If you narrowly interpreted the economic challenge as recovering from the recession and creating jobs, the profile of a successful businessman was a great profile. In fact when the president and I talked about 2012 right after the 2008 election, our assumption was that Governor Romney was the most likely nominee because it was clear that we were going to go through this economic crisis, and that someone who could run as a businessman would have an appeal. Even voters who ultimately tilted our way were drawn to this notion of a guy who'd been a very successful businessman. And maybe he could bring something to the debate, to the discussion, to Washington that would be useful.

Where Governor Romney was a vulnerable candidate was on the second-larger issue, which is economic security for the middle class. His profile as a businessman in the particular business he was in [and] some of the comments and positions that he took along the way helped paint the picture in the minds of voters of someone who was not in touch with their economic experience, who would not be an advocate for the middle class. You saw that in the exit polling and the discussion leading into the election. Of course the release of the 47 percent tape really exacerbated that problem at the end. But that was the culmination of a long process.

The second assumption that we made was that the Republican primary process was not going to help the Republican nominee. I told the president the day after the midterm election that I thought that in one way the outcome was good news, that the seeds of his reelection had probably been planted the day of the midterm election. I joked at an event last week that he probably felt like Winston Churchill when someone said to him in 1946, when he lost the prime ministership after winning the war, that it was a blessing in disguise. He said, "Well, it's [a blessing that's] rather well disguised." (LAUGHTER) The upside of the downside for us about the midterm election was that the most strident voices in the Republican Party were now very much in control of the processes of the Republican Party. It was clear that whoever the Republican nominee would be would have to pass through that toll booth in order to become the nominee.

You saw several Republicans pass on the race. Governor [Mitch] Daniels of Indiana had the temerity to suggest that maybe that some of these social issues should be downplayed if the focus was going to be on the economy. And he almost never was heard from again after that. He became a target of the right. So it was clear that that primary process was going to create problems for the Republican nominee. And it did. The positions that Governor Romney had to take in order to secure the nomination or that he thought he had to take to secure the nomination, running to the right of Governor Perry on immigration, running to the right of Senator Santorum on women's health issues and other issues, the Grover Norquist pledge, the famous "not one dollar, even with ten dollars of cuts" display in the debate, all of these things served to move Governor Romney probably farther to the right than he needed to be in order to win the election.

This was something we anticipated that came to pass. When you look at the exit polls and see that we actually increased our support among Latino voters even as the Latino voting base expanded and when you think about the impact that had in several of the battleground states, in Colorado, and Nevada and Florida, you see how important that was. Even as we lost some support among men our support among women voters was almost as strong on a percentage basis as it was in 2008. So you can see the impact of that. We won moderate voters by double digits. So we really controlled the center in the election. And I think a lot of that had to do with some of what I would call the Faustian bargains that Governor Romney had to make in order to become the nominee.

The fourth point I would make is that campaigns matter. A lot has been made of the marriage of new technology and old shoe leather that characterized our campaign. In 2008 we blazed new trails in terms of technology. Going into this election, we knew that we needed to push the envelope on that. Technology doesn't transform itself over a period of years now. It transforms itself over a period of months. Twitter was barely a factor in 2008. It was a dominating force in 2012. Eric Fehrnstrom and I had some fun on Twitter during the course of this campaign. But a lot of information and a lot of misinformation was transmitted over Twitter. And it was enormously impactful. Facebook [was] enormously impactful.

The amount of data available was much greater than ever before. Not just voting data but consumer data. The ability to marry all these things gave us a very good profile. When you married it with research as well, [the results gave us] a sense of who we needed to talk to and how to talk to them. We were able to target so many of our activities in terms of registration and mobilization, [including] our media buys, based on the very good information that we had about voters. That really came into play at the end. At the end of the day all of this is incredibly important, but it's sort of the field goal team of politics. If you don't have the right message and the right messenger, [if] you don't get far enough down the field, all of this other stuff is not going to win an election for you. But in a close election, and this was a close election, that can make a difference. And it did make a difference for us.

Finally under the category of "the message and the messenger matter" one thing that was gratifying to me was the degree to which some of the decisions the president made that looked less than politically optimal at the time [they were made] ended up being very instrumental in his winning reelection. I was in the room in 2009 when he made the decision to intervene to try and save the American auto industry. I was the guy who brought the polling data to him, not so much to make a recommendation, [but rather] so he understood what he was getting into when he made the decision. He brushed it aside and said, "Look, I understand it's not popular. But we can't let a million jobs go in the midst of the worst economic crisis since the Great Depression. If we can get the auto industry to rationalize itself, to build cars that people buy in the 21st century, and they have a fighting chance [as a result] we ought to help them do that." So I always say one of the things I like about the president so much is that he listens to me so little. (LAUGHTER) And this was one of those cases. You'd have to say that his decision to do that and the success of that project coupled with Governor Romney's position on it at the time were meaningful particularly in the industrial Midwest and particularly in Ohio, which was ground zero in this campaign. Perhaps we would've won the state without that. But I think it was very determinative.

There were other decisions that the president made, whether it was on the Dream Act, contraception and the fundamental decision to take the steps he took at the beginning of the administration, whether it was to stand up [for] the financial industry when it was on the verge of collapse, still not a popular decision, the Recovery Act, all those things that helped put a floor underneath the economy and send us back in the other direction, those things paid off. That was gratifying. But it was also, I think, important to us. Now I can't say that we made those decisions strategically. Think about the auto industry decision. If you were making a political decision you wouldn't necessarily have made that decision. But they did pay off. Elections are about choices. The president made some choices that I think were instrumental in his own reelection.

Stuart Stevens

Stuart Stevens, Principal, SSG, is among the nation's most successful political strategists and media consultants. Stevens has served as the lead strategist and consultant for some of the nation's toughest political campaigns. Beginning his

Stuart Stevens

political career in his native Mississippi, he worked on Thad Cochran's campaigns and has gone on to help elect more governors and U.S. senators than any other current Republican consultant. Stevens was educated at Colorado College, Middlebury College, Oxford University, and the UCLA Film School. Stevens has published four nonfiction books and one novel and written articles for numerous national publications including the New York Times Magazine, Washington Post, Esquire, *and* The Atlantic. *He has written extensively for series television, including* Northern Exposure, I'll Fly Away, *and* Commander in Chief, *and was a writer-producer for the HBO series* K Street.

The primary for us was obviously very important. We always thought the primary was a very difficult challenge. What we know about the Republican Party is that it's increasingly southern, populist, and evangelical. What we know about Mitt Romney is that he's not a southerner, he's Ivy League educated, and he's not evangelical. That presented certain challenges. He didn't start with a natural geographic base. He didn't start with a natural ideological base per se. It is almost unprecedented for anyone to win the nomination of his or her party without a strong geographic or committed ideological base.

I think something that is misunderstood is [that] the primary was what I would call a Le Mans start. Everybody started with the same number of votes and the same amount of money. The Governor made the decision not to put any of his own resources into the campaign. That is a decision that I and everyone in the senior ranks of the campaign strongly supported. When he announced in June of 2011 he started with a little bit under 24 percent of the electorate of the Republican primary. We started to raise money but didn't have a big jump start in money over anybody else.

The premise for the primary was that we would drive the race to the economy and force it into a referendum on who was going to be the best candidate to oppose the president, and that that would then carry that dynamic on to the general election. So you wouldn't have one of these primaries where it was about X, and then the general election was about Y. Just as the '04 Democratic primary was about who best to replace President Bush, we believed that the 2012 Republican Primary had to be about who was most qualified to replace Barack Obama. It was not really an electability argument but rather one of agenda control. I subscribe to Jack Germond's maxim that the candidates who focus on electability seldom are. We made the decision that we were going to dig the ditch that we were willing to die in, which was the economy, and that to beat Mitt Romney you had to beat him on the economy. We weren't going to fight on every hill and try to contest every segment of the vote. One of the learning experiences of the '08 campaign was that you really have to be willing to lose to win. You have to be willing to accept the fact that people may not agree with what you're saying in enough numbers to carry you to victory, but it doesn't mean what you're saying is wrong, and it doesn't mean that you should be saying something else. It's what you believe and it's what you're going to say. And if people come to you then so be it.

One of the great public misperceptions is that [after the 2008 run] the governor immediately started to run. I don't think that's true. I think that his assumption was the economy would do well and that the President would have a moderately successful first term. He immensely enjoyed focusing on writing his book. He was involved in life, intellectually many things interested him. I think that he always thought it was a possibility that he could run. But there was never a plan immediately to go and run [again]. I think that the game sort of came to him. And there was something very liberating about running and losing and seeing that your life was very good, happy. They did a very American thing. They sold the house where they brought up the kids and moved on with their lives. Then the economy didn't improve and he disagreed with the stimulus project and the whole direction of the economy. He was troubled, like a lot of people, by the President's approach to foreign policy. All of this drew him back into the race. [He decided] that he was going to run and on what he was going to run—the economy and jobs and a different direction in American foreign policy.

From the very beginning, there were many challenges to winning a Republican primary. It's hard to find anybody in the Republican Party who didn't say that he needed to walk away from MassHealth,[1] particularly in light of Obamacare,[2] to be able to win the Republican primary. There was certainly not data that indicated otherwise. There wasn't some secret sauce that you could sprinkle on this and say, "Well, if you say this, all of a sudden people will get it." His decision to stand by his record on MassHealth wasn't data-driven at all. He was proud of Mass-Health and was always going to defend it. It had problems [in the past]. It had problems now. He wasn't completely satisfied with the way that it had been executed. He said that were he governor he'd do things differently. But he was not going to walk away from the program. In May of 2011, he did an event in Michigan and said, "Here's the outline of a plan that I would use to replace it." I think that was a really seminal moment followed by the first debate in June in New Hampshire in which he got the first question on health care. He was going to defend [his Massachusetts] health care [plan]. A lot of people thought that that meant that he was going to lose the Republican primary.

One of the underestimated qualities of the Republican primary this cycle is the quality of the candidates. For the Republican primary electorate there were a lot of very good, very viable choices in that race. Governor Perry could easily have won that race. One of the realities is that the competition defines who you are in that race. Governor Perry didn't have a lot of time to prepare the way [the others] did it. But he's a very formidable and skilled candidate who had some very good days in this campaign. I don't think that what happened to Governor Perry was inevitable. If you go back and you look at Governor Perry's first debate, it's actually his best. But throughout these debates, Governor Romney set a very high standard that all of the candidates had to meet. Had Governor Romney not been in the race or not set such a high standard, the other candidates, including Governor Perry, would have been judged very differently.

One of the key lessons that we learned from 2008 was that what you're saying at that moment is never about the people that you're saying it to. It's about the larger audience you're reaching through the media, not about the room. The explosion of social media only accelerated that trend. These debates drew very large audiences. No one really knows why. No one expected it. But they did. And that [fact] created this monster that fed on itself. The large audiences meant that the networks wanted to put on more of these debates. I think this all started with the best of intentions and then spun out of control. We ended up with 20. The ultimate absurdity of it was when we had one Saturday night in New Hampshire before the primary and then another one at 9:00 the next morning. So we had a debate prep at something like 6:00 A.M. on Sunday morning. And the campaigns had very little impact or input on these debates, which is a real shame. Primary debates should be about exchange of ideas, not about the promotion of networks or cable channels or their preferred flavor of the month on air talent. Why should we have CNN- or ABC- or NBC-sponsored debates any more than we have CNN- or ABC- or NBC-sponsored rallies or press conferences? I believe that debates should be put on by leading institutions or groups like the University of Iowa or the Republican Party of Iowa or the University of New Hampshire or the New Hampshire Republican Party and top journalists, both print and electronic, should be invited to ask the questions and the debates should be covered as serious news events. Debates should not be turned into these tawdry spectacles like CNN did with its cheap promos designed to try to get attention for a dying cable network. It just demeans the whole process and turns candidates into money-making instruments instead of serious individuals seeking the presidency. In the next cycle, candidates should simply refuse to go along with the process.

I say this even though the primary debates helped the Romney campaign a great deal for one simple reason—the more people saw Governor Romney, the more they liked him. They might not agree on every issue, but they liked him.

After the debates, we would ask a question, "If your family was in trouble which of the candidates on that stage would you want to help? If your business was in trouble, if you were sending your kid across the country for their first job or to go to college, who would you want that person to be with?" And Governor Romney more often than not would be the person people would select. That really helped him through this because there're a lot of people who had ideological differences with the governor on this or that. A seminal moment occurred in those debates when this whole flip-flopping issue kept coming up. We talked about it and at its core, it's really a character issue and there was something about it that was very offensive. In an early Michigan primary debate, the Governor responded by stepping back and saying, "I'm a man of constancy. I've been married to the same woman for 43 years. I've had one job basically. I am who I am." And that really made people look at it in a different perspective. From then on the flip-flopping issue almost went away.

The primary was a rough process. It ended up, as everybody always said, with a Romney and an anti-Romney. And anti-Romney was Senator

Santorum, who in many ways was better-positioned ideologically for the Republican primary audience than Hillary Clinton was for the Democratic primary audience [in 2008]. Hillary Clinton was a pro-war candidate in an antiwar primary. We found ourselves in these situations where we had one playoff game after another playoff game after another playoff game. We had to win or go home. That happened in Michigan, Ohio, Wisconsin, state after state. We won. And finally we won in Pennsylvania. But that process of a long primary created a confusing image to much of the general electorate. When we polled after the primary, a surprising number of people thought that Governor Romney was a Catholic who opposed contraception. To use an analogy, it's like you're in a restaurant, people at a table across the way are having an argument. You're not really paying attention. But you hear snippets of it. It's annoying. Your image of it is negative and confusing. For much of the public, that was the impact of the Republican primary.

Coming out of the primary we were faced with a number of challenges. We needed to define the governor in a biographical sense. And we needed to define what he was going to do. So we did what you do in campaigns. We polled a lot. We tested a lot. We tested four main approaches. The overall Mitt Romney Story—a combination of personal and business/public service. We tested a focus on the business record— how he created jobs and grew businesses. We tested the Romney Mass record—how he turned around a faltering state. And we tested the Romney Agenda as President—what he would do as President.

Overwhelmingly, people wanted to know more about what he would do as President. It was a threshold question. People were saying, "Yes, I am interested in all of these areas of his life, these achievements, but until I have a better sense of what he will do as President, none of it really means much to me." That drove us to launch our "Day One" series of ads. Though we were only able to run those in four states in limited runs, starting in April. And that was for one reason: money.

As is typically the case, we had spent all of our money in the primary. We spent $135 million, $140 million dollars for the primary. We were raising money as rapidly as we could. But we obviously needed to recharge. We had very limited resources.

One of the great underappreciated aspects of this campaign, I feel, is the reality of having a campaign for the first time with both campaigns not taking federal funds for the general election. Federal funding was passed after Watergate because there was a general agreement in both parties that the incumbent president had a huge advantage in fundraising. Candidate Obama became the first candidate since Watergate to reject funding. I think that was a tragedy and a travesty for the political system. And yes, as everyone knew back in the Watergate days, it gave a huge advantage to the incumbent. The President had four years to raise over a billion dollars. That's a staggering advantage that the press has yet to fully grasp. Frankly the state of the current press is such that many of the reporters covering the race simply don't understand the federal financing system and how it worked. I found many of the reporters confused it with the Citizens United decisions and justified Obama's rejection of federal funding because of the Citizens United ruling. But of course Candidate Obama rejected funding in the summer of 2008, long before the Citizens United ruling. For any incumbent to have that advantage is a fundamental corruption of the system and it's a shame that Barack Obama ended one of the great post-Watergate reforms. I'd love to see us get back to a federally funded system but history shows it's very difficult to get the genie back in the bottle.

Our general election premise was twofold. First, we always said that this would be a referendum on Obama. All presidential reelection [campaigns] are [a] referendum on the incumbent. It would [also] be a choice of a different vision for the economy and the country. This whole choice/referendum thing is something that people talk about a lot. I never saw it as either/or. Because you can't have a choice without a referendum. In essence it's like a debate. You argue why you're good and the other person isn't. You go back and forth.

Meanwhile there's this whole super PAC world out there which we can speak to later that is completely disconnected, which I think is something very important for people to understand. We have no contact at all. They create a cacophony of noise that is unique to these situations that we find ourselves in now.

It's important to understand that the Obama campaign outspent the Romney campaign on television by about two to one. This reality was often muddled by the pro-Romney super PAC ads which, on paper, leveled the spending to a certain degree. However, as the campaign went on, one of the lessons we learned was that the super PAC ads—many of which were great ads—did not seem to have much impact on voters. This will be, I'm sure, studied for a long time and we can speculate about the reasons. The most obvious answer would be that we were unable to coordinate with the super PACs so that our paid and their paid messages and our earned media, our press efforts, were not in sync. We always found that our paid [message] worked much, much better when it was part of a larger campaign press effort, a lesson that is basic Campaign 101 practice. Super PACs couldn't take advantage of that synchronicity because they couldn't coordinate.

About 40 percent of the total pro-Romney advertising dollars were spent by the Romney campaign. That's compared to about 80 percent of the total pro-Obama dollars. Because the incumbent President had such an advantage in fundraising, he did not have to rely on super PACs. That disparity gave the Obama campaign a huge advantage.

The Obama campaign started attacking at the end of May and we responded. We quickly realized that we did not have the ability to control the dialogue during the summer months. Our whole goal was to get to the debates alive. We realized that we weren't in a position to win this thing until October, which is not unusual for a challenger. In most of the races I've done, be it Chris Christie [Republican governor of New Jersey, 2010–present] or Haley Barbour [Republican governor of Mississippi, 2004–2012], any of the challenger races, you rarely go ahead of the incumbent until the very end. Your polling may never show that you go ahead. I'm sure David's had the same experience. You make the play that you will be close, and that there will be enough undecided voters, that your fave/unfave with those undecided voters [will work for you], and that the universe of those undecided voters will break your way at the end. [We had to] try to control that the race would be about the economy, that those [undecided] voters would be predisposed to look for an economic alternative and we would get to those debates alive.

Before that we couldn't win. We didn't have the money to win it before that. It was very frustrating to our supporters who didn't understand how the whole money situation worked. We couldn't spend general election money until we got the nomination. So we're raising all this money and also raising lots of money that would then go to the Republican Party. They would see these big numbers. But we could only spend primary dollars, which meant money that we raised under the limits of $2,500 per person. Once someone had donated $2,500 to us for the primary, they were tapped out for the primary. So that greatly limited the amount of money we had to spend. In the summer, we made the decision to go and borrow money so that we could have more money on the air. There is some misconception and bad reporting out there that we intentionally backloaded our ad buys for the fall. Nothing could be further from the truth. We spent every cent we could under the rules, plus we borrowed an additional $20 million to put on the air during the summer. All of this comes from people not understanding how the finance system works and the reality that only primary dollars could be spent on television until the night the Governor accepted the nomination.

We obviously focused on the debates. We prepared for them. Trying to get to the debates alive [assumes] you [are going to have] a big debate. September was a rough month. We knew that whoever had the second convention always gets a better bounce. We were prepared for that. We were not expecting the 47 percent, and if you look at the tracking, they got a very nice convention bounce. But then it was trickling down. I always assumed that you guys saw that trickling down and [saw] the race resetting with the public numbers [for] the president going back to 47, 48, and then released the 47 percent [tape] to bounce it up. That release obviously was a big event that tested our campaign. Matt Rhoades spoke to this at the Harvard Institute of Politics debriefing.

There are moments when campaigns can fall apart or come together. The governor very much kept the campaign together. We dug ourselves out. We had a great deal of patience. In the primaries we had been behind Michele Bachmann [member of Congress and Republican presidential contender from Minnesota]. We'd been behind Donald Trump. We had been behind pretty much everybody. So the idea that we're having not the best day or week was not something we were unaccustomed to. In those moments, you saw the governor's leadership qualities. He takes responsibility, focuses on how this is going to get better, puts together a plan. Two days after the 47 percent tape came out, the Governor was superb in the Hispanic forum in Miami. He was much better than the President in the same forum. He has an ability to focus on solutions, take responsibility and unite a team that is remarkable.

For all the prep that went into the debates, it was really the governor. In those moments it's just the quality of the individual up there. You can't coach speed.

October was a much better month for us. We always had challenges with Hispanic voters that the party needed to address. We felt going into the storm[3] that we were in a position to close [in] the last week and win the race.

It's interesting to look at the Obama polling numbers versus our numbers. We did not think that there would be a plus seven or eight Democratic universe to turn out. We thought it would be more like plus three. We were wrong. I'm not sure what we would've done differently knowing that, but the storm was impactful for us in the sense that we completely lost control of any ability to impact the agenda. We went from these big rallies where we were attempting to prosecute the president and drive a case to literally sitting in hotel rooms watching television. There's nothing you can do about it. And [concerning what has been said] about Governor Christie,[4] I don't think it was about Governor Christie at all. He was being a good governor.

It was just the fact that all of a sudden instead of having Mitt Romney at a rally making points about the president, it was about a big national tragedy. We'd never had a presidential race where we had a big national disaster seven days before. And we did. That's just how it is. The governor was very matter-of-fact about this. Going into Election Day, we thought that we had a good chance. But the notion that we were overconfident has been overplayed. The rallying cry of "We have a shot" or "We could pull this out" is not very powerful. The last NBC/WSJ poll—

never a very friendly poll for us—showed a difference of 7 voters. That's 7 voters, not 7 points. Seven voters out of a couple of thousand. So the idea that we thought it was close is at least one we shared with Al Sharpton and Rachel Maddow and their NBC associates.

DAVID AXELROD:

You rightly said that in order to win you have to challenge orthodoxy. Where in the primary did you do that? And do you think you should have done that more? It seems to me you guys paid a big price for the Republican nominating process and all those debates that became kind of a Roman coliseum.

STUART STEVENS:

The debates spun out of control. There has to be some mechanism to control this so that they're more productive. I'm old-school about this. I don't really understand why news organizations are putting on versus covering the debates. We attempted with 100 percent failure to have serious debates, to have the University of New Hampshire put on a debate and invite people to—cover it, which seems to me how it should work. [News organizations] don't sponsor rallies. Why should they sponsor debates? At a certain point I think they were starting fires and covering the fires. That was unhelpful.

On a number of points, MassHealth being seminal, [Governor Romney's] refusing to shift was seen by most as being a killer. He was the only candidate who refused to call Barack Obama a socialist and was booed on stage for that. On the economic plans, he was attacked consistently from the economic right for the economic plan that didn't take capital gains to zero. Over and over again the *Wall Street Journal* really took us to task for that. The governor was being attacked for saying what he believed and we were letting the chips fall where they may.

DAVID AXELROD:

On issues like the phrase "self-deportation" and so on, the vehemence with which he went after Perry on the immigration issue, the Planned Parenthood issue, do you think those were costly? I understand the politics in the Republican primary. Were they costly in the general election?

STUART STEVENS:

Beth can speak to this too. Planned Parenthood definitely became problematic because it became a way to say that Mitt Romney was against contraception, which of course he wasn't remotely against. And there's two ways to look at this. On the one hand, there is a role for someone who's going to go out there and say, "Times are tough on spending. I'm going to be a truth-teller. I'm going to take popular things and say that we have to cut them because we just can't afford them, not that they're bad things, but because we're just not going to be able to afford them." And that would be emblematic of PBS, why should we be subsidizing *Wall Street Week in Review*. And—

DAVID AXELROD:

Or Wall Street, but that's a different issue—

STUART STEVENS:

That's a different issue. I can make the case for the latter more than *Washington Week in Review*. But Planned Parenthood also is an abortion provider. And that this is not a role for the federal government to be in. It's a difference of opinion. He was going to say these things because that's what he believed.

DAVID AXELROD:

We all saw your video at the convention which we thought was incredibly effective. One of the things, and it may just be that you were so occupied trying to deal with your friends who were running against you in the primary that you didn't get a chance, but why not do more in the front end [of the election cycle to] flesh out Romney? You guys obviously have great affection for him and know him well. Why not spend more time on the front end giving people more of a personal sense of him?

STUART STEVENS:

Would you have done that in the primary or in the general?

DAVID AXELROD:

I can only speak from my own experience. We had a much different situation than you did. But we spent quite a bit of time and money on the front end doing bio of Obama during the primaries and giving people a sense of who he was. But it was a much less truncated process. I'm really not asking the question to put you on the spot. I'm just—

STUART STEVENS:

Yeah, I know. I know.

DAVID AXELROD:

—curious. Because that was a great piece you did at the convention. And I'm not even going to ask you the Clint Eastwood versus the film question. (LAUGHTER) But it just seems like some of that [biographical content] would've been useful.

STUART STEVENS:

You're right. It goes back to the choices that you make. By doing that you're not doing something else. In the primary we ran spots with Ann Romney talking about Mitt and character that worked well. The super PAC ran an ad about [the] governor helping his—

DAVID AXELROD:

Fourteen-year-old, or when the kid disappeared—

STUART STEVENS:

And we ran spots about his record. But to capture the totality of him is very difficult. Whenever we would test this, which we did extensively, it never tested well. Voters would want to know what you are going to do. "Tell me more about how this affects me." They thought that at a certain point it was sort of like looking at someone's album. "Why do I care? Okay. You're a nice guy. I like you. But I've got this mortgage. I'm two payments late. My kids are telling me they're going to move home. The last thing I wanted [to hear]. And that's great that you're real successful and all these people like you and you're a wonderful person. That's terrific. But I've got this kid who's still movin' home. (LAUGHTER) And I'm two and a half months late on my mortgage."

DAVID AXELROD:

Could've offered to put the kid up.

STUART STEVENS:

(LAUGHTER) Well, he did that with some. One of the stories was about the Olympic athletes who were asking where they could train. They moved into his basement and stayed three years. (LAUGHTER) It was always sort of a Sophie's choice. When we showed voters-in-play this [biographical content] and then showed them what he plans to do, they would overwhelmingly be more interested in that.

DAVID AXELROD:

We were surprised that you had to go dark during September at points. We were impressed with the fact that Governor Romney was a man of some means. He had spent $52 million on previous campaigns. Why did he not just float you—

STUART STEVENS:

Put money in?

DAVID AXELROD:

Yes.

STUART STEVENS:

In the summer we did take a loan. I'm never big on candidates putting money into races. It's really a personal decision. I wouldn't want to speak for him. But [ironic tone] I'm confident that no one would've written that he was trying to buy the race had he put in $100 million. In a way we did. We borrowed $20 million in the primary, which ultimately he was personally standing behind. But I've never been one to go to candidates and say, "You need to put in money." I just—

DAVID AXELROD:

You're a better man than me.

STUART STEVENS:

(LAUGHTER) I just think morally, morally's the wrong word. I just never do it. But, as I mentioned, one of the great untold stories in this race is [that it is] the first we've ever had [since the passage of the Federal Election Campaign Act Amendments of 1974; FECA] with two candidates not taking federal funding. In our race, that was a huge factor. You guys had to raise a great deal of money too. But when we come out of the primary, we had to raise over $100 million a month. You have to wrap your mind around that, $100 million a month from scratch. That is an enormously difficult task that no one has ever done before in the Republican Party. And [that is what is required] just to be competitive, to have a chance to win. It meant that we were doing fundraisers into September.

DAVID AXELROD:

Right.

STUART STEVENS:

I think it is an enormous corruption of the system. I would highlight why federal funding was better and [its demise] ultimately will probably advantage Republicans more to be honest because—

DAVID AXELROD:

Yes, I agree.

STUART STEVENS:

Republicans tend to be better at these things. The incumbent president can always raise more money, Democrat or Republican. But the amount of time [it takes is a problem]. The governor would be working 18, 19 hours a day to do this and would have, say, one public event. The press would be writing, "He's not campaigning." You would get off that plane, go and raise this money, and 70 percent of it was going to the news organizations in the back [in the form of ad buys on local stations owned by the networks]. It was going to ABC. It was going to NBC. It was going to CBS. It was going to Yahoo. It was going to Bloomberg. [Meanwhile, their reporters] were writing that you weren't campaigning. It was like a direct transfer.

DAVID AXELROD:

And complaining about the money in the process.

STUART STEVENS:

And complaining about money in the process. You're literally paying their salaries. And it's, you know—

DAVID AXELROD:

You find that irritating? (LAUGHTER) We were in a much better position coming out of our primary in 2008 in part because we did not get tugged to the left by our primary. Running against the frontrunner and taking a few positions that were unorthodox—we opposed, for example, a gas tax cut when that was quite popular—was helpful to us. We did not damage ourselves in the primary process. You can't say it. I can. I think you guys paid a big price in order to become the nominee. When I asked you the question about defining him more, you gave a great answer. I think a great deal of the answer frankly is that you had a competitive primary that you had to win and you had to devote a lot of resources to struggle with the other candidates. [Where we had the chance to do so in 2008], you didn't have the luxury at the end of the day to define your candidate thoroughly. And—

STUART STEVENS:

Two things. When you came out of your primary you were ahead versus McCain. We were never ahead, which is not unusual against an incumbent. Not to be ahead is something that's difficult to explain to the press but it's not unusual. I don't know where you were in July. You were ahead of McCain—

JOEL BENENSON:

I mean, we started in May plus one. We were in single digits, three—

STUART STEVENS:

But you were ahead—

DAVID AXELROD:

But we were ahead. We were always ahead—

STUART STEVENS:

We were never ahead. We're like a football team that's behind and needs to pass and needs to run, needs to do two things at once. We had to make very tough choices. We had to believe that the governor's favorability would come up as people were drawn to him as someone they wanted to be president. And ultimately that happened at least in the public polls. In the national numbers, our favorability was fine at the end. It was comparable to the president's. The challenge that we had was introducing new information about the president. You were able to introduce new information about Mitt Romney. What is it that you're gonna tell people about Barack Obama that they don't know? The economy's bad. They know that. It's always an advantage when you have more money and you have an ability to introduce information. We couldn't fight each case. There are a 150 [Bain Capital] companies there. If we fought each case, we'd spend the entire time litigating Bain.[5] And that would be what [the election] was about.

You had to do a certain amount to defend, a certain amount to push back, but then try to turn the corner. That's why we would come back on outsourcing our sales. That's why we would come back on welfare reform. We would come back on China. We would do these things to get you to respond to. When you look at our buys versus your buys all through the summer, we're getting heavily outspent in key states, three-to-one, four-to-one in Ohio.

DAVID AXELROD:

Though the super PACs were not benign.

STUART STEVENS:

They weren't—

DAVID AXELROD:

We felt that they were hostile. (LAUGHTER)

STUART STEVENS:

What do you think was the best super PAC line of attack against you?

DAVID AXELROD:

Before I answer that question, [let me say that] I think the best decision that we made tactically was risky at the time, [the decision] to frontload our media. My reading of history was that there was no ad that ran after the conventions that ever in the modern era won a presidential race; paid media becomes largely irrelevant in the general after the conventions because the debates take over for better and worse. We did that [frontloaded] in part because we thought the combined forces of the super PACs and your spending were going to be great, but also because we knew we had to define the race before the conventions. You went into the conventions in a jeopardized position in part because of that. I always believe that the best argument against the president was what I called the gold watch argument, which is "he's a great guy, historic figure, tried his best." You did some of that. It just was inconsistent. And they [the pro-Republican super PACS] were inconsistent. Half the time they were hammering him in a very visceral and nasty way. The other half they were saying, "Yeah, he's a great guy. I'm just not sure." And there was not qualitative—

STUART STEVENS:

The problem with the—

DAVID AXELROD:

—there was no message consistency there—

STUART STEVENS:

It's an argument that works a lot better in a right track/wrong track environment of 30 wrong track, 30 right track then 40 right track. "He's a great guy. Time to retire him." The focus group showed that. It's not a to-the-barricades argument.

DAVID AXELROD:

Right.

STUART STEVENS:

Versus messages you were running in these targeted communities which were much more threatening to these constituencies. Motivating turnout. And I've used that gold watch argument in races against incumbents with great success before. He or she is nice enough but they've done the best they can and it's time for a change. Once you get people in that head space there's sort of nothing the other side can do.

DAVID AXELROD:

I think the problem is you had these swing voters who liked Obama better than they liked the current situation. And they needed a permission structure to take—

STUART STEVENS:

It was a big factor—

DAVID AXELROD:

—to give up on him. I'm not saying it was necessarily a winning path. But you asked me and I—

STUART STEVENS:

One of the realities is the right track/wrong track consumer confidence changed.

DAVID AXELROD:

It did. I remember sitting with Ed Gillespie in February. He said, "Your problem is you've lost X number of jobs." And every month that number diminished to the point where at the end we actually had gained jobs. So the argument shifted to, "Well, we've had 40 straight months of eight-point plus unemployment." Then unemployment went below eight points. The right track/wrong track grew over time. At the end the circumstances were different than when the race began. I think that was complicating.

People ask, "Well, how could the polling be different." You talked about the assumptions you guys made. The theory was that the undecided voters would break heavily against the incumbent. But their ratings of Obama were higher than their ratings of Romney. So [we were confident that] they were not going to break en masse. We thought we would get at least our share of them, that they wouldn't all come your way.

STUART STEVENS:

The number I watched very closely was the conversion of right track voters and wrong track voters. Initially coming out of the primary, we were converting a disproportionately low number of wrong track voters. Initially, we were getting about 57 percent of wrong track voters. You were getting 90 percent of right track voters. That's an unsustainable percentage. So we watched this very carefully. Our goal was always to get up to converting at least 75 percent of wrong track voters and to get you at least down to 85 percent of right track voters. We slowly crept up. On Election Day we were close to 75 percent of wrong track voters. The problem was there were fewer of them. When you look at the right track/wrong track of the undecided voters, there was always that balance where they going to be driven by the right track/wrong track or by the personal fave and unfave. And the right track/wrong track improved with undecided voters.

DAVID AXELROD:

I think people are pretty fair-minded. They did have a sense of what the president walked into. We had to be very careful and you were good at keeping us on our toes on this, to not look like we were alibi-ing. On the other hand we heard people constantly saying in focus groups, "It's not where I wanted it to be. I'm not that happy. But man, that guy really walked into a mess. You can't really blame him for all of the problems." We saw it in the polling. There was empirical evidence of this. So that was a problem for you as well. And then ultimately, [there was] the big meta issue: how people saw these economic challenges and how they saw the remedies. The whole survivability of the middle class was big. Investments versus tax cuts, a very big issue. Education, R&D, were powerful.

So this isn't all about mechanics. The circumstances shifted. I think the [issue] debate was favorable to us. It's not always just where you put your dollars on what day. There are bigger forces at play, some of which none of us have control over.

JOEL BENENSON:

On character, you tested various things that didn't test well. You had the search for his employee's daughter. You had that really compelling story of a couple with the fourteen-year-old son. When I watched that video I felt, "Why didn't they put this on [at the convention] Monday night." But that's not what my question's about. Did you have any questions on the character side of Romney that you tested or any dramatic examples [involving] people other than his family, his employees, or his church that you looked at and said, hey, these really showed you he would do things for other people? So, for example, I'm looking for something like [the argument we used in 2008 about Barack Obama] being the community organizer, which we got criticized for. He could've gone to the white shoe firm. But, his story was about going to help these people in the south side of Chicago when the steel mills had been shut down. Did you test things like that about Romney where he'd helped people outside of his orbit?

STUART STEVENS:

I was trying to think what you mean by outside his orbit?

JOEL BENENSON:

Your friends, your family, your church are very close in and they're your community. When Axe [David Axelrod] is talking about some of this stuff that worked well for us in 2008, it was the choices he [Barack Obama] made outside of his own kind of world. He rejected an opportunity for a high-paying job. We had Alan Dershowitz saying, "This guy could've done anything. He went to help people who had been shut out of the steel mills."

STUART STEVENS:

Well, there's the Olympics as an example. Other charities that he started. On the character front what people saw as defining most about Mitt Romney was his family. I think what you saw on the Pew character assessment,[6] "honest" came out as one. Whenever we would test and talk to people about it, we would always have great expectations for what the Olympic [narrative] would do or these charities. [But] the wonderful story of helping never seemed to move numbers.

DAVID AXELROD:

Did you intend to do more with Olympics?

STUART STEVENS:

People liked it. But when you did any kind of regression analysis, it just didn't move [votes].

STEPHANIE CUTTER:

What about giving Bright Horizons as the counter-argument to Bain? Bright Horizons[7] are now all over the country and have a very high Q rating.[8] Mitt started those and they're hugely successful in helping kids. Did you ever consider pushing that more—

STUART STEVENS:

We did do some of that, more than people realize. We didn't use Bright Horizons specifically. Some sensitivities there. But he won on job creation and on the business stuff. We thought it was very important to drive to what he was going to do. We couldn't stay stuck in the past. We couldn't litigate whether or not Mitt Romney was a successful business person. We couldn't litigate that much whether or not he was a good person. That was just sort of a quagmire. You had to give people some signposts to hold onto. A certain number of people were never going to believe that he was because they were not going to like Mitt Romney. You had to carry them forward based on what he was going to do, [not on] proving that he was not a bad person or proving that he wasn't a bad businessman. What always worked best for us was showing what he was going to do because ultimately that would compare to the present. We always thought that one of the biggest failings of the president's convention was not coming up with a specific agenda, and that the other was just a trap.

ERIC FEHRNSTROM:

I have a question for David. But first I'd like to take a stab at answering Joel's question. After 1999 the governor's entire career was devoted to public service. When he left Bain Capital he gave up 100 percent of the voting stock. He did have a ten-year separation agreement that continued to pay him a sum of money. But the larger sum of money is what he left on the table when he departed the company that he founded. When he went to the Olympics he did not take a salary initially. He said he would only do that if he could end the Olympics in the black. He had to run those games in the wake of 9/11. I think people overlook just how demoralized and on edge the country was following those attacks. It was the first national special security event in the history of the country. The governor did mobilize everybody. The security went off without a hitch. It restored a lot of pride at the right time in America. Then he became governor. He did not take a salary as governor. He wasn't there for the paycheck or a pension. He was there because he felt he had something to contribute.

Much has been made by the governor's critics of the fact that he only served one term. But he fulfilled his Constitutional responsibilities. He came in at a very challenging time. He turned things around in a way that put the budget back in the black and got the economy headed in the right direction. The governor is completely oriented around the idea of public service. I think his post-campaign life will probably revolve around some form of public service. I don't think he knows yet what that will be. He's not going to start a new private equity company. I think, like his dad before him, he'll look to make a contribution in the public service realm. There were many stories outside the stories about the governor pastoring to members of his church community. We started to tell those at the convention. We had Olympians come to the convention and speak. We had Mike Eruzione, the miracle-on-ice captain of the 1980 hockey team, who spoke. Those stories were out there and we did tell them.

I'd like to just follow up with David because you talked about front-loading your advertising. It seemed to me you also frontloaded your strategy for dealing with the person you thought might emerge from those primaries as your general election opponent. I'm just curious how much thought went into the decision to intervene early in those Republican primaries? Was there concern that you'd be creating some kind of a self-fulfilling prophecy by taking on Romney so directly? I remember one conference call in particular following a debate where I think you were all dissatisfied with the low level of attacks directed toward (LAUGHTER) the governor. And you decided to take matters into your own hands and help our primary opponents focus their own attacks. But was there much thought—

DAVID AXELROD:

It was all in the interest of a full debate. (LAUGHTER) There's no doubt that we introduced some of the governor's changes in position into the Republican primary process because first of all we thought it was legitimate. But we also thought it would foster more debate and discussion. It did foster more debate and discussion and I think that discussion and debate helped lengthen the Republican primary process. I don't think the assumption changed at all throughout that Romney ultimately would be the nominee of the party. I agree with Stuart. On paper Governor Perry looked to be a serious challenger. But that didn't last very long. By the time that call took place, our assumption was that Romney would work his way through the primary process. So the short answer is yes.

STUART STEVENS:

To follow up on something Eric said. I don't want to re-litigate the election. But I do think there's something that you were able to play to that's troubling. You're not the first to do this so it's not something you invented. But he [Governor Romney] was very successful in the private sector, which meant that he made a lot of money. To go to Eric's point, Businessweek did the analysis that he probably walked away from $750 million when he left Bain, which is, to me at least, a lot of money. No one has been elected president with that personal wealth. Being old-fashioned, I come from the school that [says] that should be a positive

Stuart Stevens and David Axelrod

thing, that it is a good thing that people are successful. It is very easy to press a lot of buttons, particularly with the press, to run a counter-narrative to that. And when you look at self-funding candidates who win, like a Bloomberg, more tend to be Democrats than Republicans. There are some exceptions. Rick Scott got elected [governor of Florida in 2010]. But there seems to be more of a pass given to Democrats than to Republicans. I think that this is troubling. I don't have an easy solution for it. But we're disadvantaged as a country if we send a signal that those successful people shouldn't get involved in the public sector.

DAVID AXELROD:

Our view was never that Governor Romney was wealthy and therefore subject to attack. And in fact some of the great Democratic presidents of the last century, Roosevelt, Kennedy, were people of great wealth. Ted Kennedy, who Governor Romney ran against, was a person of great wealth. [Wealth] wasn't the issue. The issue was one of advocacy and policy and how that related to the lives of everyday people, whether or not Governor Romney had sufficient sensitivity to the struggles that the middle class was going through, and whether his policies would help or hurt, and whether his history suggested that he would be someone who would [champion the middle class] in that office. That seems to me to be a legitimate area of debate and discussion.

STUART STEVENS:

I think everything's legitimate. I'm not trying to say that anything is not fair game. I think the difference between those other icons is that they inherited money. They weren't business people. There was a different process involved in their becoming wealthy. I think we're going to have a generation of people who've made a lot of money in technology. And I hope that they'll run.

DAVID AXELROD:

As do I—

STUART STEVENS:

So they can go hire media consultants, spend a lot of money. But I just hope we're not sending that signal [that self-made wealth is a disqualifier for office].

DAVID AXELROD:

I don't think we're sending that signal. The signal that was sent from this election is that we have fundamental economic challenges in this country that go beyond recovering from this recession and that we have a long-term challenge, much of which has nothing to do with anything other than the evolution of technology and the shrinking of the world that has conspired against the economic security of lots of people. The question is how do we fashion policies and what can we do as a country to address that? It may be that we just have a difference of opinion on what the best approach is. But the problem is undeniable. And it's something that courses through our electorate.

STUART STEVENS:

We talked about the problem a lot. I think we do have different approaches. But that's probably why we're in different parties.

DAVID AXELROD:

Yes.

Notes

1. In 2006 the Massachusetts legislature and Governor Mitt Romney signed into law the Massachusetts health care insurance reform law ("An Act Providing Access to Affordable, Quality, Accountable Health Care")

2. In 2010 Congress passed and President Obama signed into law the Patient Protection and Affordable Care Act (commonly known as the Affordable Care Act or Obamacare). On June 28, 2012 the Supreme Court withheld the challenged provisions of the Affordable Care Act. Many experts pointed to substantial similarities between the Romney plan and Obamacare.

3. Hurricane Sandy, which hit the New Jersey shore and New York City on October 29, 2012.

4. On October 30, Governor Christie said on the NBC *Today Show,* "The federal government's response had been great. I was on the phone at midnight again last night with the president, personally; he has expedited the designation of New Jersey as a major disaster area."

5. Bain Capital is a private, alternative asset management firm founded by Mitt Romney and other partners of the global consulting firm Bain & Company in 1984.

6. An October 29, 2012, polling release from Pew Research Center for the People and the Press found 46 percent characterizing Obama as "honest and truthful" and 40 percent saying the same about Romney, http://www.people-press.org/2012/10/29/presidential-race-dead-even-romney-maintains-turnout-edge/.

7. Bright Horizons manages child care centers for corporations and other large organizations.

8. A "Q score" is a measure of brand familiarity and favorability.

Chapter 2
Campaigns and the Press

Eric Fehrnstrom

Eric Fehrnstrom has been a key member of Governor Mitt Romney's team since Romney's winning campaign for the Massachusetts State House in 2002. A Boston native, Fehrnstrom graduated from Boston University and spent nearly a decade as a reporter at the Boston Herald, *where he rose to become State House bureau chief. He crossed over into politics as a press aide to Massachusetts State Treasurer Joe Malone in 1994, but eventually returned to the private sector. In 2002, Romney asked Fehrnstrom to join his campaign for governor as communications director, a position he held all four years of Romney's term. In the 2008 presidential race, Fehrnstrom served as Romney's senior traveling aide, then was an integral member of the strategy group for the 2012 race. He started The Shawmut Group, a consulting firm, with partners Beth Myers and Peter Flaherty. The group worked on Senator Scott Brown's upset 2010 special election, where Fehrnstrom created the ads that propelled the little-known Brown into the seat once held by Senator Ted Kennedy.*

Thank you to the Annenberg [Public Policy] Center for taking a scholarly look at the recent campaign and creating and preserving this record. I'd also like to compliment and congratulate the Obama team for what they were able to accomplish.

Of course, we went into this race knowing that we were going up against a well-organized, expert team of professionals. And they lived up to our high expectations. Standing here in front of them, I think I know what it felt like to surrender a sword at Appomattox (LAUGHTER) or maybe to be a Japanese soldier standing on the deck of the *Missouri* in Tokyo Bay. But they deserve all the credit that they get for that election. I think I'd like to start by talking about the conclusion of the 2008 campaign. There's this notion that the governor, as Stuart alluded to, immediately began planning for his next campaign. That's not the case at all.

I remember being with the governor on the plane as he returned from CPAC [Conservative Political Action Conference], where he announced his withdrawal from the primary race in 2008. He was very

Eric Fehrnstrom

busy trying to organize the lives of those he had spent time with during the campaign and on the road. And he said, "Eric, what are you going to do? What job are we going to find for you?" He was very much preoccupied with moving on at that point and leaving politics behind. And of course, following the election in November of that year, many people were predicting a permanent realignment in our politics, that Democrats would have governing majorities for the next 40 or 50 years. So it didn't seem like a very opportune time for a Republican to be thinking about staging another race. But then we had the successful Republican contests in New Jersey and Virginia in 2009. We had Scott Brown's victory in a special [election] in [Massachusetts in] January of 2010 and then, of course, the 2010 midterms.

Contrary to what some people may think about Governor Romney plotting a run for president since the fourth grade, he actually had gone into a period of some reflection and thought and study after 2008, concentrated mostly on writing a book. One thing that happens to a first-time national candidate is you learn a lot. That period of reflection was important for the governor to synthesize everything he had learned about domestic and foreign policy and put his thoughts down on paper, which produced a best-selling book.

I know we're talking about our relationship with the press in this segment. I think I'd like to just turn my attention to some of the press challenges that we faced. Of course, there were challenges every day. Some lasted one news cycle. Some persisted for several news cycles. And some went on and on and on endlessly. I think the first challenge I'd like to talk about is the health care one. Stuart covered a little bit of this in his remarks. With health care in that period following the midterm elections we knew we had a problem. Because what we were hearing about the health care law that the governor signed in 2006, his last year as governor in Massachusetts, is that it was, for Republicans, a mistake. It was a betrayal. It was, in some respects, "an abomination." This is what we were hearing from our own supporters. (LAUGH) Our own donors were asking us how were we going to deal with what they thought was this very serious obstacle to the governor's nomination.

So in the fall of 2010 following those midterms we decided to do some homework. Because by now the governor was beginning to turn more serious attention to the idea of running again. He thought he was uniquely suited in the bad economic times that we were living in to offer something of meaning and value as a candidate. But we knew we had to address health care straight up. So we did our homework. We convened focus groups in New Hampshire and in South Carolina. It was clear from that research and also from what we were hearing from Republicans that the easiest and simplest path would be to simply renounce what we did in Massachusetts.

But much like what David described with respect to the auto issue and President Obama, Governor Romney was convinced and made it very clear that he was not going to walk away from the Massachusetts health care plan. We knew that Republican voters, more than anything else, wanted to see a repeal of Obamacare. There was then, and I think there continues to be today among Republicans, a complete disdain for that law. They didn't like the fact that it raised taxes. They didn't like the fact that it cut care to seniors. They didn't like the fact that to them it represented an expansion in the size and the scope of the federal government and an intrusion into the private health care market. So based on the governor's direction and guidance, we knew we had to affirm what it was that he had gotten done in in Massachusetts and, at the same time, differentiate that from the national law, even though the national law in several important respects resembled features of the Massachusetts health care law.

We looked at different ways to do this. Obviously, there was a difference in complexity. The federal health care law was over 2,000 pages. The Massachusetts health care law was a very neat and simple 70 pages. Early on, we went through a visual exercise where we took 70 pages and put it next to 2,000. It was startling just how different visually the laws looked. We also knew that there were serious cost differences between what we did in Massachusetts and what was done nationally. We looked at those cost comparisons. We started describing the Massachusetts health care law as only having added 1 1/2 percent to our state budget. But what we found that worked for us most effectively was to describe the Massachusetts health care law as, very simply, a state plan to solve a state problem, and that we did it without raising taxes and without cutting care to seniors.

Voters, Republican voters didn't, as we talked about, didn't like those two aspects of Obamacare. So the contrast worked well for us. More problematic was the mandate itself. We talked about it in terms of personal responsibility. That goes back to the governor's days at the State House in Massachusetts. I note that the President himself co-opted that language in describing the mandate that he put in place. But it was our view that people shouldn't just show up at the hospital and expect care from taxpayers. So we continued to describe it in that way. And again, the mandate could be explained away, we found, under the rubric of state plan to address a state problem. This is what our federalist system is based upon.

We actually want our governors and our states experimenting with novel ideas and novel approaches to the problems that face them. So in May of 2011, before the governor officially announced his candidacy, two important things happened. The first is there was an interview that the governor gave to Brian Mooney of the *Boston Globe* in which he said that he was proud of what he had done with the Massachusetts health care law.[1] That was an important development in that pre-primary phase the campaign. The second, as Stuart pointed out, is that he went to Michigan and gave a very important and well-received speech about health care, the law that he passed, and his intent to repeal and replace Obamacare. So the table had been set. And the first question that the governor got in the first debate in June in New Hampshire was a health care question. We knew that this was going to set the tone for the rest of that primary. He just nailed it with his response and talked about it in the way that I just described to you, which is what carried us through the entire primary process. We discovered that we didn't necessarily need to sell voters on the Massachusetts health care plan to make Mitt accept-able to them. Rather, we just needed to convince them that this was a state plan in response to a state problem, and of course always empha-size our intent to repeal Obamacare and return to the states the power to determine their own health care futures. So that was the first big com-munications challenge that we had.

The second was Bain Capital. I get a lot of questions about Bain Capi-tal. I know Beth and other members of the team do as well. Mostly, peo-ple want to know, "Did you anticipate that Bain Capital would become an issue? And what sort of preparations did you make to respond?" And the answer to the first question is very simple. Of course we anticipated that it would be an issue. It had been an issue in every campaign the governor had ever run going back to 1994 in his campaign against Ted Kennedy for the Senate. We were somewhat surprised that it became an issue in the primary. We didn't quite expect that. But nevertheless, we were prepared to deal with it.

So how did we prepare for these attacks? Early on there was a very detailed presentation that Bob White gave to members of the senior Romney team about Bain Capital. Bob White was a former partner, a co-founder of Bain Capital, a friend of the candidate, [and] well versed in all the details of private equity, particularly as it related to the portfolio companies during Mitt's period of leadership of Bain Capital. He explained the Bain business model to everybody. Of course, just like reporters covering the campaign, most of these folks had no financial experience whatsoever. But we went through a series of anticipated attacks against Bain. We talked about the Bain companies that were going to be most problematic. We talked about their vulnerabilities. They were all identified and discussed. We would group those compa-nies into specific categories, categories like outsourcing, categories like corporate greed. (LAUGH) And to a remarkable extent, the anticipated lines of attack were the ones that actually materialized.

We also undertook to create an internal SWAT team, if you will, that included multiple researchers, lawyers, and spokespeople. We had ex-Bain employees who took part on a pro bono basis. We recruited a per-son to handle communications for this SWAT team, Michele Davis, who had Treasury background so she was well versed in matters relating to financial communications. [The swat team members] were physically located in the headquarters up in Boston. They were in constant contact and communication with other departments in the campaign. One of the issues that they had in preparing our responses to these attacks that we knew were coming was there wasn't a lot of good information on these companies. Bain Capital was formed in 1984, during the relative infancy of the private equity industry. They didn't keep very detailed records. They certainly didn't have records relating to employment information, which is why we had a back-of-the-envelope projection of job creation. We didn't have the more specific, concrete numbers that we would've desired because they simply weren't kept. We endeavored to put that together. We reached out to former CEOs and board directors for these portfolio companies. We had them searching through their attics for documents.

We were doing primary research on Bain so that we could put these fact sheets together. And we did develop detailed fact sheets that were shared with people on the communications team so that we could respond when they became issues in the media. They featured major events in the lives of these portfolio companies, investment timelines. We had contact information for ex-employees. We laid out all the potential vulnerabilities with each of these attacks. And to answer, I think, David's question, or actually it was Stephanie's question, there was an effort to look at the large number of companies that Bain invested in that represented successful growth and turnaround situations.

The creative department, under the direction of Stuart, hit the road. They produced a series of taped testimonials from Bain executives, from employees, from the companies that Bain invested in. We had business founders and CEOs and general employees all on the record speaking about their positive experience with Bain and, of course, refuting specific charges that were made about their companies. And we were very aggressive in the earned media in sharing this information with them. Those taped testimonials found their way into the information stream as web videos. The question that we get asked frequently is, "Well, why didn't you put it up on your paid?" And the answer is fairly straightforward and simple from our point of view, we were resource limited. When those attacks were occurring in the late spring of 2012 and the early summer, we didn't have the resources to do everything we wanted to do with our advertising.

Our own research was telling us that the most important thing that voters wanted to know about Mitt Romney is "What would he do? Okay, we get the fact that there's been a failure on the part of the incumbent president with respect to the economy. But what would Romney do differently?" That's what gave birth to the "Day One, Job One" series of ads. And then, we thought if we did go up on the earned media and fought Bain, then that's all we would be talking about. We had made a blood pact to avoid chasing [either] shiny objects or the distractions that our opponents would try to create [to deflect our attention] from what we felt was the number-one issue, which was the economy.

The third major communications challenge we had was the emergence of Medicare as a more prominent subject following the selection of Paul Ryan as running mate. With that pick, we were more deeply associating ourselves with his budget proposals, specifically his plan to transform Medicare into a premium support plan. A lot of commentators in the media thought we were committing political suicide for that reason alone. But this was a fight that the governor welcomed. We expected it. I think it underlined the boldness of the governor's pick. The governor himself had already brought forward a plan to retain the existing Medicare system along [with] some new options that we would add to create choice and competition, the idea being that that would lower costs. And far from hiding from the subject, Paul Ryan was our major point person in talking about the governor's plan. He talked about it in many of his speeches and rallies. He would do PowerPoint presentations in town hall-type settings to talk about the debt and the deficits and the need to reform entitlements.

Then, of course, we send him to Florida where he appeared with his mom who lives in Florida and is a Medicare recipient. And at the same time that we were very proactively making the case for entitlement reform along the lines of what the governor had proposed, we went on the attack against the President for having raided Medicare, in our view, for more than $700 billion as a way to finance Obamacare. We staged events around that subject. We ran ads on that subject. We produced video. We tried to really turn up the heat. And at the end of the day we won seniors. We won them pretty convincingly, 56 percent to 44 percent, according to the exit polls. And if you look at the state of Florida, we won seniors there too. We won them by 17 points. By way of comparison, McCain had won them in 2008 by 8 points.

So I think the lesson there and one of the positive legacies of the Romney campaign is that we demonstrated that Republicans can run on a forward-leaning, entitlement reform agenda and win, rather than always being on defense. It's a testament to the governor's courage that Medicare reform is no longer a third rail for Republican candidates. That's in part because of the decisions we made as part of the Romney/Ryan campaign to take it on as an issue.

Kevin Madden:

Kevin Madden is Executive Vice President of Public Affairs at JDA Frontline, directing the firm's Washington, D.C., operations. Madden most recently served as a senior adviser to Governor Mitt Romney's 2012 presidential campaign. He also served as National Press Secretary for Governor Romney's 2008 campaign for the Republican presidential nomination. Prior to joining Governor Romney's campaign, Madden served as Press Secretary to House Majority Leader John

Boehner (R-Oh.). In that capacity, he served as the top communications strategist
for the House of Representatives leadership office charged with directing legislative
action. Before his work as a top leadership aide on Capitol Hill, Madden served
as the Department of Justice's national spokesman on issues ranging from
national security to litigation before the federal courts. During the 2004 presiden-
tial campaign, he was a member of the communications team directing President
George W. Bush's reelection effort, serving as the president's campaign spokesman
for regional, national and international news organizations.

I join Eric in thanking my friends and colleagues from the Romney campaign as well as my friends and colleagues from the Obama campaign
and, of course, congratulate them on an incredible victory. This is part
of my therapy. Usually, I do these lying down on a couch. (LAUGHTER)
Before anybody thinks that it's not fair that Stephanie Cutter has to go
against two Republicans, Stephanie Cutter thinks that her going against
two Republicans is what she calls a fair fight. (LAUGHTER)

I think it's important to assess the changing nature of the way that
these campaigns are covered in order to understand some of the strategic decisions that we've made during this campaign. [To do so] I think
it's important to look at the last few cycles. This was now my third presidential campaign in a row. I don't know why I keep making the same
mistake. Isn't that the definition of insanity? (LAUGHTER) I want to
talk about some of what I've learned from 2004 and 2008 and how it
affected the strategic decisions that we made in 2012.

Campaigns, obviously, are moving much faster, 10 times faster than
they did the last the campaign cycle. That is something that campaigns
as well as the media are taking note of. In the 2004 campaign, we wit-
nessed the advent of blogs and their impact on [both] how voters got
and shared information and how the press got their information about
candidates. That was the beginning of the journalism paradigm being
somewhat reversed. [In the past] the big media folks set the pace and
tempo of the coverage and the discussion and the debate. And campaigns played along with that with full recognition of it. [Then] a very
top-heavy system started to crumble. A lot of the power began to come
from the bottom up. By then, [what] we were starting to call new media
[were beginning] to have a much greater impact on how reporters
themselves did their job, the competition in the news space, as well as
how campaigns dealt with it.

In 2004, we saw Drudge sneezing and the rest of the media catching
a cold. Blogs, which a lot of the big media folks used to say derisively
were run by people sitting at home in their pajamas, [began to flatten
the media paradigm]. When the person who was sitting at home with a

Kevin Madden

blog began to accrue the same sort of power that somebody sitting in the *New York Times* newsroom had, it had a tremendous effect on the information flow in campaigns and had a tremendous impact on how campaigns looked at strategy. In the 2004 campaign, there was no Facebook, no Twitter. When you wanted to watch a campaign video, you had to sit at a desktop with a bunch of people huddled around it. Remember putting tapes into VCRs? "Hey, look. It's built into the TV. You don't have to hook it up to the TV." (LAUGHTER)

All of those technologies which we believed were advanced then are now obsolete. Then in 2008 new media and social media become fused together to create another new power paradigm in how people get their information and how the press covers campaigns. Voter-to-voter contact became a more powerful way to persuade voters than a 30-second ad. We found in 2008 that you're more likely to be persuaded to vote for a candidate based on what [a trusted] neighbor says, the person who's prominent in your parish, prominent in your business, prominent in the newsroom. You're more likely to be influenced by that than you would be a 30-second ad. In many ways, folks on the consumer side were much further ahead of campaigns. [They knew that] people were much more inclined to learn what movie they might like to see based on what their neighbor said than [from] an ad for a movie. That was something in 2008 [that affected] how campaigns strategically made decisions and how the newsroom strategically made decisions on what to cover. Pack journalism essentially began to go viral.

Campaigns began to recognize this and create more unique content to affect these networks of voters as well as these networks of media, creating our own information systems, [and not just] relying on what news organizations were deciding to cover. We were creating our own news cycles. We were creating our own information networks so we could get them to voters. Instead of going to the editorial page and saying give me 750 words in the *New York Times*, you could create your own opinion editorial, put it out to your grassroots supporters, put it up on a campaign blog, ship it to a list of a million people, and have that information processed that way. And guess what? We found out the media was going to cover it then. So the power paradigm again began to shift toward campaigns. We took full advantage of that. As a result the media pace picked up dramatically. Rapid response got more rapid. It became almost instantaneous.

Campaigns then began to look at rapid response not as when your opponent would attack but instead [as] proactively defining your opponent every single day across multiple platforms. This, too, increased the campaign speed. The pace at which the media covered these attacks picked up as well. It had a dramatic impact on how we decided strategy. Remember Myspace? Believe it or not, in 2008 I signed up for Myspace and Facebook only because I wanted to find out what the candidate's Myspace account looked like and what the candidate's Facebook page looked like. I didn't even go back. I didn't learn about the impact that Facebook was having on how people got their information until Governor Romney's Facebook page was hacked. I had to log in to see what it was that was being hacked and what kind of damage we were controlling. And I find I've got 18 guys from grammar school who are looking for me. (LAUGHTER) I felt as if I was on the cutting edge of technology back then, believe it or not.

Some folks at work still hadn't even gotten Facebook accounts. But campaigns began to look at how social media and the new media were being fused to create a whole new way of how people were getting their information. And back then, in 2008, it's hard to believe [but] Twitter was only for the geekiest of the geeks. I remember calling up somebody I thought was a very good new media person. And I said, "Tell me about this thing called Twitter. I'm seeing it here and there. People that I like in media are starting to use it." And he said, "It's not going anywhere. Don't use it. It's stupid. It's 140 characters, doesn't make any sense. I can't see how people are going to share information like that." Little did we know that that as early as 2010 and 2012, it would have such a dramatic impact.

So that brings me to 2012. New media were no longer new. Instantaneous information sharing has now arrived in campaigns. We remember the old saying, "The revolution will be televised." That's gone. Now it's, "Look at me. I'm live-tweeting the revolution. Here's my Twitter handle." I described Twitter as "TNT for the news cycle." The reason I say that is because you would literally be sitting in campaign headquarters asking, "Is this a problem we have to deal with? Is this a problem that we can ignore? Is it going away? Is it staying?" And we would say, "Look, this is blowing up." Twitter would make a story go beyond just the Washington conversation and become a pop culture meme. Jay Leno would be talking about it. Rachel Maddow and Sean Hannity would be talking about what Eric was saying to David [Axelrod] on Twitter that day. So it did have a lasting impact on how the press began to cover the campaign.

Jen Psaki, a colleague of ours on the Obama campaign who did a wonderful job for them, [was on] a panel [on which] we were talking about how we used to go back and brief the reporters. Their [Obama campaign] briefings were a little bit more formalized than mine. I was on the plane with Governor Romney. I would usually go back once, twice a day and meet with the folks who were covering us. And if you've ever seen the movie Braveheart it was a lot like the scene where the Scots try to beat the British cavalry by taking these very long trees and sharpening them as spears. It was as if the press were lifting these 30 spears at me in order to derail whatever message it was that I was trying to promote that day. But we would go back there and brief the reporters, Jen on her plane, me on my plane. After 15, 20 minutes at the back of that plane, I would walk to the front of my plane, which now has wireless, and look at my Twitter feed. And I'd already made news. We are not even on the ground. We are in the air flying over America. And we are creating a news cycle, creating a news nugget that the media was then going to atomize or blow up with the news cycle. That was an incredible development during this campaign.

I'd like to take a look, too, in both a critical and clinical fashion, at what we got right and what we got wrong. And I'll start, of course, first, with what the press got wrong since they're not here today. (LAUGHTER) The message discipline required to run an effective campaign oftentimes frustrates the press. They always want more access. Their job is to never be satisfied with the access that we're giving them. My job is to be never satisfied with the message discipline that I'm providing them. I think one of the other natural tensions is that I've never met a reporter who doesn't think they could run a better campaign. And I've never met a press secretary, including myself, who didn't think I could write a better news story. That tension is real. Let's put it on the table.

Let's go about our jobs professionally. I think that's usually the best relationships that you have. But what I found interesting was that [although] the press was very unsatisfied, they did very little to try and go outside of that bubble on their own.The great David Broder would never call me from the back of the plane or ask me questions as part of a gaggle inside the bubble of the press corps that was covering that campaign. Instead, and we've all seen this, you'd be on the steps somewhere in Manchester, New Hampshire, Des Moines, Iowa, Columbus, Ohio, and he would pop up. He was there for two days doing Lion's Club meetings, two days going to Republican clubs, two days finding a Democrat focus group, listening, talking, learning about the stories that people were sharing outside of the bubble of a campaign. Then he would ask the questions.

Oftentimes, he was much more informed than we were about the nature of people's opinions, the conversations that people were having. Forget focus groups. Forget the empirical data, the anecdotal evidence that you get when you go to a staged political event. Instead, what he was getting was the real-time information that was beyond the trends that we were seeing. He was getting something beyond all of those numbers. I think that was something that the press largely, the press would [not] get on the plane. They would get off the plane. They would go to the hotel. They would go to the event. They would go back to the hotel. Repeat. Recycle. There was a sense that they were mad at what we were giving them. But there were stories out there that they could get. The best journalists during this particular campaign were the ones who did get out and do that sort of real shoe leather journalism required to inform voters nowadays.

What did the press get right? There was an acute focus on the personality contest between these two candidates—because they were very different personalities, came from very different backgrounds—and [on] whether or not that was going to have an impact on this race. Every day, in every way, some reporter would call me [and say], "Yeah, that's true. You make a good argument about this, this, and this on the economy. But people like him. (LAUGH) People like the President. And is that going to matter?" Very early on in the campaign as a strategic purpose and also to get our best message out we said that this was not going to be an eHarmony.com election. This is going to be a Monster.com election. If this was an attribute contest, we believed that we were at a significant disadvantage because this was a president with a very compelling story. He was an historical figure in many ways. And he was somebody that both the empirical and anecdotal evidence did show was somebody that people had a "connection" with.

So the press's acute focus on that connectivity as something that was going to really matter in the end to undecided voters was one that I think, as David pointed out, the Obama campaign rightly paid a great deal of attention to, and one that did have a great impact. Very early on, I started to see from the Obama communication shop this summary of their arguments: "This is about who's on your side." And it was a theme weaved through a lot of their arguments, whether it was economic, whether it was personal, whether it was just the mechanical part of what they're doing, as far as building their networks of voters in these states where it was going to have an impact. We tried to make an argument that this is not about eHarmony, which is, "Who do you like?" But instead it was about, "Who is going to be the most competent? Who is it that can do the job? Who has the better plan for the future?" That was manifest in how we made the argument at the end, which was, "Say what you want about Mitt Romney. He has a plan for the economy, and the President doesn't."

That was an interesting debate that we believed we could win. But in the end the one question, if you look at a lot of these campaigns over the years, that is answered in the affirmative is, "Does this candidate understand the problems of people like me?" The Obama campaign answered that in the affirmative. We competed on that issue in a way that said, "How Mitt Romney understands the problem of people like you is that he has an incredible command of the economy. He has a plan. And therefore, he and you should have a connection." We lost that debate, unfortunately. But it was one that the press focused on. And it did have an impact.

What we got right. In this world where we have a wealth of information, there's oftentimes a poverty of attention. Looking back to 2008 I remember riding with the governor during our announcement tour. I made the biggest mistake of any time I've ever been on a campaign. I

told a new candidate what his standing was in national polls. (LAUGH-
TER) Do not do that, future press secretaries, particularly when you're
about to get on a three-hour flight with the candidate. In 2008 we started
the race at about 4 percent. And during Governor Romney's ascent to
national name recognition creating awareness and stimulating demand
was a challenge for us. We synchronized messaging to our grassroots supporters in the fundraising world, messages to the media and to persuadable voters. What we were saying to the funders was exactly what we were
saying to the grassroots: "Mitt Romney is somebody who has a commanding control of the issues. He's somebody who's a great leader.
Here's somebody who has encountered dysfunctional entities in every
stage of his life and has turned them into success stories. He is somebody
who is uniquely positioned in this crossroads that America is at to lead
the country." And we did so by creating a symphony pretty consistently
as part of our introduction of Mitt Romney.

What we got wrong. I know today's Thursday. And usually we leave
bad news dumps for Friday. But I'll go a day ahead. While we mastered
reaching out to grassroots voters and fundraisers and synchronizing our
message, sometimes it was at the expense of a message. This goes to
David's point earlier asking about the convention video. If you looked
at the primary and the general election, we spent a lot of time focusing
on our tactics. "Today we're going to run to the right on this issue in the
primary, on either Newt Gingrich or Rick Perry." "Today, we're going to
run a little bit to the center on Social Security and Medicare in order to
position ourselves against this candidate or that candidate." And in
many ways, [in] that focus on tactics we lost an ability to drive a consistent message, [such as the one in] the convention video, which would
tell you a lot about Mitt Romney [and] position ourselves to make a better sale to that persuadable voter at critical moments. I believe that a lot
of it had to do with the state of our campaign [of] somebody who was
not as well known and was trying to create awareness while stimulating
demand. But tactic to tactic and message to message, on a day-to-day
basis, on a 24/7 news cycle, they [in the Obama campaign] did a better
job.

One of the things that we should never lose sight of is just how good
a job the Obama campaign did. A lot of that was taking advantage of the
institutional edges that they had as an incumbent. But recognizing that
was a smart thing. They took full advantage of these institutional edges
to create an environment where their plan could thrive in very unique
circumstances, as David said, that these campaigns are. As much as we
obsess over 2004 and 2008, and this is just like 1968, each campaign has
unique circumstances with unique electorates. Their plan was very well

built, very well executed. They should get credit for that. So with that, I will turn it [over] to my friend and colleague Stephanie Cutter.

Stephanie Cutter:

Stephanie Cutter *is the founder of the Cutter Media Group. Called "one of the most prominent voices in the [Democratic] party, and one of its top strategists and crisis managers" by Politico, Ms. Cutter's political and communications experience spans two decades in public service and the private sector. From the West Wing to the campaign trail and halls of Congress, Cutter has crafted communications and crises strategies for the nation's leading political figures and campaigns. Most recently, Cutter was Deputy Campaign Manager for President Obama's 2012 reelection campaign, Obama for America. She also served as Chairman of the Board for the 2013 Presidential Inaugural Committee. Before joining the campaign, Cutter was Deputy Senior Adviser to President Obama, overseeing message strategy and issue development. At the White House, Cutter also devised the confirmation strategy for Supreme Court Justice Sonia Sotomayor and helped create the First Lady's Let's Move! campaign. Prior to joining the Obama Administration, Cutter was Chief Spokesperson for the Obama-Biden Transition, and served as Michelle Obama's Chief of Staff on the 2008 Obama for America campaign. From January 2005 to March 2006, Cutter was a senior advisor to Minority Leader Harry Reid and Democratic Senator Edward M. Kennedy. In fall of 2003 the John Kerry for President Campaign brought in Cutter to develop a communications plan to reposition Kerry for victory. After the campaign's come-from-behind upset, Cutter assumed the position of Communications Director for the Kerry-Edwards 2004 presidential campaign. From 1994 to 2001, Cutter held various positions in the Clinton Administration. Cutter was a Fellow at Harvard's Institute of Politics, taught at Johns Hopkins University, and has lectured at Smith College, American University, and the University of Pennsylvania.*

I'm going to talk about three things. One, I'm going to agree with Kevin about how media treated this campaign. It really was almost wholly lacking any analysis of what was actually going on in the country or going on the ground. There was a herd mentality of our captive press corps without much enterprising or investigating or going out there and doing the hard work and talking to voters and seeing what's actually going on in the country and how they're perceiving what these campaigns are doing. [Although] there's a little bit of that on every campaign, I think it was exaggerated on this campaign. So why was that? This is my third presidential campaign in a row also. So I'm as (LAUGHTER) I don't want to say demented as Kevin. But I consider myself demented for doing it.

Stephanie Cutter

There has been an evolution of how people communicate. In '04 we saw the first introduction of blogs. Because I was very much entwined in the Swift Boat controversy, I saw up close and personal what blogs could do. We didn't pay attention to those blogs. We didn't think they mattered. But they spread information below the radar among the Republican base before we even knew it was happening. And then it popped up on Fox News. Unless you have tens of millions of dollars to go up with advertising, it's almost uncontrollable. That was the blogosphere in 2004. In 2008 we had much more capability to communicate online. We had millions of supporters that we were able to mobilize and communicate [with] online. And we really used that as a tool to get our message out. Facebook was around in 2008. But it was a tenth the size it is today. [Although] Twitter existed, I think we only sent our first tweet in the last week of the campaign. It wasn't a primary communication tool.

So fast forward to today: there is news everywhere. People are getting their news in so many different sources. You know, those bloggers are now reporters. Reporters now are tweeting. So whether you're on the investigative beat, on the financial beat, every reporter is basically a wire reporter. Because you're tweeting out 140 letters every hour, which is like being a wire reporter. It's hard to get down to any substance of what's going on in an election if you are filing a tweet every hour on the hour. So what did we do about it?

I want to talk about our overall strategy but then our techniques for delivering that strategy. So David mentioned before that elections are always about choices. We firmly believe that. We sure as hell were going to make sure it was about a choice. What was that choice? It was a choice about economic values, who was going to get up every day and fight for the middle class, help reclaim the security that the middle class had lost. In a nutshell, as Kevin said, whose side were you on, basically. We set out a strategy to do that. Not only did we have to make it about a choice, but we have been dealing with our own press corps and national media for years, since we took office, basically, saying, "You're going to lose. You're going to lose reelection. No president has ever been reelected with unemployment over 8 percent. No president has ever been reelected with consumer confidence this low or with this amount of job loss. You're going to lose. Look at these statistics." [However] we knew, thanks to Joel's great research, that people didn't look at the economy based on statistics. It wasn't about GDP. It wasn't about unemployment rates. It was about what was going on in their lives. So how do we communicate to them, in a very personal way, about what's going on in their lives? That was a challenge but also an opportunity for us.

We also knew that people got their information from many different sources that also varied by demographic. Young people, obviously, get their news primarily online or from friends. Latino Americans, online. Older Americans, an increasing number of them getting their information online. So we knew we had to be varied with how we communicated our message, but also continue to be creative about how we deliver that message because in a 24-hour news cycle with things moving so fast, you had to grab people's attention.

We spent much of the end of 2011, the beginning of 2012 making sure that everybody understood that, in the face of very dire circumstances, the worst economic recession since The Great Depression, working in Washington without willing partners across the aisle, [President Obama made] these tough decisions, often unpopular, but it was the right thing to do, they had real impacts on people's lives. The automobile rescue saved a million jobs but created hundreds of thousands more jobs, really revitalized the Midwest, the industrial Midwest. Health care, we battled for, I'm looking at my colleagues because they all have the wounds. As soon as that law was passed, we battled to try to change the impression of that law and [communicate] how it would positively impact people's lives. That really started to turn during this presidential campaign, as more and more of the law got [implemented] and people were more and more comfortable with it.

You know, there's always going to be a segment of the country that's not going to like the law, until it is fully implemented and the sky doesn't fall because there's so much else caught up in in it, basically Barack Obama. But a huge swath of those in the middle just want to see what it's going to do to their lives. That was starting to come to fruition during the course of this campaign. No more discrimination [based] on pre-existing conditions for kids. Contraception for women, which, obviously, we talked a lot about during the campaign. But it's something that women really wanted. More than $1 billion of rebates got mailed out over the summer. The automobile bailout. The health care law. The Lilly Ledbetter Act.[2] Cutting middle-class taxes. Reforming education: with a fraction of what we spend on public schools every day, we were able to increase standards in 47 states. These are just a few of the examples of the accomplishments that we spent 2011 and a lot of 2012 pushing out. The sum of all that is that Barack Obama took the steps necessary to save this economy [and is] rebuilding the economy in a way that will help the middle class reclaim the security that they had lost. It always came back to the middle class, no matter what we were communicating.

Now, the converse of that is Mitt Romney. We spent the end of 2011 and 2012 up until really the conventions rolling out three phases of our messaging on Mitt Romney. The first was Bain. We were determined to make sure that Bain was not about job creation. It wasn't about Mitt Romney being able to turn around a company to create jobs, [but] about turning around a company to create wealth for himself. There's nothing wrong with that. We weren't demonizing it. But that's not a qualification to be President of the United States, particularly in an economic downturn where so many people were looking for help. So that was number one. If that Bain experience was not about creating jobs, it was about creating wealth for himself and his partners, which is what private equity does, then what type of values, economic values, does that give you? We can tell you what it doesn't give you. It doesn't give you a first priority about how you're going to help the workers at that firm or how you're going to make sure that everybody gets ahead, not just the investors. We were able to tell that story through different Bain deals and other circumstances around it.

So we set the conditions with the economic values. We applied that to Massachusetts. So he told the same story in 2002 that he's telling now, that because he understands the real economy he can turn the Massachusetts economy around. So let's look at what happened when you take those economic values [during his time as governor] and you apply them to Massachusetts. We debated his record pretty fulsomely [detailing] how he left that state. Like anything else, there are statistics on both sides that we both can point to and we both did point to very vigorously. And then [as the third piece of the strategy we said], "Okay, you've got this set of economic values. You saw how it worked in Massachusetts. Now he wants to do it again. Look how he's going to do it. Look at this set of policy proposals and what they're going to mean for you. They're not going to mean greater economic security, the ability to have a fair shot, to get ahead, if you work hard, play by the rules, build a better life for your kids." So those were the three stages of our Romney messaging. We worked very closely with [our] paid media and our online department to communicate that.

So now I want to move to the techniques of communicating. I had mentioned that Facebook was a tenth the size of what it is today. Given our challenges in dealing with the [traditional news] media, we saw an opportunity to go around that filter and directly to our supporters and those that we needed to persuade, which was a much more valuable communication to them than reading something in a newspaper. We had 33 million people on Facebook following Barack Obama. Those 33 million were friends with 90 percent of Facebook users in the United States, more than 90 percent. So we could communicate with 90 percent of Facebook users in this country, which in sum total is more than the people that voted for us. So we did that very diligently. It was largely a positive conversation online. Because when you're communicating with people on Facebook, as everybody in this room who is on Facebook knows, it's about getting them to share something with their friends. They're more likely to share something if they're proud of it. So our conversation on Facebook was largely positive. So that's in a big way how we got out what the President had done over the course of four years, what the President stood for, who he was as a person, the values that [informed] the decisions that he made. Facebook was an important tool. We would post a picture of Michelle and Barack on Facebook, and it would get 10 million views. For just one click of the mouse, we'd get 10 million views. So it was an incredible communication tool for us.

We had about 21 million people following Barack Obama on Twitter, more if you counted the other accounts, Michelle Obama, the Vice President. We used those accounts to continue that positive conversation. Obviously, we used our accounts for different (LAUGHTER) purposes, you know, battles between Axe [David Axelrod] and Eric or, you know, largely driving negative. But our principal accounts were largely driving a positive conversation. The last thing is YouTube, which became almost a TV channel for us. By the end of the campaign, 133 million views of our YouTube videos. Some negative. You know, I personally did some. (LAUGHTER) But they were largely positive.

We used every communication tool on the campaign to communicate our message in a very disciplined way. We weren't out to win a news cycle, unless it fit into our message. If it didn't fit into our message, we were going to communicate what we wanted to communicate in different modes of communication. Here's an example. You're all familiar with "Dinner with Barack," which was a big very successful fundraising tool for us. We filmed one of those dinners, it was Barack and Michelle and a few other couples. During this incredible conversation about parenting among the couples sitting at the table, you saw the President of the United States and the First Lady not as the President of the United States and the First Lady but [as] parents. That was an invaluable conversation for us to send to our supporters, so that they could share with others. It was one of the most successful videos that we did. Now, that started as a fundraising tool. We raised a lot of money off of Dinners for Barack. But then we ultimately used it as a communications tool.

So we used every aspect of the campaign as a communications tool as much as possible. People trust their information when it's coming from a Facebook friend much more than if it's me on TV saying something. They trust information if it's [from] somebody knocking on their door who happens to be a community member [more so] than a piece of mail from our campaign. So we tried to take advantage of that as much as possible. We were really running ward races in communities all over the country. We were also running ward races online among Facebook friends, online followers, YouTube, very localized, personalized campaigns. It proved to be very effective, not just in getting people to vote for us but getting people to work for us to get that vote out.

ERIC FEHRNSTROM:

Can I start it off? When you said that we didn't get much real analysis from reporters, I had to agree. We spent a lot of time at the campaign brainstorming how to get reporters interested in the economy as a story. We would look at things like the ADP report, the Consumer Confidence Index. There's a lot of economic reporting that takes place on a weekly basis. But business reporters don't even like to write about that stuff. Durable factory orders: that's a news brief deep inside the business section. But the one metric that we could use to focus their attention was the monthly unemployment report. And I'm just curious what it was like at the Obama (LAUGHTER) campaign in Chicago—

Eric Fehrnstrom, Stephanie Cutter, Kevin Madden

STEPHANIE CUTTER:

Oh, my God.

ERIC FEHRNSTROM:

—the first Friday of every month. Did you have some kind of a heads up about what was coming and what kind of a pins and needle experience was that for you?

STEPHANIE CUTTER:

Well, we didn't have a heads up on the numbers. Legally, we couldn't. But, of course, we had lots of economic experts giving us their forecasts. And we had the ADP numbers[3] that came out a couple of days before. Yes, pins and needles is a light way of putting it. You know, I was thinking that tomorrow is the jobs report. And it is the first time in four years that—

ERIC FEHRNSTROM:

You're not holding holding your breath?

STEPHANIE CUTTER:

—I'm not thinking through what we're gonna say—

JIM MARGOLIS:

We care deeply. We care deeply.

STEPHANIE CUTTER:

We care deeply.

ANITA DUNN:

Yeah, we care deeply. (LAUGHTER)

STEPHANIE CUTTER:

But I don't have to think through what we're going to say this time. You know, through the campaign, it always felt like the job [report] days fell on really inopportune days. It was the Friday after the end of our convention. It was the Friday before the election. They always popped up at just the wrong moments. And—

ANITA DUNN:

It was the Friday after the first debate—

JIM MARGOLIS:

After the first debate.

STEPHANIE CUTTER:

Friday after the first debate, right. And you know, through the summer, there were some concerns that we could see a negative job report. What in the world were we going to do about that? And there was probably not much we could've done about that except come out and react strongly and aggressive about what we need to do as a country to turn that number around.

KEVIN MADDEN:

Did you ever put together a plan that said, "Okay, we're going to respond aggressively. And we're going to pop this out on offense against the Romney campaign." I found that oftentimes you used the Sunday show after the Friday, where we were sitting there looking at the transcripts. And we're [saying], "They only asked one question about jobs. It was all the Obama guys out there dumping on us."

STEPHANIE CUTTER:

Well, we did a lot of downplaying of the number. We were fortunate not by pure luck, but blood, sweat, and tears, that that number was on a steady trajectory. It wasn't growing by leaps and bounds. But it was on a steady trajectory moving up. So we lived by the first Friday of every month. And reporters had been dealing with it for four years, too, which worked to our benefit, in that they were conditioned to it. And certainly, the American people were conditioned to it. They were so conditioned to the unemployment figures, GDP, consumer confidence that it really didn't have an impact in economic approval ratings. For them, it was a very personal experience. "Was the drycleaner down the street open or closed?" "Do I have more money in my paycheck?" But we knew that if we got a bad job number that could all change very quickly. So we conditioned people to [the notion that] that number was not indicative [of] how people felt about the economy and then tried to change the conversation into a forward-looking [direction], "How are we going to grow the economy?"

ERIC FEHRNSTROM:

The economy, of course, is what compelled Mitt Romney to get into the race in the first place. It seemed to us, in the thick of it, that we were winning every month, that job growth was just weak enough so that we could continue to make the case for change in the White House. But then you look back at the long-term trend line, and it was positive. We had 10 percent unemployment when Romney announced his candidacy in the spring of 2011.

STEPHANIE CUTTER:

Who could forget?

ERIC FEHRNSTROM:

A year out, in November of that year, it was 9 percent. And then for the last month of the campaign, it was 7.8 percent. I remember when we got that September report where we had the precipitous drop from 8.1

percent to 7.8 percent that we were of two minds, that this either aug-
ured something really strong that was happening in the economy or it
was a complete anomaly and they're going to pay a price for it.

KEVIN MADDEN:

At that point, we began to mirror the messaging that you just talked
about, which is that, "Look, the unemployment rates, this isn't about
numbers going up and down. This is about whether or not you feel this
is having an impact in your community." And you know, the numbers
guys will always tell you it takes six months of good economic numbers
just to reverse the trend on how people's opinions were being formed
about it. But what was happening very slowly during this entire time,
which showed up on Election Day, was the wrong track/right track had
gone to about 42/50-something-or-other. So this gradual trend had
begun to take hold in the electorate.

ERIC FEHRNSTROM:

Everything improved. The right track/wrong track numbers that were
totally lopsided a year out were much more evenly divided on Election
Day. The President's job approval was negative a year out. He was − 5.
He was + 9 on Election Day. And it tracked the improvement in the
economy. Was the economy going great guns, the way we thought it
could? No. But I think it had improved enough that people were willing
to stay the course. And of course, they didn't tend to blame him in the
first place for the situation that he inherited. So when people ask me
what happened, I say, "Well, the central rationale for our candidacy was
we had a guy who could fix the economy." And when he announced, we
were at 10 percent unemployment. Things were really bad. But it got
better. It got better just enough for the President to make a persuasive
case for staying the course. And even though we won on the subject of
the economy it was only marginal, I think by four points, which is basically margin of error. If we had won on the economy the way we won on
debt and deficits, which was by 30 points or more, we might've had a
different outcome.

DAVID AXELROD:

The trajectory of the unemployment rate in the year before the election,
I think, was the fastest drop since 1995. I think trajectory's really important. You know, that 7.2 that everybody says, that was Ronald Reagan

before he won a landslide. That's still very high. But it was much lower than it had been. And there was—

KEVIN MADDEN:

It's never the number. It's the trend.

DAVID AXELROD:

The trend line was good. I don't wanna cut into your cross-questioning. But I feel like we gotta get this in before you guys are done, especially since I'm sitting next to Mr. Jackson [Brooks Jackson, Director of Fact-Check.org] here. (LAUGH) Can you guys talk about two things, the impact that you think public polls had on the coverage of the race and the impact that fact checkers had on the nature of the coverage of the race and the race itself, and whether you think they played on the balance a positive or negative role. And [to Brooks], I want to ask you to leave the room. (LAUGHTER)

ERIC FEHRNSTROM:

Let me take your question about fact checking. I thought they did a great job when they went after you guys. (LAUGHTER)

STEPHANIE CUTTER:

That's essentially it—

ERIC FEHRNSTROM:

Of course, a lot of the problems arose when they came after us. Look, I think they play an important role. We always welcome the scrutiny. We felt it was important to present our evidence and our side of the case, even though we knew going into the exercise that things may not turn out the way we had hoped. I think one of the issues with fact checking is there's been a proliferation now of organizations that engage in it. And I think we're very soon going to arrive at the moment where you'll have conflicting fact checks out there. I mean, obviously—

STEPHANIE CUTTER:

We're there.

ERIC FEHRNSTROM:

—the best-case scenario would be you get all your fact checkers. And they all agree that this particular ad went too far. But when you have fact-checking organizations kind of splitting—

DAVID AXELROD:

Maybe we need FactCheckFactCheck.org. (LAUGHTER)

KEVIN MADDEN:

So that you can rate the fact checkers.

ERIC FEHRNSTROM:

Yeah. But I think that they play an important role. And it wasn't something that necessarily found its way into the earned media all the time. Sometimes it did. But it was very useful on the paid side to help destroy an argument that your opponent was making against you by being able to cite the Annenberg [Public Policy] Center or the *Washington Post* fact checker or whatnot—

KEVIN MADDEN:

Yeah, just real quick—

ERIC FEHRNSTROM:

And just one example, because we talked about Bain earlier. This wasn't an issue for the general election, but the "King of Bain" mini-movie that came out during the primary, that was a case where all the fact checkers lined up in support of the arguments that we were making about some of the outlandish charges that were included in that film. But there were other times when the fact-checking organizations would go in different directions.

KEVIN MADDEN:

I agree, there was a proliferation. And in many ways, it contributed to this sentiment among voters and, I think, even many in the observer class in this. It was like the final scene of Reservoir Dogs, where everybody's standing there pointing a gun at each other. And they all shoot

at the same time, and they all fall down. (LAUGHTER) They all die. So
it kind of canceled it out a lot because of the proliferation, I think. The
problem I had with a lot of the fact checkers was they had very arbitrary
standards. I joked that if Ronald Reagan's ad "Morning in America"
ever had to go through a fact check, they would've given it a pants on
fire. Because "Somewhere, right now, it's not morning. (LAUGHTER)
Therefore, this is half true." I'm like, "How do they apply the standard
'what he meant to say?' How do they know what he meant to say?" It's
not a fact check. This is an opinion piece. Put an editorial on it. Put it
on the back page of the paper. From the tactical standpoint, I was always
arguing, vigorously, to stop sending them out, even against the Obama
campaign. Because I just wanted to just be rid of them. They're sending
out ones that are good on for them. And we're sending out ones that
are good for us. And it's just a big, giant waste of time. What was the
other question?

DAVID AXELROD:

About public polls.

KEVIN MADDEN:

I'll let you answer the fact checking and then the polls.

STEPHANIE CUTTER:

I think that it got into almost the realm of ridiculousness. Because fact
checkers were disagreeing with each other. And a lot of it, they were
just making subjective assumptions about what they thought happened,
where objectively you could see it both ways. One example of that, and
I'm sure there'll be plenty of people in this room who disagree with me,
whether some Bain deals were fair game after 1999 because Romney
had, according to Romney, left Bain to go to the Olympics and was no
longer involved. Our argument was, "Well, he was involved because he
was taking a salary from Bain. He was the president/CEO, sole stock
owner, and chairman of the board. So he's still responsible for what's
going on at Bain. He's still profiting from it." That was a real argument
that we had with fact checkers about whether or not, you know, some of
those deals that happened after 1999 should be part of the discussion. I
believe that whether or not he was responsible for those deals really was
a subjective argument that is part of a normal political campaign. That
was one of our biggest battles. And if you didn't agree with us about
whether he was responsible for those deals, everything that we did was,

you know, five Pinocchios, knocked down. And we spent hours upon hours dealing with it.

DAVID AXELROD:

One thing I—

STEPHANIE CUTTER:

So the subjectiveness—

DAVID AXELROD:

—would say about it, and Joel can speak to it is, I think it all swirled around in a place where voters had no, I mean, I think voters were discounting all of that stuff.

STEPHANIE CUTTER:

I think it was definitely—

QUESTION:

Do you think that's right?

STEPHANIE CUTTER:

—the inside Washington chatter. It provided fodder for each campaign to use things in their advertising. We didn't completely ignore it. Obviously, we had staff solely dedicated to it and didn't consider it insignificant. But we had problems with it.

KEVIN MADDEN:

Public polls definitely had an impact. The narrative that would emerge was probably as frustrating for the folks that put the numbers together as it is for those who have to react to it. They treat every poll as an event, not a process. "48/40, you've lost Ohio, right? It's over." And it's like, "Buddy, it's September. (LAUGHTER) You've got 60 more days." Public opinion is not an event. It is a process. We have a great deal of time where we can still impact and persuade voters. And reporters oftentimes, looking at just those top-line numbers, would never investigate the data. And everybody knows that you have to investigate that data.

Where are the trend lines on it? What opportunities still arise [or] are still baked into those numbers for persuadable voters? How soft is that 48 or that 40? That was something that really did dramatically impact how reporters covered the race. When you would walk to the back of the plane after a bad poll everybody was asking a question about that poll. And the next 15 to 20 stories that were either a blog post or would find themselves into a hard copy would be talked about ad nauseam for the next 48 hours on the news were about that poll, treating it only as an event, not a process. So it did have a great impact.

JOEL BENENSON:

They also treated them all as if they were tracking polls. So on Tuesday, one organization would come out and say, "You're down eight in Ohio." But the next day, they say it's even. And they would write, "Obama's lead disappeared." Two different polls, two different methodologies—

KEVIN MADDEN:

It was even worse in the primary in 2008. We were in a knife fight with the McCain folks. And the press back in 2008 had such an affinity for the president of New Hampshire, John McCain and the Straight Talk Express. They were rooting for him in many ways. And when he went down really fast [in the polls] after the immigration debate and we had risen up, the natural tightening of the race was occurring. In these public polls, with a margin of error of about 5 percent, Governor Romney went down 3 percent, and McCain went up 3 percent. And I'm literally talking from 23 percent to 20 percent. And McCain went from 10 percent to 13 percent. A reporter called me up and said, "I'm doing a story on how you guys are losing voters, and they're all going to McCain. (LAUGHTER) You lost three. He gained three." And I said, "That's not how it works," you know? But the story got written. I had to give a comment explaining that. For a lot of folks who don't cover statistical methods and how that stuff works, it did create other stories. And a blog would pick it up. Somebody on a cable news station would then atomize that story and use it as their own. That became something that you had to very aggressively combat before it would begin to take hold.

JOEL BENENSON:

I think those were a bigger pain in the ass than the jobs reports.

ANITA DUNN:

Absolutely.

ERIC FEHRNSTROM:

On the public polling, I think reporters were genuinely confused by what they were seeing and what they were hearing from the two campaigns. And a lot of the public polling tracked our wrong internal polls both nationally and in some of the battleground states. It turns out that that polling was flawed because we made assumptions that didn't turn out to be to be correct. Your polling, apparently, internally was more accurate than ours. But for the reporter covering the race, I mean, they would hear you very adamantly talk about our move into Pennsylvania or Wisconsin. You guys were describing that as a tactic because we knew we were going to lose places like Florida and Ohio. So [in that storyline] we were looking for electoral votes elsewhere. But we genuinely believed that we were on the march, that we had already locked down Ohio and Florida and Virginia. And we were going to be adding to our total. And this was going to be a plus-300 electoral victory for Mitt Romney. That was not spin. Our opinions were informed by the polling that that was done.

ANITA DUNN:

I have one quick question. And I'm glad to see that we can all still find bipartisan agreement around the role of the press here. So there's nothing that gets us all together. But my question for Eric and Kevin is you both worked for him in 2008. I think one of the things that I was surprised by was that he didn't clean up those personal financial disclosures and tax returns before he ran. But one of the reasons the wealth issue really did hurt him was because of this sense that he was hiding stuff. And if he didn't have anything to hide, why wouldn't he just release them? I've worked on plenty of campaigns where I did not take the kind of preemptive action that I should have. So I'm not being critical or trying to put you on the spot. But I am curious about whether you had a discussion after 2008 about that, or whether that was one of those things where it was just like, "It's his thing. The accountants take care of it."

ERIC FEHRNSTROM:

Well, we never made tax disclosure in 2008. We—

ANITA DUNN:

Right, I know you didn't. So—

ERIC FEHRNSTROM:

We did personal financial disclosure. I think this is an area where I tip my hat to the Obama campaign for using issues like the governor's wealth and the tax returns and some of the disclosures in those tax returns, and also Bain Capital, as a way to paint the governor as somebody who didn't care about the concerns of average voters. With Bain in particular in the past, we always had to defend the business decisions that were made at Bain. And at the end of the day, we thought this was a good thing, particularly in tough times where budgets need to be balanced that the governor makes these types of tough decisions. And if it results in layoffs of public employees, well, that's just part of the pain that we have to go through to achieve a balance. But you guys did something that none of our opponents had done previously on Bain. You made it a character issue. We hadn't confronted that before. But that is a place where you were able to achieve something.

JIM MARGOLIS:

Could you unpack, though, the decision not to release on taxes? I mean, this was something—

STEPHANIE CUTTER:

Because that's why it actually started during the primaries—

JOEL BENENSON:

—to frame it. You said you didn't do public disclosure in '08. But it was publicly known—

ERIC FEHRNSTROM:

Well, we did the personal finan—

JOEL BENENSON:

—you had 23 years that you had given to—

ERIC FEHRNSTROM:

We did personal financial disclosure in '08.

JOEL BENENSON:

But the tax returns—

ERIC FEHRNSTROM:

There were no tax returns.

JOEL BENENSON:

As you answer Jim's question, everybody knew you had given 23 years of tax returns—

ANITA DUNN:

—tax returns to McCain.

JOEL BENENSON:

—to McCain. So you had them. The governor even said, "I'm a pack rat. I had them all."

ERIC FEHRNSTROM:

We talked about what our theory in the race was, which is it was going to come down to the economy. And it did come down to the economy. As I said, things improved enough that you guys were able to make a case to stay the course. A corollary to that is that we weren't going to be distracted by shiny objects. And the shiniest of all the objects was the governor's tax returns. So we put out a level of information that we thought could withstand press scrutiny and also satisfy a legitimate public interest to know how much money the governor made. But we weren't going to get drawn into a protracted debate about Swiss bank accounts and the like. We wanted to keep reporters and voters, of course, focused on the main issue, in our eyes, which was the economy—

KEVIN MADDEN:

I think one of the main issues was, "Was it ever gonna be enough? If we did 10, where's—why not 12? Why not 15? Why not 20? Why not 30," right? So we there was a certain level of strategic retreat there, which is, "We're going to put out the two and that's it. And it's going to satisfy what we believe is the requirement."

The second was, would it matter? One of the main arguments I made [was that] if this is an election about Mitt Romney's finances and tax returns, we've already lost. We can't win it. Then it becomes about an issue about wealth and whether or not that's a good or bad thing. And if it's a bad thing because you have a lot of money and your tax returns are getting a certain level of scrutiny, we're not going to be able to win it. Where we think we can win it is that this is going to be about the future, the state of the economy, and whether Mitt Romney is perfectly positioned as a candidate to help build a better, more prosperous future for the country. Giving into that in any way would in some way give into the exact kind of race that you all wanted to run and abandon what we thought was the bigger, larger argument. One of the reasons that this was a competitive race was because we didn't do that. And we did make it a case about the future and Mitt Romney's unique position to help build a better future. Now, we've litigated that and we lost. But that was the kind of thinking behind a lot of it. It was debated. The governor likes robust debate, likes to hear from both sides. But ultimately, the decision was made and fully and faithfully executed by the team without reservation.

Notes

1. Brian Mooney, "Romney and Health Care: In the Thick of History," *Boston Globe*, May 30, 2011.

2. Passed by the Democratically controlled House and Senate in January 2009, the Lilly Ledbetter Fair Pay Act was the first piece of legislation signed into law by President Barack Obama. The Ledbetter Act protects against pay discrimination by extending the statute of limitations for filing a lawsuit challenging unequal pay.

3. Employment numbers as reported by Automatic Data Processing, Inc.

Chapter 3

Looking Back, Looking Forward

DAVID AXELROD

One of the utilities of exercises like this is that we get to spend some time with our colleagues on the other side. Campaigns are a very ferocious process. Eric [Fehrnstrom] and I went hammer and tongs from time to time. Stephanie [Cutter] had her moments with both you guys [Eric and Kevin]. And you know, the tenor of our politics sometimes gets very raw.

This is a great opportunity to address each other as professionals and as people who are in this process because we believe deeply. It's clear that you felt as strongly about your candidate as we did about ours, and in a very positive way. And I think that's important, especially for the young people who are here on this campus and young people who are watching. Because, as raucous and raw and sometimes trivial as this whole process is, there's a lot of nobility in it. It's a great calling. It's important because the outcome has a tremendous impact on the world in which you live.

And so, I think it's important for us as professionals to set a good example for you and make it clear that we have enormous respect for the individuals on the other side. I have a sense that we have a lot of commonality of experiences. And I think at the end of the day we ought to resolve that whatever divides us, there are things that unite us that are even larger. So I appreciate the opportunity just to be with these guys in something other than an adversarial proceeding.

Let me make three points about the election. I spent some time asking Stuart [Stevens] about whether the Romney campaign had thought about doing more in terms of fleshing him out for voters. Here's my observation based on these two presidential races and a career of doing this, including a career of covering it. I think in a presidential race, more than any race because it's a unique office with unique power, biography is very, very important. We did spend a great deal of time in 2007 and 2008 really tying Obama's story to the things that he wanted to do. And that authenticated the things that he was saying, the commitments he was making. And it gave people a sense of identification with him. It's not an easy thing to do, especially in the midst of what was a very hot shooting war that they were in in the primary campaign. But I do think that it was advantageous to us that these guys never had the opportunity to do that because I don't think Governor Romney was ever fully fleshed out. And it probably contributed to message difficulties down the track for him. They had resource issues and other issues. But one of the things that gave us comfort when we saw that [biographical] video at the convention was that that was the first time we had seen it. And that we hadn't seen it earlier.

So the topic I was given that I'm only marginally abiding by was looking back and looking forward. I think that if I were to advise future candidates in campaigns (and I'm retired from the campaign business) based on these experiences, I would say make sure that you closely tie your own personal story to the larger story you're trying to tell. And really develop an authentic sense in voters as to who you are, what motivates you. I'm convinced, for example, that George W. Bush won in 2004 because ultimately people felt more comfortable with him. They thought they knew who he was, and [that] he was an authentic person. They didn't have to guess who he was or who he would be. And I think we benefited from that as well in this election. So that's one lesson that I would draw from this.

The second thing that I would say is [that] there's been a lot of discussion about whether this [election] was about big things or small things. I think this election was actually about big things. I think it was about very big things. And we are sort of talking about it in fits and starts here. But you know, for all our complaints about the system, at the end of the day, it was a race about our economic future. And these two candidates had starkly different views on it. And I say that without prejudice. The election's over. I obviously have one point of view. I share the President's point of view. Governor Romney had a different point of view. These guys share his point of view.

But they were both legitimate points of view about how we move forward. One was if we do less, essentially, an unbridled private sector would lead us out of the morass. And if I'm doing injustice to the governor's position, then you should correct me. But I think that's roughly it. And ours was that there are certain things that we had to do as a country through the government on issues like education and others that were necessary in this twenty-first-century economy to prepare people for jobs and to create the kinds of high-wage jobs that we were looking to create. Very legitimate debate, and it's going on in Washington still. So as much as we denigrate the process, I actually think that it was a very good debate and a healthy one for the country to have. We shouldn't get lost in all the noise and all the tumult and miss that point.

Third, I think we have to think through how we approach the coverage of these races. I thought Kevin was very compelling. I was a young reporter back in the day when there were some real giants covering political campaigns, who had been doing it all their lives. Johnny Apple and [Jack] Germond and [Jules] Witcover and Curtis Wilkie[1] and just a whole array of people. They reported exhaustively. As Kevin said, they would disappear and they'd go and talk to voters. They didn't simply jump on planes, go to the event, get fed, go back, [and] report what happened that day. This is not in any way to denigrate the wire services. But there are plenty of people who can report what was said. It's tougher to go out and do the reporting about what's really going on. I think that the economics of the news business is such that there's less of a premium on that. First of all, there aren't these giants, and perhaps that's an economic [dimension] as well. But they don't assign people to just go out and find stories as much as they used to. And that's my one concern.

[Earlier] I asked a question about public polling, because I think the proliferation of public polling was a perversion of this process. These things are related. If you're not going out and doing serious reporting, the easiest and laziest thing you can do is wait for the Keokuk Junior High School poll to come out, and then write a piece observing how Iowa's going. And the fact is that there's absolutely no discrimination among these polls. Every poll was treated [by the press] as if it was equally valid even if each said something different. There were days in this race on which we were 6 points behind in one poll and 13 points ahead in another, neither of which was true. But they both were covered as if they were real. News organizations have come to invest in these things as a way of branding themselves.

So [reporting on these polls] took over the process in this campaign in a way that it hadn't before. And I hope that's something news organizations examine, how they deal with these public polls. And Joel [Benenson] will speak later. I'm sure Neil [Newhouse] will have some views on this. There are real fundamental, methodological reasons why a lot of these polls were wrong. But nobody asked those questions. And we, in fact, and you guys probably have, too, [have] gone to news organizations and said this poll is wrong and this is why. And they would politely listen, but they would use the poll anyway. The most noteworthy is the Gallup Poll, which was just profoundly wrong almost the entire race. There were really good reasons why they were wrong. And those reasons were apparent during the race. Yet, news organizations were using Gallup. They paid out a contract. And they were going to write the story. That is a real issue for coverage in the future. And we need to examine it.

I think this fact check issue is also a tricky one. There's no doubt that there's plenty of policing to do. The truth gets brutalized in the political process. But as Stephanie pointed out there's a lot of subjectivity that goes into those judgments. To authoritatively rule on these things is an enormous responsibility. And it's often discharged differently by different people. And that creates a lot of confusion. I don't know the answer to how to approach this. But I can tell you that, as was said, the fact check process became sort of a parody of itself, and a phenomenon of the news media. And voters tended not to ascribe much credibility to any of them. In fact, you guys probably know this. We were better off running a news clip of a newscaster or a *Meet the Press* someone saying something. That tended to be believed more than any of the fact check organizations. So this is something for you to consider as you move forward in your work and what role you're going to play in future campaigns. I wish I had an easy answer. The polling thing is easy, let's not give bad polls lots of attention. Let's not cover presidential campaigns like they're horse races.

On that point, and I should have made it during my critique of the polling, I said at the beginning there are big things at stake in these elections. But so much of the coverage is about who's gonna win and who's gonna lose. And it's all based on these tea leaves. So those are my three observations in my non-address.

KATHLEEN HALL JAMIESON:

The deal struck was that I got to ask the questions. (LAUGHTER, OVERTALK)

DAVID AXELROD [POINTING TO SPRAY OF FLOWERS ON TABLE]:

Why do I feel like I died here?

KATHLEEN HALL JAMIESON:

You deserve a much wider spray of flowers than that. And we will ensure that if it ever happens, that—

DAVID AXELROD:

Thank you.

KATHLEEN HALL JAMIESON:

—we will provide it.

DAVID AXELROD:

Yes—lovely.

KATHLEEN HALL JAMIESON:

And it will be from FactCheck.org.

DAVID AXELROD:

A lovely arrangement.

KATHLEEN HALL JAMIESON:

Which we hope will not have died before you. My first question is based on what we think we learned after 2008. We think we learned that behavioral economists advised your campaign in ways that were different from the past, different, first, because they were there. But could you tell us what they told you, and did it matter?

DAVID AXELROD:

Well, we got a lot of input from various places. Was the advice we got determinative? No. Was it helpful? Probably. But the most helpful advice we got was from technologists about the possibilities of using social media, the data dives and so on. Interestingly, technology has allowed us to return to a version of good old shoe leather politics because we can have an individual dialogue with people. But we can do it in a much more efficient way. And that became important because of what these guys said. Because there is such cynicism about political ads, news media, even fact check organizations, hearing messages from people who are trusted, which is something that I think is more and more prevalent in consumer work, was really important to us.

What guided us more than anything else were deep studies. Joel perhaps will talk about the ethnographic study of these swing voters in which this issue of the viability of a middle-class life came screaming through. And we learned much more from that. Not to denigrate the contributions any of your colleagues made. But it was really the research that was most helpful in terms of shaping our message.

KATHLEEN HALL JAMIESON:

Let me ask you two specific things. There was in the academic world the notion that the 2008 Obama campaign had tried to create a sense of historical inevitability, and that you as a voter were either going to be part of this or you were going to be out of it. If you were in it, it was going to be a major life experience for you. And as a result, that vote was going to be a very special vote. The academic world thought that that may have come from the behavioral economists, since it was consistent with things that they knew. Was that there? Did that happen? If so, did it matter?

DAVID AXELROD:

Well, I think there's no doubt that it happened. But in certain ways, it happened. It wasn't something that was the calculation, a calculation that we made, or made in conjunction with any academics. And it also became a great challenge for us. I mean, we knew when we were traveling in 2008 and 100,000 were waiting for us that even in the best of times it would be impossible to meet the expectations that people had. And we knew we weren't moving into the best of times. We knew we were headed into very challenging times.

And that, in a sense, was something that we had to solve for in this election because there was a sense among people that somehow the President's election in 2008 was historic and somehow a panacea for all that ails us. People imputed to him many of their hopes and dreams and expectations, some of which wasn't even based on anything that he said. And so it created a very high bar. And given the set of circumstances that we faced after he took office, meeting that bar was difficult. But I know I'm diverting your question to something else. But that's what we're trained to do.

KATHLEEN HALL JAMIESON:

Yes. You—and you do it well. In the 2008 debriefing, you told us that as of the first debate you thought you had the election. And let's assume that you're correct.

DAVID AXELROD:

Didn't quite work that way this time.

KATHLEEN HALL JAMIESON:

Let's assume that there's a common understanding that [in 2008] that was right, that basically it was over for McCain after the first debate, barring something very, very unusual. Did you calculate the effects of having heightened expectations on an electorate at that point, and try in any way to downplay the expectations by suggesting that it was going to be a difficult presidency, and that we were going to have sacrifices and [tough] choices? Or did you abet the assumption that we were going to have change we could believe in with a fierce urgency of now and, as a result, set yourself up for some disappointments as president?

DAVID AXELROD:

It's a fair question. We tried. I traveled with the president when he was running in 2008. In every speech, there was a very big disclaimer saying change is going to be hard, it's going to take time. I'm not going to be a perfect president. But it was not an easy lift for us to make that happen. I thought you were gonna ask a different question, which is when did we feel secure in this race? I talked earlier about these public polls. One of the confounding things about this race is we were really never behind in our own polling. And the race kept trading within a very consistent band of two to four points.

The only time that it got larger than that was in the post-convention 47 percent tape time, when Governor Romney lost some independent voters who were Republican-leaning. And then, [when] the first debate happened. Obviously, a great debate for Romney, a bad debate for the president. Those voters came back to him and the race snapped back into the range, a three point race. And that's where it remained. It sounds preposterous, but we were very confident based on the data. We were confident based on what we saw in these battleground states. We became more confident in mid-September because Florida looked real to us, which we were wondering whether that was possible. So we were always confident. I thought the other question you might ask is what the hell happened in that first debate. That question comes up a lot.

KATHLEEN HALL JAMIESON:

I think we're gonna save that for the debate panel.

DAVID AXELROD:

Oh, the debate panel? Yes.

KATHLEEN HALL JAMIESON:

Unless you have a different answer from the one Anita's going to give, in which case please share it.

DAVID AXELROD:

Well, I'm not going to advance the altitude—the altitude excuse. No, I'll leave it for that panel.

KATHLEEN HALL JAMIESON:

Let me go back to the first theme. The behavioral economists say that if you give people one lump sum, they're going to save it. They're not going to spend it. But if you give it to them gradually, they're more likely to spend it. So you gave the tax cut that you promised, but you gave it across a whole series of iterations. It didn't just happen in one lump sum. Did the behavioral economists basically trap you into doing what they said was the right thing (which probably succeeded because people did spent it) and, as a result, make it very difficult for you to get credit for having delivered on your promise?

DAVID AXELROD:

I don't want to strip the aura away from whatever exists there of our operation. But when we got to the White House, we were really very much a triage unit. Around December 16, 2008, I was part of an economic briefing that was nothing short of horrifying, in which Larry Summers said there was a one in three chance that we were going to have a second Great Depression. And we were just pushing buttons when we got there to try and stop the free fall and turn it around. And we could have done, from a marketing standpoint, a better job on, for example, the tax increase—

KATHLEEN HALL JAMIESON:

Tax cuts.

DAVID AXELROD:

The tax cuts. But we wanted to get it into the bloodstream as quickly as possible. And all the other steps we took weren't driven by strategic concerns as much as they were by economic concerns about how do we get the biggest bang as quickly as we possibly could. Because there was a genuine fear. You don't expect to hear words like a second Great Depression. You think of that as part of history. There was a great deal of concern when we got there about just doing the things that were necessary. Some of those things I mentioned earlier, the auto bailout was not popular. The Recovery Act, not popular. Standing up to the financial industry, continuing the TARP [Troubled Assets Recovery Program], expanding it, was less than not popular. It was calamitous in terms of our own politics, but necessary. Perhaps we should have been more attentive to the advice of academics and others. But we were trying to bail out the boat there.

KATHLEEN HALL JAMIESON:

It struck me as interesting that a campaign that did so well at communicating to get elected managed, in one public poll, not to get credit for the tax cut it actually delivered that it promised.

DAVID AXELROD:

Yeah.

KATHLEEN HALL JAMIESON:

And so, what happened to that disconnect?

DAVID AXELROD:

Well—

KATHLEEN HALL JAMIESON:

You warned us in 2008. "Everybody says that we're geniuses now that we won, but—"

DAVID AXELROD:

Well—

KATHLEEN HALL JAMIESON:

—we're not actually. But—

DAVID AXELROD:

We discussed [whether we] should do what Bush did and send the tax cut to everybody, signed by Barack Obama. And the thought was that it wouldn't get into the bloodstream of the economy fast enough. So we sacrificed that opportunity in order to try and you know, save the country from the disaster. So it turns out that it's easier to run for president in an election when you have the wind at your back than it is to be president in the midst of a once-in-a-generation economic catastrophe.

KATHLEEN HALL JAMIESON:

So with this amazing communication team, was there not some way to do what was the best thing: get this into the bloodstream and do it in a way that people would spend, and also get the credit for it? In retrospect, if we were now going to rerun that for you so that you got credit could you have done that?

DAVID AXELROD:

You know, first of all, sitting here now, reelected, I don't really care that much. But second, I am proud that the principal considerations that we made at the time [were based on] what to do to have the maximum impact on what was a terribly difficult problem for the country. And if we were guilty of not being self-interested enough, I'll take that.

KATHLEEN HALL JAMIESON:

That is a great sound bite. Let me ask what, in 2008, you would have known about me if I were an undecided voter in Ohio who was a target for you that was different from what you would have known in 2012? So what specifically did you [not] know about that target voter in 2008 and what would you have known in 2012 about exactly the same person?

DAVID AXELROD:

Yeah.

KATHLEEN HALL JAMIESON:

And then, how did you know it?

DAVID AXELROD:

Because of the prevalence of Facebook, social media, and so on, there's a lot more information available about consumer interests, and so on, of voters [including information from] cable and, is it satellite boxes? Yeah. (OFF-MIC CONVERSATION)

DAVID AXELROD:

These guys will talk [about] it later.

We have much more refined information about viewing habits. So, for example, we were able to target our buy in a much more efficient manner to reach target voters in a way that we wouldn't have been able to in 2008. We knew a lot about millions and millions and millions of voters. We knew a lot about their interests, their viewing habits. When we polled, we polled from voter lists. One of the reasons we had more success in terms of the accuracy of our polling is we polled from voting lists. Those voting lists were updated all the time based on registration, so they were current. We could append that information to the voting history of voters to the polling list. And we could make some suppositions. If someone might say they're probably going to vote, but you can see they voted in the last 10 elections, you can pretty much assume that they're going to vote.

But if you just use a barometer of voter interest and they say "probably," a lot of polls would drop them out of the likely voter model. And Joel did some good work, which he'll probably talk about. And the deduction that we were able to make was that about 20 percent of voters were being excluded from some of these public polls, because their self-description didn't match up with their history. They ended up being voters. And those voters were disproportionately, by about 60 percent to 40 percent, our voters. So there's just a wealth of additional information. And aggregating all that information, both in terms of persuasion and in terms of evaluating where you are in the race was very important.

KATHLEEN HALL JAMIESON:

Should we worry that with all of this enhanced capacity to speak to individuals where they live, based on everything that you can amalgamate of consumer data and voting data and polling data, that we're going to see campaigns that are going to be increasingly deceptive because they're targeted to the narrow interests of specific individuals outside any form of mass mediated scrutiny?

DAVID AXELROD:

Well, first of all, I think there's always going to be a broad discussion. And apropos to what I said before about authenticity, I think that even within the realm of tailoring your message to individuals, if it's gonna be effective, it's gonna be part of a larger message. I think it's a fair question. But if your question is can you be all things to all people because you can so tailor your messages that you can have lots of discussions, I suppose—you know, there's always been that capacity through things like direct mail and otherwise.

I think in a presidential race, it's very hard to do that. You know, one thing about presidential races is they're so rigorous and they're—there's so much attention paid to them, that ultimately I think everything gets flushed out in a way. That if you're doing things like that, I think that will catch up with you.

KATHLEEN HALL JAMIESON:

So if we knew everything we could know about your campaign and about the Romney campaign, we wouldn't be finding any suspect messages that didn't get some public scrutiny?

DAVID AXELROD:

I give the benefit of the doubt to the Romney campaign. But at least as far as I know, and I think I know the messages that went out, there was no message that went out that you would find shocking, dissonant, inconsistent with who we are.

KATHLEEN HALL JAMIESON:

Are you confident that you know enough about what the third parties were doing to say that what was being microtargeted by the third parties basically got enough scrutiny that people knew that it was there, so that you and they could evaluate the messages?

DAVID AXELROD:

I would never suggest that third party actors in this process are getting enough scrutiny. Let's start with the scrutiny of knowing who they are and where the money's coming from. [The fact that] these 501(c)4s in campaigns, [their] lack of transparency is very, very concerning. I can't tell you precisely what Mr. Rove and others were doing beyond what they were doing on television. I think that's a little harder to track. And there is this sense that, well, you know, they're not us, so there's a detachment from what they do.

From a process standpoint, there are big problems associated with this. There are also, by the way, strategic problems. I've heard Stuart talk before about the fact that you really can't control what they do, and they're on the battlefield. They're ostensibly trying to help you. And that isn't always the case. You know, we had a case with one ad that created a lot of problems for us that never even ran but was a huge media story. I'm sure there are plenty of ads that ran that, you know, caused you guys to scratch your heads and say why the heck are they doing that.

So it's a crazy patchwork system that invites prodigious spending. In this case, I think prodigious spending, in many cases, to no particularly productive end. But nonetheless, it's a source of concern, because all this unregulated money in the process can't be good for politics and undisclosed.

KATHLEEN HALL JAMIESON:

There was a targeted cable and radio ad that said that Barack Obama supports a UN treaty that will take away your guns. I assume you knew it was there. And I didn't see any effort to respond. So I assume you decided that either you shouldn't respond in a mass media environment or somehow you were going to get a correction to those [who saw or heard the ad]. Or it didn't matter; they weren't going to vote for you anyway. Can you give me some sense when something like that happens of how the campaign decides whether it's going to respond or not, and whether there's any concern about letting it be unrebutted with a part of the electorate that may not vote for you anyway, but nonetheless is being reinforced in a kind of mindless fear?

DAVID AXELROD:

Well, that's where we rely on FactCheck.org. But—

KATHLEEN HALL JAMIESON:

FactCheck.org, by the way, won't go after something that doesn't look as if it's not going to have an impact. Because we don't want to legitimize it.

DAVID AXELROD:

Well, didn't you go after that? (OFF-MIC CONVERSATION)

KATHLEEN HALL JAMIESON:

We did.

DAVID AXELROD:

Obviously, we evaluated all the communications that we saw that were aimed at us. We'd make assessments of what was a hit to the main engine, what wasn't. Jim's [Margolis's] people were excellent at tracking all the media that was running in a market. We would poll rigorously in those states and with large enough samples at the end so we could tell if there were trends. There were times we were being attacked in Ohio on coal. We felt we had to respond to that. Those were targeted kinds of appeals. And we responded to them.

So that's part of campaigns. You have to evaluate the efficacy and the reach of various media. Are they simply persuading people who were already persuaded? It's a mixture of art and science.

KATHLEEN HALL JAMIESON:

Big question. We've now had the first African American president reelected. What across this period do you know about the effects of that, if any, on perceptions about race and racial stereotyping?

DAVID AXELROD:

I don't have a measure of that. And we haven't really delved into that. I think it's human nature, however, that breaking these barriers changes attitudes. And it changes attitudes not just on those who might have had a negative reaction to the prospect of an African American president. But it also changes attitudes. I remember when we were talking about running in 2006—late 2006. And Senator Obama was asked, well, what do you do that no one else can do? He said, "One thing I'm pretty sure of is that if I get elected, there are millions of kids who are going to look at themselves differently." I think that that's true. And I think his ability to win reelection was very important in that regard. But has race been exacerbated as an issue in the country? I don't think so. Has it been resolved as an issue for the country? Clearly not.

This I may—this may aggravate some of my friends. But were there elements of race[ism]? Yes. But you know, I suspect that that's been true with Democratic candidates since the Civil Rights Act of 1964 or '65. '64? This has been a strain between Democratic candidates and Republican candidates. So we have a long way to go on the issue of race. But I think that the notion of an African American president in the future is obviously going to be less noteworthy than it was in the past. I think you'll see the same thing when a woman gets elected president.

KATHLEEN HALL JAMIESON:

And did you see any elements that were involving religion with the Romney campaign? What was your internal discussion about that as a potential issue?

DAVID AXELROD:

Well, our internal discussion was that we wanted to stay as far away from it as possible. It would be supremely ironic if, given who Barack Obama is and his message, we were trying to exploit those kinds of passions. And I think that they did pretty well with the evangelical voters out there who were thought, at first, to be resistant to a campaign.

One question I didn't ask you guys, though, is how you thought that issue through. Because one of the things that I thought was difficult if I were sitting in your chair was that the governor's faith is obviously very important to him. It's central to his life. And yet I don't know how free he felt to talk about it. And I'm sure you guys had long discussions about how much he could introduce it into the discussion or not. But as far as I'm concerned, from our standpoint, we thought we had a pretty good argument. It turned out to be a winning argument. And that argument was very much separate from the issue of faith.

KATHLEEN HALL JAMIESON:

Please join me in thanking David Axelrod. (APPLAUSE)

Note

1. R. W. ("Johnny") Apple was a correspondent and editor for the *New York Times* from 1963 until his death in 2006. Jack Germond and Jules Witcover are veteran journalists who co-wrote the syndicated column "Politics Today" for 24 years beginning in 1977. Curtis Wilkie served as a national and foreign correspondent for the *Boston Globe* from 1975 to 2000.

Chapter 4
Debate Strategy and Effects

Beth Myers

Beth Myers *has a long history of involvement in public issues and campaigns. Most recently, she was Campaign Manager for Mitt Romney's presidential race and before that served as his Chief of Staff through all four years of the Romney governorship. She previously worked as a litigation associate at Akin, Gump, Strauss, Hauer & Feld LLP in Dallas, Texas. Beginning with the 1980 Reagan presidential campaign, Myers has worked for a slew of candidates. Working for Market Opinion Research, she developed and implemented GOTV campaigns in California, Texas, Massachusetts, Louisiana, and Missouri. She was Deputy Campaign Manager for Ray Shamie's 1984 U.S. Senate race in Massachusetts and on the 1986 Bill Clements for Governor campaign in Texas. She also spent a stint as Chief of Staff to Massachusetts State Treasurer Joe Malone, and worked on Malone's 1998 campaign for governor.*

A central part of Mitt Romney's debate success at the Denver debate was preparedness. Where was the campaign when the debates began? To put it in perspective you have to understand what the September race was like for the Romney campaign. We started August, the month before the Democratic Convention, in a pretty good place. Then the Democrats had their convention and got a nice bump. The Embassy was attacked in Benghazi and some of Mitt's comments on the statements from the Embassy in Cairo were controversial. That was followed shortly by the release of the 47 percent video and Governor Romney's 2011 tax returns, which made it a bumpy month for us. So we were not going into the first debate on a particularly high note. But we always sort of expected that.

We knew that October was going to be our make or break month. And although we weren't going into October from a strong place, we always suspected that we would go into it as the underdog. What this meant for us was there was a lot of pressure to perform. And the expectations were very high for both camps. They were high for us because we needed a

Beth Myers

good debate to stay in the race. And they were high for the Obama campaign because a good debate for the President might put Mitt out of the race once and for all.

So then . . . rewind back to the spring when we were anticipating that we would be coming from behind on October 3rd in Denver when Mitt walked onto the stage. At one of our very first post-primary strategy sessions Mitt put it to us that he wanted the debate prep to be the "Manhattan Project" of the campaign. I think that's probably different from a lot of other campaigns. But that was his idea, his point of view on the importance of the debates to his campaign. He asked me to be the point person because he knows that I could manage his calendar and was probably the only person on the campaign who could get the time on the schedule and keep it on the schedule without having the time bumped for other things, especially by Spencer Zwick for fundraisers, which we needed to have in the fall because the campaign wasn't taking federal campaign funds.

On our debate prep team Stuart Stevens was the strategist, Lanhee Chen organized the policy, Jim Perry focused on debate answers and formulating the attacks on President Obama's record, and Austin Barbour handled logistics. I coordinated and drove the process.

We had our first formal session on June 23rd. Why did we feel it was so important to have all this prep and start it so early? Mitt is a candidate that we knew had the ability to win big, to hit a long ball. We wanted to make sure that we gave him the opportunity to do that. He is at his best when he's relaxed and comfortable. And to get him relaxed and comfortable, this guy has to be prepared. He has to have mastery of his material. And he has to be comfortable that he understands the lay of the land. The easiest way to get to that point was to prepare, prepare, prepare, and then prepare some more.

So how did we prepare? The first thing we did was made sure that Mitt was solid on policy. We'd had a lot of practice in the primaries—22 debates over the course of the primary season. But those debates were, for the most part, candidate forums. They were not the kind of debate where you walk on the stage and there's another person there waiting for you and you get to bat around the ideas and think big. They were sponsored by networks. And the networks were promoting themselves and their newscasters. They were looking for a big moment. So those primary debates were really a very different animal. And while Mitt was familiar with President Obama's policies and his record, he did not have the deep dive understanding that he wanted to before he walked onto the stage in Denver.

We didn't want to overwhelm Mitt with volumes of materials which would have been impossible to read given how busy he was with the campaign. So we had to synthesize then synthesize some more. We started off with big, thick volumes that got smaller and smaller and smaller. He read pretty much all the materials we gave to him. We came up with the schedule and we gave the materials to him before he'd take long plane rides or over the weekend so he had the opportunity to review and digest. We followed up with numerous small group discussions where Stuart, Lanhee and I would meet up with Mitt on the road. We got intimately familiar with the conference rooms in Marriott Courtyards. Over the summer our goal was to get our policy settled and President Obama's policies into his head.

The second thing we did was to make sure that the debates were negotiated fairly. The Romney campaign had Ben Ginsberg negotiating on our side. The Obama campaign had Bob Bauer. In advance of the first meeting, Bob and Ben had spent a long time developing our respective points of view on numerous debate logistics. Ben was loaded for bear. And then Bob and Ben met with the Debate Commission and were presented with a completed Memorandum of Understanding indicating how the debates were going to be. Here's who the moderators are. Here's where the debates are going to be held. Here's everything. Both sides were dissatisfied with that. There were a few points to be determined like coin tosses (LAUGHTER) for who would go first. Where the location of the time clocks would be, whether the candidates would be seated or standing. That was really, at the end, the extent of the debate negotiations. I suspect both sides feel there's a lot of room for improvement on the way the debates are negotiated.

The third thing we did was to develop strategic goals and approaches to the debates that were comfortable for Mitt. In our first meetings in June we began talking about how we would approach the debates, always aware that President Obama's a very good debater. We watched his previous debates. We watched his debates with Hillary Clinton. We watched his debates with John McCain. He is an excellent debater. We also watched all the debates with challengers to seated presidents in past election cycles. We watched the Kerry versus George W. Bush debates. We watched the Clinton versus George H. W. Bush debates. We watched the Reagan versus Carter debate. And we put our ideas together of what we thought were strategies that each of them had employed successfully or unsuccessfully. Mitt watched the tapes too. It was an iterative process.

Fourth, we had a total of 16 mock debates: ten before the first debate, four between debates one and two, and two before the last debate. All of them involved Senator Rob Portman (R-Oh.) as the stand in for President Obama. Rob was thorough, thoughtful, unflinching, and eerily able to channel President Obama. It was kind of scary. Their body types are similar. They're both kind of long, tall guys. If you close your eyes, (LAUGHTER) you could almost imagine Rob had morphed into President Obama during our mock debates. While our policy discussions were held with very few people, we expanded the debate prep group for the mock debates. We got a lot of great input, particularly from the communications team. They were vital in giving us feedback. We kicked off the mock debates at "debate camp," which was held in rural Vermont during the Democratic Convention. Several days before each of the actual debates we did a full dress rehearsal mock debate. We recreated the stage, the seating, the lighting just as it was going to be at the live debates.

The fifth thing we did was develop an offense, an attack on every issue. We understood that particularly in the first and second debates, we had to be aggressive to win. Interestingly, when we had our debate prep at debate camp Mitt was not very good at that. He was very good on the policy. He had studied all summer long and he understood the policy. But he was not consistent in pivoting to offense. So we spent a good portion of September focusing on how to attack and then parry attacks from President Obama on all of the issues.

Sixth, the campaign approached the debates holistically. We looked at late September through mid-October as "debate season." Starting from perhaps a week before the debate until the days after the last debate, our campaign was going to be about the debates. This was understood by our campaign manager, Matt Rhoades, who pretty much put everybody at the disposal of the debate prep team. We all worked as a unit. Communications had pre- and post-debate strategies developed with intense use of surrogates. We had full cooperation from the scheduling department. When we needed more time, they gave it to us. Digital did a full debate build out. No detail was too small. Although for the first debate we did find out that we were at a hotel far away from the debate venue and near a train track that wasn't conducive to restful sleeping for the candidate, which made me a little crazy.

We didn't have our VP selected until early August, so the seventh thing we did over the summer was create a turnkey VP debate prep package so that when that person was selected, everything would be ready to go. We also decided that we would take two of our top campaign team members, Dan Senor and Russ Schriefer, and dedicate them to the Ryan debate prep team.

So those were the seven ways we prepped. Our prep wasn't just mock debates; it was a comprehensive exercise involving the whole campaign team. Now I'll talk in a little greater detail about some of the things I outlined.

Debate Camp. Leading up to the first debate we had a three-day debate camp. In those three days, we conducted five full mock debates. Our dinner discussions were with whiteboards going over pivots and parries. Lots of wine. But those were a pretty serious three days. That's what we did during the Democratic Convention. Paul Ryan was out there on the stump, but Mitt was out only once during the three days. Following debate camp we had thirteen additional sessions including five more mock debates between the convention and the first debate. The Univision forum, which fell in the middle of that window, was good live practice and we thought Mitt did really well there. We were very happy. We saw a lot of the prep that we had done in debate show through in the Univision forum.

Focus. All the distractions that occurred in September made it tough for us to keep focus on the necessary prep. But we were very disciplined. We did not blow up Mitt's schedule. We stayed very focused on the debate. Stuart started traveling with Mitt. Others of us met up with them all over the country. It was a crazy time for all of us. But as I said, we stayed very disciplined. We also needed to devise our debate strategies for dealing with the "September issues"—the 47 percent video and Benghazi. We suspected that that would be a bit part of the first debate, although that ended up not being so. But we were very ready for it.

Clearly defined debate goals. During the many, many primaries debates, we found it very helpful to articulate specific goals for each debate. We did this a week or so out. Our goals for the debates may surprise you. Our first goal for the Denver debate was to articulate a credible vision for job creation and economic growth. That's not really a surprise. Second, we wanted to present the case against Obama as a choice, in a way that was fresh in both policy and phraseology. What specifically you get with Obama versus what you get with Romney. The third goal [was] to speak to women. Not women's issues per se. But to speak as a husband or a father or friend. Speak to issues as you would around the kitchen table. We thought the Obama campaign had done a superb job of this during the entire campaign. We really encouraged Mitt to start thinking that way and to talk as if he was talking around a kitchen table and not before an audience of tens of millions of people. We also wanted to make the series of debates an ongoing conversation between the candidates and the voters. We knew that we weren't going to win the election at the first debate. What we wanted to do was open a discussion.

The debates begin. In the final few days before the Denver debate we felt really good about things because Mitt was relaxed. We knew he felt prepared. We knew he felt ready to go on stage. The last day all we did was work on a closing statement. His family came to Denver. They watched movies. His sons were there. Ann was there. They ordered take out and hung out in the suite and made each other laugh. We felt pretty good about that because we know that Mitt is at his best when he's relaxed.

At the Denver debate, it was clear in the first minutes that Mitt was in command of his material and was on a roll, in a groove. He stayed consistent throughout. The president was defensive. The strategies that came together, I think, worked better for our candidate in that particular debate. Mitt did what he needed to do—he changed the equilibrium of the race. Going into that debate, we were at a disadvantage. Coming out of that debate, we were not. The coverage was near consensus that Mitt had won the debate. We saw immediately in our crowds in the days after

Denver that the entire feel of the race was very different. Our fund-raisers were energized. The Denver debate really helped the campaign in so many ways. Before the debate, we had had some concerns about funding the media at the level that we knew we needed. That problem really resolved itself after Mitt's stellar debate performance. In our track-ing, Mitt's image was at its strongest point after the debate. Interestingly enough, our numbers also showed that Obama stayed the same. The movement was similar in the info flow. Mitt's shifted a positive 22 points. And Obama's information flow directly after the debate was slightly neg-ative. My takeaway is that this was really more of a positive for Mitt than a negative for the president, although he was taken to task by his base and by the media for not coming with guns loaded.

The next event was the VP debate. I don't have too much to say on that other than that Vice President Biden's supercharged presentation gave us a sense of just how seriously the president would be coming at us in the Town Hall debate. In the run up to the Hofstra debate, we conducted four mock Town Hall debates. All the stages were built to scale. The reason we did so many mocks in such a short period of time was primarily to get Mitt accustomed to the geography of walking around that stage with the audience so close. When we watched the clips from 2008, we observed how President Obama was masterful at the Town Hall format. He didn't just answer the questions; he really owned the stage. We worked really hard on getting Mitt comfortable coming up out of the chair, walking around, not getting too close to the people where it was kind of creepy but (LAUGHTER) not too far back. Believe it or not, there is a geography (LAUGHTER) to that stage.

So we built several models of the stage in several cities. And our advance team was great. Senator Portman was extremely helpful in iden-tifying the range of audience questions. When you're getting questions from a live audience Lord only knows what's going to come off the floor. And so whenever we were doing our mock debates, we always had one or two crazy questions. Mitt seemed to really like answering them. He really got into that. He'd say, "I hope I get that question." We'd respond, "I don't think you're going to get that. That's just the sort of question that we didn't think you'd know the answer to. But you han-dled it well."

Our goals for the second debate were very different from the first. Our first goal was "Just do it like you did on the last one." The second goal was to meet the attacks from the president head on. We knew they were coming. We didn't want to seem as if Mitt was stepping back. Walk into it. The third goal was don't simply answer the question, speak to the questioner. And fourth, make the contrast on the big issues. You'll get a lot of questions. You can answer those. But make sure when you get a big question on the debt, on Obamacare, on taxes, on certain foreign policy issues, that you make the contrast on those issues. That was very important. At the Town Hall debate at Hofstra, the president had a strong, more aggressive debate. [He] had a strategy and clearly executed on it. Mitt was solid. Although his answer on why Barack Obama didn't deserve a second term was very strong, I think his answers were less consistent at that debate. The president scored some points on taxes in the second debate that he was unable to score in the first one. My personal opinion, that the only gaffe was made by the moderator who gave the president an extra four minutes, forgot to give Mitt a rebuttal twice, and did your job for you, Brooks, by doing a fact check in the middle of the debate.

Final debate: every campaign should get to spend three days in Boca Raton during the home stretch. This debate at Lynn University was on foreign policy. Over the course of the summer, we had not done as much foreign policy briefing as we had on the domestic issues because we knew that everything could be changed by the time of the debate. And we were right: there were a lot of new developments on the foreign policy front. The week leading up to the foreign policy debate. Benghazi, which hadn't even existed over the summer, was a huge issue. Iran and Israel both had a lot of moving parts. So we had intense policy discussions during that week. We squeezed in two mock debates in Florida. But we spent most of the time that we were together in the six days between the last two debates going over foreign policy.

Mitt was a lot less aggressive in the last debate. We had four goals. The first was to reassure American voters of his knowledge and competence as commander-in-chief. Second was not taking the bait and going into areas in which it was easy for the president to demonstrate his strength and knowledge as commander-in-chief. Third, look for first downs not touchdowns. The fourth was pull in the economy wherever possible. Mitt didn't buy into that fourth goal. He didn't think that was going to be easy to do in this debate. So our goals were very different from those in the first debate, and we took some heat for not going after the president aggressively enough, on Benghazi in particular. But we felt very good after the third debate. An analysis by Rick Klein (ABC News) said, "In a debate about who should be commander-in-chief, Mitt Romney was just as much in command as the man in the job now. President Obama came into the debate with a record to boast of and he used it to play offense. . . . But Romney also had a strong debate in pursuing different goals than the president. He sought to come across as reasonable rather than confrontational—a candidate comfortable with the campaign's trajectory."[1] So while we may not have satisfied the folks who wanted us to get in the president's face and attack him on the controversial issues on foreign policy, we felt that Mitt had accomplished his goal of presenting himself as a strong leader and a commander-in-chief.

The final pre- and post-debate numbers on the president's image and info flow didn't change that much after the first debate. We found the same thing after the third. Mitt's info flow and his image improved significantly in the ballot and our numbers closed a bit too. So we felt very satisfied that the debate season did for our campaign what it needed to do.

The lessons learned? Some candidates aren't going to be as amenable to putting in as much time as Mitt did during the campaign—there are many, many other demands on their time. But for this candidate, it was important to start early. It was worth committing the necessary time and resources. It's a pain in the neck and it takes away from other things, but important. Second, debate prep doesn't happen in a vacuum. Do the work that you can do early. Be ready to be flexible to prepare other things that pop up—for us the 47 percent video—later in the run up to the debates. Develop a solid line of attack on every issue. Our most effective strategy was that we didn't let anything lie. We picked up the sword on every issue.

Small group sessions work better for policy discussions and the structuring of the answers. It's a temptation on a campaign to have a lot of people be involved in debate prep. That sometimes was counterproductive. The number of voices heard by the candidate should be as few as possible on game day. I tried to make sure that for the last couple hours before the debate, Mitt really was alone with just Stuart. We really tried to keep as few people from getting in Mitt's head in the last minutes. Finally, no detail is too small. And all the facts that you put before the candidate better darn well be right. It's as if the candidates are standing up on that stage naked. And if they use the wrong facts and the opponent comes back and says, "No, that's not right," which is what happened in the second debate regarding the President's comments on Benghazi in the Rose Garden, then that can be very problematic for your campaign. A small factual error can magnify.

Anita Dunn

Anita Dunn, *a managing director of SKDK, has previously served as a senior communications strategist for President Barack Obama for both his campaign and the transition to the White House. As White House Communications Director, she directed both conventional and new media operations. As Senior Adviser to the Obama campaign, Dunn was responsible for the strategic direction and management of Communications, Research and Policy. She has advised a wide*

Anita Dunn

range of other national political leaders. In 2001–2002, she served as senior Political Advisor to Senate Democratic Leader Tom Daschle, as well as consultant to the Senate Democratic Caucus when they gained the majority. Among other Senate representations, she has developed strategy and produced the media campaign for Senator Evan Bayh, who won reelection in 2004 with the highest percentage of support in recent history. In the House of Representatives, Dunn has advised Speaker of the House Nancy Pelosi and also served as chief strategist and media consultant to senior Democratic embers facing challenging reelection battles.

So that was fascinating for me to listen to because I've been involved in debate preps for other campaigns as well. What is really interesting is how similar our processes are. But you got much more time than we ever did. I just have to say that. (LAUGHTER) And it wasn't just because you didn't have a day job the way the president did.

As a preface, I'm going to go back to 2008. In 2008 we did not have difficult general election debates. The first [2008] general election debate, which was supposed to be foreign policy but then ended up having domestic policy added to it right at the beginning because the economy had collapsed that week. Some of you may recall [that because] Senator McCain said he was suspending his campaign to go back to Washington to try to get the TARP bill passed, it wasn't clear there would be a debate. There was all this drama. The first debate was supposed to be foreign policy, which was the one thing the commission had let us agree to back then, [but] it ended up being half domestic policy because of the economic meltdown. We were facing a Republican nominee who had spent, as far as I can tell, maybe 15 minutes preparing for the debate. The McCain campaign was nothing if not spontaneous in many respects. He was open about the fact that he didn't like to prepare. [Senator McCain] clearly had not prepared and didn't go in with a strategy. Candidate Obama went in with a strategy and did a very good job in what was supposed to be his toughest debate, foreign policy.

The second, the Town Hall debate, was one where, again, I think Obama was very prepared. It was the best of the three, in my opinion. McCain had not spent the time even on just the geography of the stage. You saw him chasing around. It was a poor debate for him. By the time the third one rolled around, which was supposedly the domestic policy debate, there was so much water under the bridge I think the viewership had dropped rather dramatically [Nielsen estimate of 59.2 million].

So fast forward. Governor Romney's had 20 debates. Whether they're candidate forums or debates, he's been on a stage. He's had to deal with it. He's had to prepare. On the other hand, Barack Obama has been the President of the United States for four years at this point [and] incumbent presidents historically don't always do very well in their first debate. If you go back and look at the polling after the Bush-Kerry 2004 first debate, you'll see Kerry clearly won the first debate. And it gave Kerry's campaign a bit of a boost. In 2000 Gore, who was a semi-incumbent, versus Bush in the first debate lost. [Governor G. W.] Bush over-performed expectations. [Vice President Al] Gore had a few exaggeration-size eye rolls and told one anecdote that turned out not to be 100 percent factually true, which the Bush campaign used against him. So he lost. [President G. H. W.] Bush 1992 versus Clinton. Bush lost. Just out of touch. In a race in which he won 49 states, [President Ronald] Reagan lost the first debate against [Vice President Walter] Mondale. And of course, [President Jimmy] Carter 1980 versus [Governor Ronald] Reagan, a disaster. The one, the only, the bad debate.

Challengers win those first debates, in many respects, when they walk on stage. For the first time, most of the time, they have the same stature as the President of the United States. Suddenly, they seem more presidential, just because they're there. Challengers [also] have been campaigning full time. Honing their arguments and answers for 18 months. It's hard to underestimate the value this has. Whether you have been in 20 forums or 18, you've had to go in front of groups. You've had to talk to people. You've had to do four or five events a day. You've had to be out there. Whether or not you've been accessible to the press, you're still answering questions all the time. You're answering questions from donors, you're answering questions and doing a lot of give and take. Your campaign messages are far more ingrained in you. Presidents have a very time-consuming day job governing the country. They tend to have a lot going on besides preparing for the debate. And they have not been on the campaign trail as long. And so they don't have the same level of automatic preparedness when it comes to some of the answers within their message frames.

Challengers do have the advantage of debates during primaries. In 2008, we had at least 15 of these during the primaries.

MALE VOICE:

Oh, like, 22.

ANITA DUNN

Something like 22.

We went through this process, too, with a large field and then a shrinking field and then several one-on-ones with Senator Clinton, who was quite formidable. It is a huge advantage. It does force a degree of preparation. And then finally if you look at the list of presidents or semi-presidents such as Gore who have lost their first debates, they've been making really tough decisions for four years. And sometimes that means it is hard for them to take themselves out of their presidential mode and put themselves back in the candidate mode. Which [requires] a very different kind of answer. So presidents tend to have difficult times in their first debate. Now fortunately, first debates are never [with the exception of Carter in 1980] last debates.

If you look at the spectrum, presidents tend to have poor first debates and then get dramatically better. It's almost as if they get their wakeup call or get back in the saddle. But this was a very real concern for us. You know, Governor Romney was not John McCain. We'd watched him in 2008 when he was running for the nomination. A very disciplined, very smart, and very effective debater. We watched him throughout the primary process. He went in with a strategy and would execute the strategy. He's very articulate. He's very smart. He understood his issues. He was a very good debater. In a couple of really critical times during the primaries in 2012, when it looked as though he was in trouble, he had really gone in there and just blown away his opponents in debates, which is something that's very rare in the primary process. So we had a very, very healthy level of respect. We knew he was disciplined. We knew he worked very, very hard. We knew he went in well-prepared, well-rehearsed, with a clear strategy. We also knew he was a great salesman. It's what he had done. He was good at convincing people of things.

So we had a healthy degree of concern around overall preparation and a huge expectations problem which had to do with the fact that the president is a very, very effective communicator in some formats. Beth, I appreciated your kind words about his debating ability. But I think if he were standing here, he would say it's not his preferred format. There are lots of things he likes better. He had this image with the American people of being a great communicator. In terms of the expectations, we felt that the press was going to score the two candidates very differently. There are two phases to any debate. There's the debate itself and then there is the press interpretation after the debate. You can win a debate and lose the press coverage. If you ask Al Gore about a few of his debates, he'll tell you that. So we were very concerned about the fact that the press would score the two candidates differently. We felt that Romney would be scored on a basic likeability factor. Now, we'll come to his September in a minute. He was aggressive without being nasty.

Sometimes during the primary debates, Romney would get overly aggressive, which I'm sure that they had worked with him on, and cross that line to unlikeable. We knew that that was one of the things he'd be scored on. He'd [also] be scored on whether he could articulate a plan for the future. It was actually the single biggest strategic goal for both campaigns. And we had the same one. We too wanted to articulate a plan for the economic future and [indicate] how our economic approach would create jobs and strengthen the middle class from the middle out as opposed to the top down. We also felt that a strategic goal on their part would be to see if they could get under the president's skin a few times to try to evoke that snappish, peevish moment that you sometimes saw with presidents in first debates. You certainly saw it with [President George W.] Bush in 2004 when [Democratic nominee Senator] John Kerry got under his skin on foreign policy and he got very snappish. "How dare you do that?" So we felt that would be a strategic goal as well.

For the president, we felt he would be scored on whether he got pulled down into a kind of tit-for-tat schoolyard brawl or whether he could rise above that. We felt that he would be scored on whether he sounded patronizing or condescending. That that was something the press was actively looking for. And if you go back and you look at the press coverage leading up to the first debate, they were all writing, "We want to see if he's going to be condescending and patronizing." They told us what they were going to score him on. Most importantly, was he going to be effective at articulating and communicating his vision for the future, his plan to grow the American economy. And could he do that effectively in contrast with the Romney plan. That was where we put the bulk of our preparations time.

We, too, began earlier. We began earlier than we began in 2008. Both sides use the same iterative process. You start with the thick notebook and it gets smaller and smaller. And hopefully by the day of the debate, it's one page. But we did not start that process until the end of August in 2008. We started it much earlier this time. The president does read his notebooks as well and comes back with some very, very, very detailed questions. This time, we didn't have to spend as much time, obviously, on issues. He's been president for four years. He knows his record and he certainly has a deep understanding of issues. What he didn't know and what he hadn't followed was the Republican campaign. He was not as familiar with the day-to-day stuff that was being said about him on the stump by Governor Romney and with the overall issues as they were framed against him. He really needed to be brought up to speed on Romney's record and also on the arguments Romney was using against him. We actually spent the bulk of our time during the summer on getting him up to speed on Governor Romney.

Expectations for the first debate became more problematic, due to the Romney campaign's problems in September. As a matter of fact, one can look at September as a brilliant expectations-lowering exercise on the part of the Romney campaign, beginning with their convention (LAUGHTER) and all of the memorable moments from that. Going right into the Benghazi issues. And then culminating with the 47 percent tape, which played almost continually for the three weeks after it was released. Parts of it were looped over and over again. The dominant image of Mitt Romney throughout September was him talking about the 47 percent of the people in this country. To say they lowered voter expectations around these debates, that these issues did, would be an understatement. We saw it in our own research. We saw it in our focus groups, where people would get asked who they thought was going to win the debate. According to Gallup on October 2nd 57/33 people thought that Barack Obama would win that debate.

JOEL BENENSON:

The best thing they ever said about us.

ANITA DUNN:

So voter expectations were that Mitt Romney would probably stand up and in his opening answer insult half the country. We felt that was a pretty darn low bar at that point for Governor Romney, who we knew was going to come in and do a good job. Now I'm going to quote a few notable people who are in this room right now, as an example of the degree to which campaigns at that point were frantically trying to lower expectations for themselves and raise them for the other person. Beth Myers said, "Obama's widely regarded as one of the most talented political communicators in history." And Stephanie Cutter said, "We're coming into this debate very realistic that Mitt Romney's likely to win if he plays his cards right." And I think [Obama-Biden Campaign traveling press secretary] Jen Psaki actually at one point said, "The president's just really bad at this." At one point, we actually said, "People, let's pull back a little on running down of the President of the United States."

Then the final thing that we took into account was that we felt from a press and an overall narrative perspective, the press was dying to write the Romney comeback story at that point. They'd been writing "Romney's down, Romney's down, Romney's terrible, Romney had a bad convention, Romney this, Romney that" for six weeks. In modern politics, you just can't sustain. I mean, they get bored with writing, "You guys are winning, you guys are winning, you guys are winning." We felt everything in the press dynamic was gearing toward the Romney comeback, which he could accomplish simply by standing up and not insulting 47 percent of the Americans in the country. So we felt that the perfect storm was brewing. In addition to that, the choice was being defined so much more dramatically than it had been in July when we started serious debate prep. Our strategic memo from July had said one of our goals is to really make this a choice and not let Romney keep this a referendum. [After the two conventions], it was very much a choice about the two visions moving forward.

As a strategic team, we felt that the president really is a great communicator who is at his strongest when he's talking to the American people directly about what he believes, about the joint journey we're on, about the country he thinks we can be, about why he does what he does, why he's made these decisions and what he wants to get done for the people of this country, for the families of this country. We felt that was the person who could rise above whatever Romney would be throwing at him.

So our counsel to him was probably less engagement than you saw in the second and third debates. As it turns out, given the Romney strategy, it ended up being an interesting debate in the sense that the president didn't make a mistake. He didn't commit a gaffe. He didn't do anything wrong. And frankly, his answers are pretty good. If you go back and read the transcript you think, "This isn't such a bad debate. Why did everyone get so hysterical?"

It's still a pretty darn good question because as Beth pointed out, even in their own data he didn't lose any ground, really. Romney made up a lot of ground. But the first debate ended up being a strategy where we probably counseled less engagement than we should have, with a very excellent, well-executed performance by Romney. One thing we had not expected was that he [Governor Romney] would totally walk away from his tax plan and say that he wasn't going to give tax cuts to the upper 1 percent. We had plenty of video, 18 months of tax cuts for everyone being his policy. And that the people at the top tier are the job creators. If you don't give them more money, how are they going to create jobs? We had plenty of material where he had said that on tape during Republican primary debates and other times. So what the president was not prepared to hear was that he [Governor Romney] actually wasn't cutting taxes for the top 1 percent plus a few other things that he said in the course of the debate, in particular that his health care plan would cover preexisting conditions, which is not true, and his outsourcing comments.

We listened to MSNBC the moment it ended with people screaming at us about how terrible it was. It wasn't like we didn't know what was going on. We had dial groups too. But we also felt that in terms of the overall press coverage the next day that we'd been left a significant opening from the Governor around issues that were important to us. Particularly around trust and around whose side he really was on and whether he was leveling with the American people. We'd already laid some ground on [those issues] during the summer. So the first debate was not a good debate. We lost it. Now, the press, which had been wanting to write the comeback story, went overboard. So, "historic loss." "A Romney surge."

Of course, the reality, as Joel will probably mention when he talks about our polling, is that we didn't collapse. We didn't lose [ground]. It wasn't a surge. Romney helped himself, particularly on attributes, a lot in this campaign. He did a very good job. He did show up as the person that I like to think of as Massachusetts Mitt, the pragmatic, problem-solving governor, as opposed to right wing, "I have to win the primaries" Mitt. And because of that, that was a Romney that people really hadn't seen a lot of. He was a very attractive candidate. For many of the American people who had not been following all this stuff closely, this is really the first extended time they'd watched him. So it was a very good debate for him. In our opinion and in Joel's data, it didn't move a lot of voters. It didn't change the dynamic out there. In the press briefing the next morning David Plouffe encountered 10,000 questions about "Don't you suck? Didn't you lose the race tonight?" Which is kind of the level of press coverage these days, the kind of thoughtful analysis that you get after an event. "Aren't you guys terrible? How come you didn't raise the 47 percent?" Oh, you think they weren't prepared for that? At the end of it, Plouffe basically said, "We don't think anything structurally is changing. And we would just humbly request," and those were his words, "Humbly request that some of you actually go look at states like Iowa and Ohio and New Hampshire and see if anything has really changed structurally. Because it hasn't." Which was the truth. It didn't affect anything.

So if you look at the campaign and the three levels of narrative on the campaign, as Stephanie outlined in her presentation, you had the national press narrative, which was driven primarily by bad polling. You had the battleground state narrative, which was the same thing we'd seen in 2008 when we were doing fake cable ads to drive that national narrative. But the battleground narrative is very different. It's where campaigns are spending 3,000 points a week on television. It's where all of the super PACs are playing. It's where the organizers are. It's where 130 field offices exist for us. It's where everything is actually going to be won or lost. And the battleground narrative was very different. Because people knew a lot more in the battleground states. [They] had an enormous amount of information from our campaign, from their campaign, more from our campaign, quite frankly. And we really did not see a lot of changes in the battleground states because frankly, a lot of voters had made up their minds about both these candidates a long time ago.

The third level of narrative, which was what our campaign was putting out, and what Stephanie's unbelievably brilliant and effective shop was doing, was very much focused around the places where we felt that the governor had not been, shall we say, entirely candid. I think the fact that the Romney campaign had to go into the press room right after the debate to say he actually isn't covering preexisting conditions gave us a great opening with the press. We drove that outsourcing and the tax thing very, very hard to help set up [the Biden-Ryan debate]. In 2008 the vice president had the toughest debate. The debate against [Republican vice presidential nominee Alaska Governor] Sarah Palin was probably the one thing that could've dramatically changed the dynamic of our race. He worked his tail off [in 2008]. He worked his tail off again this time. But his race against Paul Ryan didn't have the same dramatic intensity that his debate against Sarah Palin did. Having said that, he did a great job. He went in there and did exactly what our supporters needed, which was basically standing up and pushing back. And everyone was very energized.

[Vice President Biden's debate performance] really did help set the table for the Town Hall meeting. The conventional wisdom about Town Hall meetings, of course, is that you can't do contrast in them. If you go back and read some of the coverage leading up, [it says] "People in the Hall don't wanna hear negativity." No, the people in the Hall want facts, as both candidates knew. They want facts that serve larger points, that drive their arguments. They don't want gratuitous nasty, negative stuff. But you should never have your candidate delivering that stuff anyway. So we went into the Town Hall debate with a very different strategy from the first one. We did feel that we needed to engage directly much more. We felt it was the president's strongest format. He had done beautifully in 2008 in the Town Hall. He's great when he's with people. That is where he's a great communicator. He loves to talk to people. He likes to communicate to people. So he went in with a strategy that he was not going to allow Romney to misrepresent his record or the Obama [administration] record.

There were certain places in particular that were very important to us. In particular, taxes and health care. There were certain offensive places where we felt Romney's record was either all over the map or gave us huge opportunities. In particular, college loans, higher education, education at any level. He'd been all over the map in the Republican proposal to cut student loans [and his plan to] cut Pell Grants was so unpopular. So we went in there with an offensive strategy that we had not had in the first debate. And the president, of course, was very good, very effective. Very good at talking with people. Comfortable in the Town Hall. And then at the end, of course, the fact that Governor Romney made a factual error that not only did the moderator catch, but the president [caught as well]. Go back and look at the tape, [when] he says, "Continue," or (LAUGHTER) whatever he said. But, like, "Dig your hole deeper, Governor." He was very prepared for Benghazi and he was very prepared for the attack. If you go back and you look at the polling, you will see that the president was seen to win that debate. It did not change the national narrative, which said "Yes, he won. But we still think there's this huge surge for Romney." Which was fine, but we were seeing in our data that everything was holding firm. And so I think there was a high degree of comfort. And the metrics on the ground in particular were great.

The third debate was one where we wanted an outright win and we felt we could get our outright win because it was foreign policy. We remembered from 2008 how terrible it is, having to bring a challenger up to speed for a foreign policy debate where, you know, wonder if Africa comes in or some issue that you haven't studied. [With an incumbent] it's just very different. You've been the president. You've gotten a daily briefing every morning for four years. You've been in the Sit[uation] Room. You have done these things. Plus, the president's record in foreign policy is so exceptionally strong. He kept his word to end the Iraq war. The troops are coming home from Afghanistan. We led on Libya. He had a very strong record. He looked forward to having that discussion.

As we went through our debate preps we did mocks, although nowhere near as many as yours. It became clear that this was not a place where Romney was going to engage with us. The debate included six topic areas. The only one we felt potentially he might come on aggressively was Libya, Benghazi because the Republicans had been making so much noise. It was very clear that this was a losing proposition for him [Governor Romney] in terms of the debate. So we felt that that was all the more reason to be aggressive. Because at the end of the day, commander-in-chief is the number one thing people expect from a president, to keep America safe. And so the president went in with a very aggressive strategy of things he wanted to accomplish. And we did feel that part of their strategy for this one would be to try to take it back to the domestic policy and economic policy as much as possible.

National security, at the end of the day, depends on your economic security. That was Romney's sweet spot as opposed to having to defend either the Republican overall foreign policy from the last eight years, which is still very unpopular in this country, or defend some of the statements he had made in the course of 2008 and then [in] his primary campaign in 2012. That was something we were looking forward to. So the president won the final debate decisively.

I'll make three quick points to wrap up. One is that we think the final debate actually did matter. If you look at polls and you look at late deciders, we actually believe that debate mattered. We watched Romney in the final debate. To quote the president, I felt like, "Hey, Governor, Denver's calling, it wants its first debate strategy back." We were like, (LAUGHTER) "Come on, why did you steal our bad strategy? You had a much better one for the other two." But the lesson from the debates in one line is, if you're not on offense, you're on defense. It's that simple. Anybody who's going to be involved in this in 2016, if you're not on offense, you're on defense. You will lose. It's that simple.

Memorable moments from the debates. Big Bird. Which I think Stephanie's shop did a great job with. Binders of women, which exploded on Twitter. Exploded. Twitter gave us a lot of guidance as to what we wanted to drive in terms of the press coming out of the debate. And it let us reopen the entire discussion around women and attitudes around women, which involved much more than contraception. The Benghazi moment, obviously, from the second debate was very critical. And then the "horses and bayonets" [comment] got a lot of attention on both sides but did crystallize that the president was going to stand up and be tough, which people needed to see. The final thing I'll say is that the debates were in bad locations. Two were in swing states. The Town Hall that actually had audience participation was in New York. A state—how much did we win New York by?

JOEL BENENSON:

Doesn't matter. (LAUGHTER)

ANITA DUNN:

Let's put it this way, we won it by a lot. The Town Hall debate was in New York on Long Island. It was in a very Democratic area. It was difficult to find undecided voters. Stuart talked this morning about [why] the networks shouldn't sponsor debates. I think the fact that the commission chooses the dates of these things [is a problem]. Who ever thought it was a great idea to have the final debate so close to the general election? We were given dates, we were given locations. Also, why wouldn't you have a town hall meeting in a swing state, as opposed to a state that has voted reliably Democratic? It's the same thing if we were doing a town hall meeting in Utah. Doesn't make a lot of sense. I would hope for the future that everybody rethinks the entire [general election] debate process in terms of locations, formats, moderators. Everything should be on the table.

BETH MYERS:

When you were preparing and looking mostly at our materials, what materials did you look at? How did you prepare for that?

ANITA DUNN:

Well, we had those big binders. Lugging them around was probably the source of your cracked ribs. (LAUGHTER) The first materials that went into the president were basic issue notebooks. Here's what the administration's done on these issues. Here are some of the Republican attacks. They were not as Romney-specific. Here are the top 15 issues that we know will be the centerpiece of these debates. And here's everything you need to know about what your administration's done. Here's what you need to know about the other side.

The second set of materials were the Romney materials. And they were very, very detailed: his quotes, his positions, where applicable, congressional positions. Once Ryan got picked, we did start imputing a lot of Ryan positions to Governor Romney just because he bought him. The second piece was the Romney record. That was very substantial. The president had a DVD of Romney clips from primaries, both good and bad. We showed him a little of [the debate against] Senator [Edward] Kennedy. We showed the president much less video than you showed Governor Romney. But we did send the [1980] Carter/Reagan debate home with him. We felt that was a model for what you might try to do, get him very into defending every detail of every program he'd ever done. We felt that presidents naturally fall into wanting to defend what they've done. One of the things we saw with incumbent presidents is that they see that first debate as the vindication debate.

BETH MYERS:

We were happy with the order, with the economy coming first and foreign policy coming last because we had the same thought that you did. Foreign policy and the commander-in-chief role were from the get go very hard for a challenger to impute. We were happy that we didn't have to do that first. Would you have preferred that the debate [topic] you were strongest on be first? Should the debates be mixed up? Should there be a foreign policy debate? An economic debate? What do you think?

ANITA DUNN:

It's a great question. I think we were perfectly happy to have domestic policy first. We thought it should be our debate. And he had an off night. We didn't have a great strategy. Your guy had a great night and you had a great strategy. But we felt that should be a great debate for us. One of the things that Joel's polling consistently showed is that when you tested those two messages, our message of what we felt was the way to grow this economy for the middle class and to move forward versus Governor Romney's message, we won. So we actually embraced this. We felt that if we went out there and effectively delivered that message and drew the contrast, it was a winning argument for us with the voters we care about. So we were fine with that. I think from our campaign perspective, [and] I suspect with yours, [the fact that] the timing of these debates knocked out two of the four weekends in October for campaigning was just crazy.

BETH MYERS:

Right.

ANITA DUNN:

Yeah.

BETH MYERS:

And in the case of the middle one, in a state that really neither of us cared to be in.

ANITA DUNN:

Yes.

I am interested in what the thought process was for the Ryan debate because I felt that was a very defensive debate on his part. We had expected him to be more aggressive.

BETH MYERS:

Because that came between debate number one and debate number two, I only attended a couple of his debate preps, but I was not expecting the Joe Biden that showed up. At the time, I thought it was a bad strategy to be as over the top as he was. But I don't think he paid a price for being as, "super-charged" would be the word I'd use.

ANITA DUNN:

Energetic.

BETH MYERS:

Energetic. (LAUGHTER) And he got a lot of benefits from energizing the base.

BETH MYERS:

Absolutely.

BETH MYERS:

I think if we watch that debate a year from now, everyone'll say, "Really? That guy looks really crazy." But it was probably the right approach at that moment, kudos for contemplating it. And Vice President Biden actually pulled it off. I thought that SNL's (LAUGHTER) skit was actually very, very funny for both. Paul had a very good night that night. He was encountering a guy that was not what he expected. They had run a whole range of personas that were going to come. That was not the persona that they expected.

ANITA DUNN:

Interesting.

BETH MYERS:

He [Republican vice presidential nominee Representative Paul Ryan] was a young candidate. He needed to show that he was serious, that he could stand up to the Vice President of the United States and not get outgunned—it's interesting that you say he was defensive. You probably think he was more defensive than I did. But he had some tough issues to stand up to. And I think he did a good job, particularly on Medicare.

ANITA DUNN:

We felt that, in particular, the exchange at the end around choice and a woman's right to choose was, first of all, the Vice President was terrific on that. But we felt that was actually something that, coming out of the debate, was extraordinarily useful to us, to bring that entire issue back. We saw these things holistically. As how do they play into our overall campaign strategy.

BETH MYERS:

Somebody asked me at a forum that I did a few weeks ago what I regretted most in our campaign. I regretted not going a little bit more crazy about your spring campaign focused on women. Now, we could've done it differently. We did not engage on women's issues early enough, in my opinion. We gave you free rein to talk to the women of America. And to frame it to them, particularly in the states you were advertising in. On the three levels of communication, particularly on that second level, where in the battleground states you were able to address the women in the collar counties and in swing counties. By the time we got to the debates, it was very important that we talk to women and that Mitt hone his communication skills to them. Women receive information in a different way than men do. That was an important thing for him to do. Perhaps Paul Ryan didn't hit a home run on addressing that issue. But I think he did a superb job given the amount of time he had to prepare for the role. Four years ago, that was the toughest debate. And—

ANITA DUNN:

Oh, absolutely.

BETH MYERS:

The attention paid to this year's VP debate wasn't as much as was paid four years ago.

ANITA DUNN:

I know Stuart said there was some sensitivity around Bright Horizons. First of all, I was remiss in not saying that Ron Klain, who has done debate prep and managed it and is brilliant and one of the smartest people in the world, was a driving member of the team. And that Karen Dunn, my sister—not really, has a child at Bright Horizons and was a critical member of the debate team. She kept saying, "I'm surprised he doesn't use Bright Horizons more." 'Cause we felt that was—

MALE VOICE:

Bright Horizons is what?

ANITA DUNN:

Bright Horizons is child care. And, you know—defensive.

BETH MYERS:

A fabulous child care model.

Anita Dunn:

—it would've been a wonderful, Bain thing for him to be able to talk to women about. So I don't know what—

Beth Myers:

We always talked about it. I think there was sensitivity there to being pulled into a controversy. We talked to a lot of the business owners from Bain. Bright Horizons is a nursery school. They really didn't want to be—

Anita Dunn:

Yeah, political.

Beth Myers:

They didn't want to be a political football. We respected that. Some people such as Tom Stemberg from Staples [said], "Fine, you can use this example all you want." The Bright Horizons people never, ever said, "Don't use our name." We used it all the time. We talked about it all the time.

Male Voice:

They were Democrats.

Beth Myers:

They were hands off. A lot of the Bain companies said that. "We don't want to do this."

Anita Dunn:

That's interesting.

Anita Dunn:

Which is exactly what Stephanie told me.

Anita Dunn:

Well—

ANITA DUNN:

The deal I'd cut with Stephanie, which turned out to be a great deal, was that I would do the debates from Chicago and run the communications back there. (LAUGHTER) And she had to go do TV in Denver. I was really happy we'd cut that deal. (LAUGHTER) For the first debate, we had Axe and we had Plouffe and we had Stephanie. And we had Messina. We had senior campaign people. Debbie Wasserman Schultz. But Stephanie afterwards came back and said, "Never again." She said, "We are so seriously outgunned."I said we were fighting Twitter wars, we're doing this, we're doing that. And she said, "It's the foreign press. There're just not enough of us." The reason we had cut back was that in our experience in 2008, the spin room was labor intensive and expensive to get people there.

Nobody really wanted to talk to them that much and they didn't influence the stories. Even in 2008, the stories were being written so much more real time, based on what people were getting. What influenced the stories much more were, (1) the instant polls, and (2) what you chose to pick up and drive out of the debates, which is why both sides produced ads. We got that video out right away. So if we just take away the foreign press credentials, (LAUGHTER) we don't have to do a spin room.

ANITA DUNN:

For the Obama people—

ANITA DUNN:

—to get there in the first—

ANITA DUNN:

—debate.

ANITA DUNN:

Right. So in the second debate, Stephanie brilliantly made sure all our surrogates got there before it ended, as a sign of how well we thought we'd done. And there were stories about that.

Note

1. Analysis by Rick Klein on the ABC News blog "The Note," October 23, 2012.

Chapter 5
Vice Presidential Selection

JOEL BENENSON:

[On] the selection of Ryan, I always assumed that Governor Romney really wanted someone he had a high comfort level with and that you may or may not have assumed that we were going to make you wear the Republican Party Ryan budget positions anyway. And when I heard that—

BETH MYERS:

We had already supported it.

JOEL BENENSON:

You had supported it. He'd said it was fabulous or marvelous, whatever the word was. Was there any consideration of trying to create distance from that position as you went into the fall? Because at the time you picked it that Saturday night, I was actually betting on one of the other two finalists. And I wondered, are they just making a decision here to double down because they're already there and they figure we're going to make them own that [the Ryan budget] anyway?

BETH MYERS:

As everyone from the Romney team here can attest, Mitt made this decision and kept his counsel very close. He gave two simple criteria: someone who's immediately qualified to be president and someone whose background is not going to create such a distraction that the campaign would derail. He wanted to make his selection from a choice of qualified candidates. So we gave him a number of dossiers of people who met both qualifications and who would've been excellent VPs. He then asked everybody their opinions. In part of the dossiers were narratives.

He was well aware that the narrative of Paul Ryan would be precisely what it was. That the focus would be on the Ryan plan that he'd endorsed. But he always felt that the Ryan plan wasn't the Romney plan. We would never run away from it and he would embrace it and I think we handled it, as Eric talked about in in his section, in a very proactive and a very confident way. The narrative of the Romney/Ryan candidacy certainly included that. That was a hurdle and a challenge but also had some advantages in that we were able, for the first time as a party, to seriously talk about entitlement issues. While it may have seemed an interesting or controversial pick, Mitt wasn't that concerned about it. In the primary, I remember he came back from Wisconsin and he just said, "Gosh, that Paul—." He really liked Paul Ryan. That was a huge part of his decision making.

JIM MARGOLIS:

Admitting a bias that generally, I think, when people are voting for president they vote for president not the vice president, Ohio was very, very close. And at least an argument could be made that [Ohio Senator Rob] Portman could've been a little bit more helpful. How [important] for you guys was the potential assistance the vice presidential candidate might be in giving you a little lift in one of these states?

BETH MYERS:

We very consciously said we were not going to make a decision about the vice president based on winning an individual state. There are no bigger fans of Rob Portman than the folks who worked with him on the Romney campaign. I consider him to be one of the greatest patriots living today. He works hard. He's an amazing public servant. He would've been a superb vice president. We made a case for and against the Rob Portman candidacy, just as we did with the others. That was ultimately Mitt's decision. I think he [Portman] would've been an excellent vice president but I think Paul Ryan was an excellent vice presidential candidate. We never really said, "If we pick this guy, we've got a better chance at this state." We didn't pick Paul Ryan to put Wisconsin in play. It really didn't come into—

JIM MARGOLIS:

Subsequently did you think you'd picked him for all the right reasons? Did you think that it actually gave you a little lift in Wisconsin? Or again, pretty irrelevant to what would happen? Neil? I don't know.

NEIL NEWHOUSE:

I think it gave us a lift in Wisconsin. I think we ran closer in Wisconsin than we would've otherwise. It put it in play for a good couple of months. Politics-wise, I think it helped us. But it obviously didn't make the difference in the state. I thought Paul brought issues to the campaign. He brought a sense of seriousness. The governor wanted a partner when he's elected to get done what he wanted to get done. And I think he saw Paul as fitting what he wanted.

MALE VOICE:

Joel, who did you think he was gonna pick?

JOEL BENENSON:

I actually thought he would pick Portman. Let me go back a second, actually. I said Ryan. In my head politically, we actually had a pool at one debate prep session on who (LAUGH) everybody thought he'd pick. And I was the only one who picked Ryan. Actually, my reason for it was my sense of the governor was that this personal comfort level was really important to him. I did not think Ryan was going to come across as presidential. I thought he was very good on things like Meet the Press. I never thought he was very good in other settings. Or not coming across as presidential yet. Now, maybe he will going forward. Maybe he did better than I thought he would have. But I thought the personal comfort level was important. I was surprised on the political side for a couple of reasons. I don't know how you guys mapped out the race. But we decided pretty early on and then really nailed the strategy actually the day you guys picked Ryan. That Saturday. We kind of identified Ohio as our ultimate roadblock. We looked at the map in every which way. And on that Saturday it was very clear that if you didn't win Ohio, you weren't going to be able to—

BETH MYERS:

If Mitt had picked Portman, would that have changed that?

JOEL BENENSON:

I tend to agree with you, that you don't pick a VP to win a state. There's no history of winning a state because of it. And he would've come with his own baggage because of being the Bush budget director. But I thought it gave you your best shot at Ohio. I didn't think Ryan would add anything. But that's just my view. I was a part of our vice presidential selection team last time. So I'm looking at it as a political kibitzer.

BETH MYERS:

People argued for and against. Nobody was passionately personally for or against anybody. But everyone put their best thoughts on the table. Mitt solicited them regularly and widely. But probably on this decision more than any other, he kept his counsel close. He didn't talk about his own thinking. And he made that decision for reasons that were very personal to him. And probably to Ann.

JIM MARGOLIS:

There was a period of time where I thought you closed in Wisconsin a little bit more, frankly, than I thought Wisconsin would close. It got a little closer than I thought. And given the judgment that it probably was going to stay with us and by some relatively significant margin, I did think that Portman might give you, if that got down to a one point kind of race, that there was the potential that he could help you a little bit more there. If for no other reason than, "How are we gonna deal with this auto issue?" There's that understanding of the state, the kind of connections that he might have to the—.

BETH MYERS:

And probably more than any other elected official for the last two or three months of the campaign, we were attached at the hip to Rob Portman. And he did have that insight into Ohio. He was very, very forceful in saying, "Look, you've got to do this in Ohio." And I think he does understand that state brilliantly.

NEIL NEWHOUSE:

And the other thing is, I think, Beth, it would've been easy for Rob after not having gotten VP to have stepped back.

BETH MYERS:

Yeah, he didn't.

NEIL NEWHOUSE:

And if anything, he stepped forward.

BETH MYERS:

A real class guy.

NEIL NEWHOUSE:

Yeah, I mean, a real soldier.

BETH MYERS:

Every way.

STEPHANIE CUTTER:

He was a great surrogate.

MALE VOICE

He really was.

STEPHANIE CUTTER:

Why did you roll out the VP over a weekend?

BETH MYERS:

Well, that was not the intention. The intention was to roll him out on Friday in New Hampshire. And then the unfortunate murder of the Sikhs in Milwaukee precluded that because the funeral was that Friday. And it was in Paul's district. Our schedule simply got crazy. We wanted Mitt and Paul to campaign together for a couple of days. We had fund-raisers in states that weren't battleground states. It was a scheduling thing. And then oddly enough, somebody said, "Okay, it's got to be Saturday morning because we are actually campaigning at the Battleship *Wisconsin*." So that's why we picked that event.

STUART STEVENS:

Do you think it matters? I mean, you guys did the—

STEPHANIE CUTTER:

I don't think it matters that much.

STUART STEVENS:

Four years ago you did—

STEPHANIE CUTTER:

Biden?

STUART STEVENS:

On a Saturday, right?

MALE VOICE:

I think that's right.

STEPHANIE CUTTER:

I can barely remember.

BETH MYERS:

We didn't want to push it any further. We held it for six days as it was. I felt that was like a fruit ready to burst. I mean, it was—

JOEL BENENSON:

The only difference with that four years ago, Stuart, is that part of that deal was an organizing tool. People could get the text of who we picked first.

STUART STEVENS:

That's how I remember it.

JOEL BENENSON:

So the date was secondary to how many cell phones we thought—

STEPHANIE CUTTER:

We announced it at midnight via text.

Chapter 6
Advertising

Jim Margolis

Jim Margolis, president of GMMB, has worked for years at the intersection of politics, advertising, and advocacy on behalf of candidates, foundations, government agencies, and corporate clients. In presidential politics, Margolis served as a senior advisor to Barack Obama in his 2008 and 2012 campaigns for the White House, leading advertising efforts for Mr. Obama as part of the core strategic team. Overseas, he has helped direct political contests in Latin America, Africa, Europe, and Asia. Margolis has been recognized nationally and internationally for his work.

It's a lot more fun sitting on this side of the table than sitting on that. (LAUGHTER) We've been on that side as well. If it's any consolation, you did give us a lot of sleepless nights along the way. Stuart will particularly understand, I think, sitting in those little studios at about 4:00 in the morning trying to get out an ad before the morning shows begin. I also would like to do one little piece of housekeeping. We actually formed within the campaign an Obama Media Team. We had a terrific group of people who came together to create the advertising. Most of them are competitors in senate races and governor's races.

But we've come together a couple of times now as the media team to do the work for the President. The group includes Larry Grisolano who helped organize the media operation. Mark Putnam and Putnam Partners, David Dixon and Rich Davis, Mike Donilon, AKPD, which is Axe's old firm and was one of the other lead agencies along with my firm, GMMB. Fuse [Advertising] helped us with the African American advertising, MAP [Message, Audience & Presentation] helped us with our Spanish language spots. It's important that we acknowledge a lot of these different firms in the same way that we had a very large polling team that Joel can talk about who were pretty instrumental and who did terrific work.

This is now the entertainment portion of the program. What I thought I would do is walk you through the strategic overview, a little bit

Jim Margolis

of what we thought was important strategically, then take you through ads. Believe it or not, we didn't do a whole lot of talking earlier regarding what we would present. You'll find, fortunately, some symmetry between what Axe was saying and what I'm going to share. That's always nice when it happens. We did believe that this election was about big things.

And ironically, it was exactly one year ago today that the President was standing in Osawatomie, Kansas, with what was really one of the foundational speeches from a message perspective of the campaign. It was at the center of what we tried to communicate throughout the election. It was at that speech that the president said, "This isn't just another political debate. This is a make or break moment for the middle class. At stake is whether this'll be a country where working people can earn enough to raise a family, build a modest savings, own a home, and secure their

retirement . . . I believe this country succeeds when everyone gets a fair shot, when everyone does their fair share, and when everyone plays by the same rules. These are American values and we have to reclaim them."

Now, pretty much everything you're going to see in all the advertising, whether it's positive, whether it's negative, in much of what we did at the doors and what was communicated online in some form or fashion, flows from that speech he gave exactly one year ago today on a snowy afternoon in Kansas. I think one of the things that we were relatively successful [at] was being pretty focused on and staying with our core message. Although we did have some challenges.

One year ago today as he was giving that speech, you would've said, here we are: unemployment stuck at over 8 percent, partisan gridlock after the mid-term elections. Wrong track, as we've talked about today, was over 60 percent. The president's job approval rating was at about 48 percent at this point. Republican floodgates had been opened up on the money side with the Supreme Court decision in Citizens United. So we were looking at some trends that didn't feel all that good. Although there was this fundamental confidence that David talked about a little earlier today, regarding the structure of the election and some of the things we knew we needed to do.

President Obama: Osawatomie, KS (12.6.11)

"This isn't just another political debate. This is a make or break moment for the middle class... At stake is whether this will be a country where working people can earn enough to raise a family, build a modest savings, own a home, and secure their retirement... I believe that this country succeeds when everyone gets a fair shot, when everyone does their fair share, and when everyone plays by the same rules. [These are] American values, and we have to reclaim them."

OBAMA ● BIDEN

Challenges – 1 year ago

- **Unemployment stuck over 8%**
- **Partisan gridlock after midterms**
- **Wrong track over 60%**
- **POTUS job approval under 50%**
- **Republican floodgates opened after Citizens United**

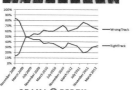

OBAMA ● BIDEN

Assets

- **President still personally popular**
- **Voters believed he understood and cared about them**
- **Voters understood he inherited a bad hand**
- **Real, meaningful accomplishments:**
  - Auto Rescue, Iraq, Bin Laden, ACA, Economic Uptick
- **Vulnerabilities for Romney:**
  - Tacked to right during primary raising concerns among key constituencies:
    - Women, Hispanics, Young Voters, Moderates, etc…
  - Profile out of touch with voter preferences

OBAMA ⬤ BIDEN

We had some assets. The President was still personally popular, and that was something that I think was a life raft for us throughout this campaign. The fact that people like this guy, that they felt he understood their problems, was something that buoyed him even in the darkest days and was a real asset. Voters believed that he understood and cared about them. Voters understood that he was dealt a bad hand, that what he walked into was unlike anything that most any president, certainly in modern political history, had been handed. That he had to work his way through these challenges that weren't of his own making. There were real meaningful accomplishments. Sometimes, they were forgotten. They were particularly forgotten by our base. (LAUGHTER) A lot of the time our own people were saying, "it just doesn't seem like he did anything."

Then, when you'd start to roll through the accomplishments—the stimulus, healthcare, the auto rescue, bin Laden, Iraq—there were actually a lot of things that got done. And for certain constituencies, the fact that we had the first Latina Supreme Court justice [mattered]. There were a lot of things that actually were resonant with key constituencies as we moved into this election year.

There were also significant vulnerabilities for Governor Romney. He had tacked pretty far to the right during the primaries. We've talked about that this morning. And that he had done [so] with some key constituencies that were going to be important in this election, particularly

4 Key Message Elements - Ads

- **Context**
    - o Reminding voters what POTUS inherited
    - o Longer-term struggle of the middle class
- **Progress**
    - o Moving FORWARD but much more to do
- **Define Romney**
    - o Failure as Massachusetts Governor
    - o Out of touch
    - o Not "Mr. Fix It" on the economy
- **The Choice**
    - o Top down vs. middle out
    - o Who understands you?
    - o Who is going to fight for you?

OBAMA ❂ BIDEN

on women's issues, Hispanic issues, some things that we could talk to young people about, and moderates.

Finally, as CEO of Bain, was Romney's profile the winning profile in this kind of a year? So, there were some good things going on as we began to put together the messaging—the narrative arc for the campaign—and there were really four major message elements that we thought were important. And again, they were present in varying degrees throughout the entire campaign.

At different times, we would emphasize each of these in different ways and at different volume levels. One was context. We needed to remind people of what the President had inherited. We were losing 750,000 jobs a month the day that he raised his hand and took the oath of office. The kind of struggles that middle-class people were confronting as they moved into this election year were struggles that had been building over decades. This wasn't something just of the last 24, 36, or 48 months. We wanted to talk about the progress that had been made, but it had to be done in a way that was tonally correct.

If we overshot the runway, if we had tried to pretend that everything was okay, we were going to be in big trouble. People were going to shut down. If we talked about it in terms of making progress, still more to do, then we were in a much better position. As the campaign progressed, we felt better and better about leaning into it more and saying you know what? We're actually moving forward and this isn't a time to turn back to the same policies that created the problems in the first place.

We felt that it was going to be critical to define Romney. We began to talk about that earlier today. We made the decision to define him early, to push money forward, to try to do that in the early summer, before he really had the opportunity to define himself with general election voters. We wanted to burn in that he was a failure as Massachusetts governor, that he was out of touch in terms of the kind of problems and concerns that people had, and that, probably most importantly, he wasn't Mr. Fix-It. That if you were concerned about the economy, if you were concerned about where this country was going economically, this man was not the solution.

And finally, that all led to a choice. There were two different views about the economic path of this country. Were we going to go top down as Governor Romney had suggested, or middle out? Our argument was that we need to build the middle class in this country. Who understands you? Who's going to fight for you? So those four elements were things that you will see through the course of the campaign in virtually all the communications that we did, whether it's what Stephanie was working on in her free and earned media efforts, whether it was what was going on at the doors, or whether it was what we were doing in terms of the advertising.

Advertising. I put this ad in because this was a question for us early on. We talked earlier today. This is the only one I'm going to show from early. This was November of 2011, one year ago, the period where we were trying to "help" the Republican conversation that was beginning to take place across the country as the primary began. Who was the real Mitt Romney? And did he have some of those more progressive tendencies in Massachusetts that you all might want to talk about as you have your conversations and debates? Or was it the new Mitt Romney? This ad ultimately got about a million hits but really pushed people toward a much longer video that told the story from our perspective.

TV advertisement: "Mitt v. Mitt"

ANNOUNCER: From the creator of "I'm running for office for Pete's sake" comes the story of two men trapped in one body: "Mitt versus Mitt."

MITT ROMNEY: I will preserve and protect a woman's right to choose.

MITT ROMNEY: The right next step is to get *Roe v. Wade* overturned.

ANNOUNCER: Two Mitts willing to say ANYTHING.

MITT ROMNEY: We put together an exchange and the president's copying that idea. I'm glad to hear that.

MITT ROMNEY: Obamacare is bad news.

ANNOUNCER: See it all, at MittvMitt.com. The Democratic National Committee is responsible for the content of this ad.

But the point here, and it's an interesting one is, gee, which is the real Mitt? What's the real position? Subsequently, as we moved from the primary to the general, we wanted him to own all of the positions which he had been pushed to embrace during the primary, to "own" those conservative positions, whether it was on women's issues, immigration, so on.

All right, so now we're into May. It is the beginning of the general election campaign. We ran a very significant flight of positive advertising at the front. This was the initial opening ad of the campaign. It was to try to do those things that I just talked about. What did the president face as he came to office? To demonstrate that there was progress. Listen for tone. "Still more to do. We aren't done yet." And listen to whom he credits. It's about you. What Americans have done. Not him thumping his own chest.

TV advertisement: "Go"

ANNOUNCER: 2008, and economic meltdown.

NEWS ANNOUNCER: Worst financial collapse since the Great Depression.

ANNOUNCER: 4.4 million jobs lost.

NEWS ANNOUNCER: American workers were laid off in numbers not seen in over three decades.
announcer: America's economy spiraling down.

NEWS ANNOUNCER: The biggest point drop that has ever been seen in a day.
announcer: All before this president took the oath.

BARACK OBAMA: . . . So help me god . . .

ANNOUNCER: Some said our best days are behind us, but not him.

BARACK OBAMA: Don't bet against the American worker.

ANNOUNCER: He believed in us. Fought for us. And today our auto industry is back. Firing on all cylinders. Our greatest enemy brought to justice by our greatest heroes.

SOLDIERS: Go. Go. Go.

ANNOUNCER: Our troops are home from Iraq. Instead of losing jobs, we're creating them; over 4.2 million so far. We're not there yet. It's still too hard for too many. But we're coming back, because America's greatness comes from a strong middle class. Because you don't quit. And neither does he.

BARACK OBAMA: I'm Barack Obama and I approved this message.

A month solid of very significant positive advertising, focused on context, and what he faced and the kinds of things that he had accomplished. Moving into, now, early summer 2012. This is where we begin to try to define Governor Romney. It begins in Massachusetts. Basic argument, he says he's "Mr. Fix-It. Hey, we've heard this before. That record isn't one that worked out very well in Massachusetts. Maybe you shouldn't have confidence that it will work for you."

TV advertisement: "We've Heard It All Before"

BARACK OBAMA: I'm Barack Obama and I approved this message.

ANNOUNCER: It started like this.

MITT ROMNEY: I speak the language of business. I know how jobs are created.

ANNOUNCER: But it ended like this: One of the worst economic records in the country. When Mitt Romney was governor, Massachusetts lost 40,000 manufacturing jobs—a rate twice the national average—and fell to 47th in job creation, fourth from the bottom. Instead of hiring workers from his own state, Romney outsourced call-center jobs to India. He cut taxes for millionaires like himself, while raising them on the middle class. And left the state $2.6 billion deeper in debt. So now, when Mitt Romney talks about what he'd do as president . . .

MITT ROMNEY: I know what it takes to create jobs.

ANNOUNCER: Remember, we've heard it all before.

MITT ROMNEY: I know how jobs are created.

ANNOUNCER: Romney economics. It didn't work then, and it won't work now.

STUART STEVENS:

Jim, a 60-second negative is extraordinarily unusual.

JIM MARGOLIS:

It is. Part of it was pushing through as we went into some of these different areas and tried to make sure that people paid attention. We weren't trying to do it just in 30 seconds. We needed a little more time to breathe and to make a broader case. Underneath the 60 would be the 30s. A framing 60 and then 30s that popped underneath. I'm giving you the highlights, the title card, so to speak. We went from there and a whole series of spots that looked at Massachusetts to the Bain record, to what he had done as CEO [arguing that] he, in fact, wasn't the solution, that he was the problem. And this was one of those.

TV advertisement: "Firms"

BARACK OBAMA: I'm Barack Obama and I approved this message.

AUDIO: Mitt Romney singing "America the Beautiful"

GRAPHIC: In business, Mitt Romney's firms shipped jobs to Mexico.

GRAPHIC: . . . And China.

GRAPHIC: As Governor, Romney outsourced jobs to India.

GRAPHIC: He had millions in a Swiss bank account.

GRAPHIC: Tax havens like Bermuda . . .

GRAPHIC: And the Cayman Islands.

GRAPHIC: Mitt Romney's not the solution.

GRAPHIC: He's the problem.

One of our best advocates and one of our best communicators was the president himself. In almost every ad test that we did, when the president was speaking directly to people it was about as strong as we could ever get. One of the most important assets that we felt we had was him.

This was a spot that ran in July. It was the first time voters had really seen the president in a spot. We had done a few things where he was in interviews, but not where he was speaking directly to camera—to begin to lay out the choice; to begin to move to the two different paths that we could go as a nation. It turned out from our data to be one of the more effective spots.

TV advertisement: "The Choice"

BARACK OBAMA: Over the next four months, you have a choice to make. Not just between two political parties or even two people. It's a choice between two very different plans for our country. Governor Romney's plan would cut taxes for the folks at the very top, roll back regulations on big banks; and he says that if we do, our economy will grow and everyone will benefit. But you know what? We tried that top-down approach. It's what caused the mess in the first place. I believe the only way to create an economy built to last is to strengthen the middle class; asking the wealthy to pay a little more, so we can pay down our debt in a balanced way. So that we can afford to invest in education, manufacture, and home-grown American energy. For good, middle-class jobs. Sometimes politics can seem very small. But the choice you face? It couldn't be bigger.
I'm Barack Obama and I approved this message.

STUART STEVENS:

Did you give pause to having the president himself carry the whole message the whole time? That's what you did at several points in time during that campaign. Do you think he was that strong that he could actually carry that message the whole time?

JIM MARGOLIS:

We did. We used him, I think, four times over the course of the campaign. We spread it out over a fairly significant amount of time. One at the front that was the set up. We used him a little bit later on in September. We used him to do our closing just before early voting started. And we always used him in longer formats. The one- and even a two-minute spots.

Our data would suggest that he was our best guy. When we were actually having a conversation with people, when we were actually talking with them in a way that wasn't a 30-second or 24-second clip—that produced a lot of response. It feels like maybe you had a different view of it lookin' at—

STUART STEVENS:

No, no, I just thought it was just a very interesting decision to do that. For any candidate to be able to carry a two-minute spot as you guys did is pretty extraordinary. It doesn't happen much.

JIM MARGOLIS:

He is extraordinary. Not only does he always conclude a take on time— exactly at two minutes. He comes in at one minute, 56 seconds every time. And you just shake your head and say, that is the most amazing thing I have ever seen. (LAUGHTER) Left us four seconds for our disclaimer. You need to write for him, but he has a really good sense of how to do it.

We're now into August. We're moving from some of the Bain record spots to the tax plan and the tax issue.

TV advertisement—"Stretch"

BARACK OBAMA: I'm Barack Obama and I approved this message.

ANNOUNCER: You work hard, stretch every penny, but chances are you pay a higher tax rate than him. Mitt Romney made $20 million in 2010, but paid only 14 percent in taxes, probably less than you. Now he has a plan that would give millionaires another tax break and raises taxes on middle class families by up to $2,000 a year. Mitt Romney's middle class tax increase: he pays less, you pay more.

When Representative Ryan was selected, they leaned into the Medicare issue. And we wanted to lean back in a lot of our key states like Florida, where we had an older population. We ran what was essentially a Medicare track all the way through. I think it'd be good to have a conversation later between you guys about how that Medicare issue played out. We felt it was very important to continue pushing on Medicare. This is one of those spots.

TV advertisement—"Promise"

BARACK OBAMA: I'm Barack Obama and I approved this message.

ANNOUNCER: It's a promise that was made long ago. You work hard, pay in. Your Medicare benefits are guaranteed. But Mitt

Romney would break that promise . . . replace your benefits with a voucher.

Insurance companies could just keep raising rates. Instead of a guarantee, seniors could pay 6,400 dollars more a year. AARP says the plan Mitt Romney supports undermines Medicare.

Mitt Romney. An end to the Medicare Promise.

I'm not sure they really had anything on the other side that was as big a benefit as Bill Clinton. As they went into their GOP convention, we put up this Clinton spot. We felt he would be very strong. It would [be] the set-up to what he would do at the convention. He just does an awful lot of work for us when he's talking to voters.

TV advertisement—"Clear Choice"

BILL CLINTON: This election to me is about which candidate is more likely to return us to full employment.

This is a clear choice. The Republican plan is to cut more taxes on upper income people and go back to deregulation. That's what got us in trouble in the first place.

President Obama has a plan to rebuild America from the ground up, investing in innovation, education, and job training. It only works if there is a strong middle class.

That's what happened when I was President. We need to keep going with his plan.

BARACK OBAMA: I'm Barack Obama and I approved this message.

We are in September. The 47 percent tape is released. We actually let that roll for about a week before we went up with this spot. It was working itself very nicely through the earned media. And then, at the point that it began to subside a little bit, we popped up with the ad to carry it further. It was interesting to us that this was one of those instances where 80 percent of Americans had heard about the 47 percent comments. That doesn't happen very often. And so, we didn't feel we needed to do a lot. We just needed to touch on it. This is how we did it.

TV advertisement—"My Job"

BARACK OBAMA: I'm Barack Obama and I approved this message.

MITT ROMNEY: There are 47 percent of the people who will vote for the president no matter what . . .
. . . who are dependent upon government, who believe that they are victims, who believe that government has a responsibility to care for them, who believe that they are entitled to health care, to food, to housing, to you-name-it . . .
. . . And they will vote for this president no matter what . . .
. . . And so my job is not to worry about those people. I'll never convince them they should take personal responsibility and care for their lives.

One of the lessons here, and I think it was true for you as well, is when you have the candidate or the president, whoever it is, on tape saying things versus us doing another production spot where we're having a faceless announcer making the charge, it makes a big difference. That had power.

The spot that they did after the first debate where you could see the president not, shall we say, terribly engaged in the debate, those were things that I think had a lot of impact with voters. I wanted to give you just a quick example of what you might be experiencing if you were in a target state like, say, Ohio. Here we are in Cleveland. This is week one, the week just before the election.

Targeted Media Tracks

- **Markets had up to 9 tracks of TV targeting different voter segments with relevant messaging:**

Cleveland DMA - Week 1 TV Tracks				
Track	Buy	Length	GRPs	Ads
Persuasion	National & DMA	:30	3350	4
	National & DMA	:60	750	1
Women	DMA	:30	600	1
Youth	DMA	:30	850	1
GOTV/Dems	DMA	:30	200	1
Jewish	Cable-Zip (Shaker Heights)	:30	250	1
Tire Workers	Cable-Zip (Akron)	:30	600	1
AfAm	National & DMA	:30	*	1
Spanish Language	DMA	:30	**	1
Seniors Track	NA	NA	NA	NA

OBAMA ❀ BIDEN

We were running upwards of nine tracks of advertising in some of these key battleground states. Most of them, not nine, usually six or seven. But if you were sitting in Cleveland that week before the election, you were getting four spots. This is a huge number of GRPs. And the other side had even more collectively.

Four spots focused on persuasion that were coming through, one 60, four 30s, five total. We had a women's track, a youth track, a get out the vote track. We took a [sound]bite from the president from the foreign policy debate where he vigorously defended Israel and [addressed] the problems that were being confronted by Israel. It ran in specific cable zip codes particularly focused on the Jewish community in and around Cleveland. In the zip codes right around the tire factories, in Akron, we were running a spot that dealt with the position of Governor Romney on imported tires.

We had an African American track, a Spanish language track. In a lot of states we had a seniors track. [The weight of the advertising] was overwhelming and crushing. And that's just our side. We had a women's track that really began in the end of May, beginning of June, all the way to the election. We felt that this was going to be a key voter group for us.

TV advertisement—"What He'll Do"

ANNOUNCER: Which do you believe? What Mitt Romney's TV ads say about women, or what Mitt Romney himself says?

MITT ROMNEY: Do I believe the Supreme Court should overturn *Roe v. Wade*? Yes.

MITT ROMNEY: And it would be my preference that they reverse *Roe v. Wade.*

MITT ROMNEY: Hopefully reverse *Roe v. Wade.*

MITT ROMNEY: Overturn *Roe v. Wade.*

MITT ROMNEY: Planned Parenthood. We're going to get rid of that.

MITT ROMNEY: I'll cut off funding to Planned Parenthood.

ANNOUNCER: No matter what Mitt Romney's ads say, we know what he'll do.

BARACK OBAMA: I'm Barack Obama and I approved this message.

We thought they were running some pretty good ads right then that were pushing back on us. We needed to get a response going toward the

Targeted Tracks – Spanish Language

Organizer

Cristina

POTUS DTC

Negative

OBAMA ⬥ BIDEN

end. Spanish language we did a lot of different ways. We used some that felt very, very local, using organizers who carried a story in Spanish language.

We used some celebrity types such as Cristina, who had a lot of credibility within the community. The president direct to camera getting through his Spanish; people appreciated the fact that he was giving it a shot. And then, obviously some tracks that were hitting pretty hard on Governor Romney in a more traditional production way. We did come back and do some things around the Jeep issue at the end in Ohio. We did some work around get out the vote. Here would be an example of something we would do in the markets on programming where we just focused on turnout.

TV advertisement: "537"

ANNOUNCER: Five hundred and thirty-seven. The number of votes that changed the course of American history.

NEWSCAST: Florida is too close to call

ANNOUNCER: The difference between what was . . .
And what could have been . . .

So this year, if you're thinking that your vote doesn't count, that it won't matter. Well, back then, there were probably at least 537 people who felt the same way.

Make your voice heard. Vote.

BARACK OBAMA: I'm Barack Obama and I approved this message.

In the 2012 presidential race, over the general election—this does not include primaries on their side or anything that we might've done, which wasn't much during the primary period—staying in Cleveland if you were an average viewer, you got 1,450 spots. Just presidential.

Not Senate, not Sherrod Brown, not congressmen, just presidential. It came from 30 different advertisers. It wasn't just them and us. It was all those super PACs and everybody else. There were 190 different ads that you would've been exposed to potentially. Compared to 2008, it was about double. A little more than double in terms of the overall volume. And you can see what 2004 is. All right, candidates. Obama and Romney. We spent about $415 million on regular paid advertising. This doesn't include all the digital.

Media Buy – Unprecedented Clutter

- **In the 2012 General Election/Presidential Race, the average TV viewer in Cleveland saw the following:**
  - o 1450 TV Ads
  - o 30 Advertisers
  - o 190 Different Ads

- **General Election TV volume in 2012 was 129% higher than 2008**

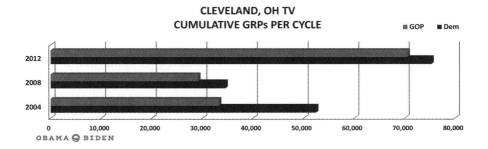

Media Buy – TV Spending

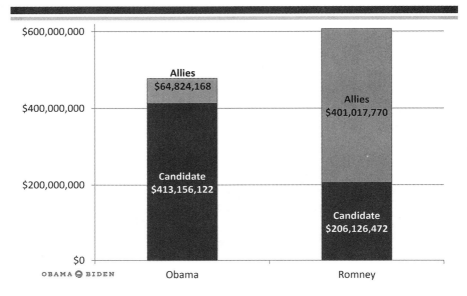

The Romney campaign spent $206 [million]. This was for all sorts of reasons that Stuart will undoubtedly reinforce when he gets up. It was a huge advantage to us because [it just reflects] candidate-to-candidate spending where we could control our own message and where they had a harder time controlling message because they were more dependent on allies, the super PACS, to help them. They couldn't control what the super PACS did. We had some help and we appreciate it from the super PACS. But overall, they outspent us collectively. But we had more candidate money available which also gave us more gross rating points because we [Federal candidates] can buy at a lower rate than the super PACS can. We'll save that for another day, but it's an important point for two reasons. First, we get more gross rating points for every dollar we spend than the super PACS. And second we get to control our message.

In our buying, we bought early. We bought at lowest unit rate time. We bought more national cable—figuring that there were some efficiencies in doing that. We used some new tools to more effectively actually purchase the advertising. We did those targeted tracks, tried to speak more directly to individual voter groups about issues that they cared about in the same way that we tried to talk to people at the doors on issues that they cared about. Where we could, we tried to avoid political clutter. For example, doing some network buys put us into different

Media Buy - Strategy

- **Buy Cheap:**
  - o Early Placements
  - o LUR Placements
  - o National Cable
- **Buy Smart:**
  - o New tools to identify most cost efficient programs to reach swing voters
  - o Targeted tracks: Women, Hispanic, AfAM, Youth, Dems
  - o Avoid political clutter:
    - OFA: 30 networks

OBAMA ☰ BIDEN

placement pods in advertising, rather than being dumped in with eight other spots in local markets around TV news. I think I'm going to save Rentrak for later just because we've got a lot to do.

Here are some of the analytics. If somebody wants to ask a question later about how we used some of this new data and set top boxes and all of that, I'm happy to answer it. I'll leave you with the last spot that the president did. This was the closer, which we felt was a strong way to go. Focused on you, focused on the kind of problems that you're facing, whether we're making progress.

TV advertisement: "Determination"

BARACK OBAMA: There's just no quit in America and you're seeing that right now. Over 5 million new jobs, exports up 41 percent, home values rising, our auto industry back and our heroes are coming home.

We're not there yet. But we've made real progress and the last thing we should do is turn back now.

Here's my plan for the next four years: Making education and training a national priority; building on our manufacturing boom; boosting American-made energy; reducing the deficits responsibly by cutting where we can, and asking the

wealthy to pay a little more. And ending the war in Afghanistan so we can do some nation-building here at home. That's
the right path.

So read my plan, compare it to Governor Romney's, and
decide which is better for you. It's an honor to be your President and I'm asking for your vote. So together we can keep
moving America forward.

BARACK OBAMA: I'm Barack Obama and I approved this
message.

One note as I conclude. Probably one of the most important lines anybody had in that spot was the invitation to read Governor Romney's
plan, compare it, and make a decision for yourself. That was something
that people over and over again in our focus groups talked about. The
fact that he was saying I'm just asking you to look, they didn't feel it was
negative. They felt that he was issuing the invitation and it made them
more confident about the President's program.

STUART STEVENS:

In the debates, too. Which is like, "Don't take my word for it.'

Media Buy – Rentrak

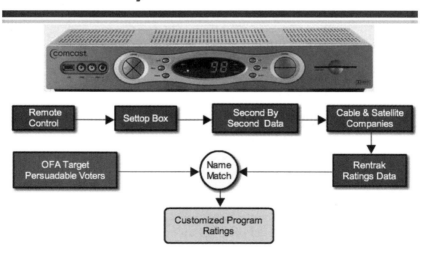

JIM MARGOLIS:

Don't—yeah. Exactly. We used it a couple times once we figured it out. (LAUGHTER)

STUART STEVENS:

Let me just start by giving credit to a bunch of people. We set this up in-house with teams. Ashley O'Connor moved from Washington to organize and run the advertising effort. She did a fabulous job. Ashley had worked for SSG, the firm I'm associated with, since college, but also had left at various points and gained extensive Madison Avenue experience. Under Ashley's direction, we put together teams of Madison Avenue and political people. From Madison Avenue, we had Tom Messner who is sort of a genius. He was part of the Tuesday Team that created "Morning in America." An absolutely brilliant guy.

We also had from Madison Avenue a top director, Bruce Van Dusen. Bruce has directed many of your favorite ads. A fabulously talented guy. From the non-political world we also had Jim Ferguson, who had headed up this team we had in 2000 when he was head of Young & Rubicam called "The Park Avenue Posse." He helped us find an art director and creative director type name James Dalthrop who is from Texas and works in LA. As a copywriter, we had another really interesting big talent. Harold Kaplan, who came from Young & Rubicam.

Those guys formed the nucleus of our nonpolitical ad teams.

And then, from the political world, we brought in Vinnie Minchillo, who had worked with Scotty Howell a lot. Really top talent. And Bob Wickers, who works out of California. They both moved to Boston.

Ashley O'Connor had the idea to set all of our production and editing up in-house. We had four edit suites in-house. We tried to do as much as possible in-house, in part because we liked to have an environment where people could come in and stick their finger in the cookie dough. And it saved us a lot of money.

In the Romney campaign, we believed that the future of campaigns is much like Smartphones. Functions of campaigns that would have previously been done by outside vendors at greater cost can now be brought in-house, like apps on your phone. We did that with ad production, with ad placement, with our internet services, etc. I think in the future you will see other campaigns inevitably adopt this model. It just makes sense and it is being done in the non-political work by smart high-tech corporations every day.

We also had other teams that focused on the web. Tim O'Toole made some extraordinary web videos. And a woman named Clare Burns. We had all these different plans for a convention film in the works. And basically, it ended up being made by this twenty-five-year-old woman who came to work for us as an archivist to keep track of video but was so talented we realized she should be doing lots more. She put together that video, which I think was extraordinary work.

Because we had to win the primary, we had a very different campaign operation and challenge than the Obama campaign. Republican primaries are a unique beast. This one was very different than the one four years ago largely because of the debates.

We didn't go on television until after Thanksgiving, whereas before four years ago we went on television sometime in February or March. We did not have the resources to do that this cycle and we quickly realized that the debates were going to be critical. The first debate that Governor Romney participated in was in June 2011 in New Hampshire and it drew an unexpectedly large audience. So did the second debate. And that made it pretty obvious that the debates were going to have more impact than advertising for a long stretch in this race.

Strategically, from the very beginning we believed that to win this race we had to win it on the economy. We felt that for the primary and for the general. Because ultimately as a perfect match for Republican primary voters a governor from Massachusetts would never be an ideal fit. We had to let voters focus on choosing who they wanted to go up against Barack Obama. And it wouldn't be just in win-ability. I'm a great believer in the old Jack Germond saying that those candidates who focus on win-ability seldom do. It had to be on who they thought was best qualified to face Obama. And that that would be based on a set of skills that would go to the candidate's ability to turn the economy around.

In the Republican Party, there's always a slot for the business guy. We felt the value of that slot was enhanced in this economic environment. On the cultural front, rather than trying to stress one or two specific issues, we would let voters get a sense of the Governor's personal values and personal conservatism. He embodies family values and is very much a cultural conservative. That would carry us through. We wouldn't try to get to the right of a lot of people on a lot of different issues.

When you look at our advertising for the primary, we focused on the Governor's record as Governor more than any one aspect of his background, as we found it was the information voters were most looking for. It proved he was serious about balancing budgets without tax increases, changing the status quo, taking a fresh approach to old problems. The primary was long and hard but there were a lot of factors that made that almost inevitable. The most dominant of those is the new reality of super Pacs that kept campaigns alive for a lot longer than in previous cycles.

Before we look at spots, one area I want to touch on is Hispanic voters. The Republican Party obviously has a lot of problems with Hispanic voters. We had a lot of problems before the primary and a lot of problems after the primary. You look at GOP generic numbers with Hispanics before the primary. And after the primary, they're pretty much the same, which wasn't very good. But I don't think the primary was definitional for hurting Governor Romney with Hispanics.

To change [those numbers], one would've had to adopt a very aggressive approach toward immigration and really taken it on as a mission, which in the primary would have been a daunting task and wasn't really motivation for why, in Governor Romney's case, he's runnin' for president. Governor's Romney Election Day problems with Hispanics were really a generic Republican problem more than a candidate problem. Which actually is a more daunting message for Republicans because it just indicates the long-range challenges ahead which we need to address and must address. And when you look at the success Republican governors have had with Hispanic voters, I think that is indicative of a path for success for Republican presidential candidates.

What I want to do is show some spots and take you through a chronology. Very early we did a web video, which got over a million hits, called "Bump in the Road."

Web advertisement: "Bump in the Road"

GRAPHIC: Millions Have Lost Their Jobs Under President Obama

GRAPHIC: Long Term Unemployment Is Now Worse Than The Great Depression

GRAPHIC: June 3, 2011 Unemployment Hit 9.1 percent

GRAPHIC: President Obama Called It a Bump in the Road

BARACK OBAMA: There are always going to be bumps on the road to recovery.

AMERICAN CITIZEN 1: I'm an American, not a bump in the road.

AMERICAN CITIZEN 2: I'm an American, not a bump in the road.

AMERICAN CITIZEN 3: I'm an American, not a bump in the road.

AMERICAN CITIZEN 4: I'm an American, not a bump in the road.

AMERICAN CITIZEN 5: I'm an American, not a bump in the road.

AMERICAN CITIZEN 6: I'm an American, not a bump in the road.

AMERICAN FAMILY: We are Americans, not bumps in the road.

AMERICAN CITIZEN 7: I'm an American, not a bump in the road.

AMERICAN CITIZEN 8: I'm an American, not a bump in the road.

AMERICAN CITIZEN 9: I'm an American, not a bump in the road.

AMERICAN CITIZEN 10: I'm an American, not a bump in the road.

AMERICAN CITIZEN 11: I'm an American, not a bump in the road.

AMERICAN CITIZEN 12: I'm an American, not a bump in the road.

AMERICAN CITIZEN 13: I'm an American, not a bump in the road.

AMERICAN CITIZEN 14: I'm an American, not a bump in the road.

AMERICAN CITIZEN 15: I'm an American, not a bump in the road.

ENTIRE GROUP: I'm an American, not a bump in the road.

This shows how we believe we needed to frame the race. This very much was a battle for the middle class. We had to get those voters who believed the country was going in the wrong track to invest in Mitt Romney and believe in Mitt Romney and believe that he'll take [the country] in a different direction. By the end of the campaign, we succeeded in winning the vast majority of those [who] believe that that country's going in the wrong track. The economic situation improved such that that wasn't a winning majority.

There had been talk about referendum versus choice. Let me show you "Conservative Record." We ran this spot in the primary a lot, as I mentioned.

TV advertisement: "Conservative Record"

MITT ROMNEY: I spent my career in the private sector. In Massachusetts when I came in we faced almost a 3 billion dollar budget gap. And there were some that said why don't we just raise taxes or why don't we just borrow money. We actually cut spending. I balanced the budget every single year, and by the time I left we had established over 2 billion dollars of a rainy day fund. The principles of business work in government and it's high time to bring those principles of fiscal responsibility to Washington, D.C.

MITT ROMNEY: I'm Mitt Romney and I approve this message.

This was shown by us more than any other spot in the primary. There was always a lot of talk in the campaign about a choice versus a referendum. Frankly, a campaign against an incumbent is always some of both. An ad like this helps establish Mitt Romney's record and credentials. Is that a choice or referendum? It shows he is a conservative choice for this referendum on a more liberal President Obama

Once we got out of the primary, we did a lot of testing of various forms—focus groups, online ad testing, survey research. We approached this with a totally open mind with one driving question: what did undecided voters want to know that was critical to making them vote for Mitt Romney? We tested various bio elements—personal bio, business record, Mass Gov. record, Olympics, and in different combinations –stressing Mitt Romney as a change agent, turnaround guy, etc. And we tested a Romney agenda—what he would do as President. What we discovered was that overwhelmingly, voters wanted to know what Romney would do as President. It makes sense. It was a threshold question they wanted answered before they would focus on anything else. So we created a series of ads we called "Day One."

TV advertisement: "Day 1"

ANNOUNCER: What will be different about a Romney presidency? From day one President Romney focuses on the economy and the deficit, unleashes America's energy resources and stands up to China on trade. President Romney's leadership puts jobs first. But there's something more than Legislation or new policy, it's the feeling we'll have that our country is back, back on the right track. That's what will be different about a Romney Presidency.

MITT ROMNEY: I'm Mitt Romney and I approved this message.

We ran a series of these. We only had the money to run them in four states. And we ran state-specific ones as well.

TV advertisement: "Virginia"

ANNOUNCER: President Romney's first 100 days, what will they mean for Virginia? Day 1: President Romney moves to repeal Obamacare and attacks the deficit starting with 20 billion dollars in savings. By day 100 President Romney reverses Obama's offshore drilling ban, creating thousands of new jobs for Virginians. President Romney's first 100 days: for the people of Virginia they mean new life, new energy for our state.

MITT ROMNEY: I'm Mitt Romney and I approved this message.

We also tested different approaches to presentation. This is something we had started back in the summer of 2011. The governor on camera. The governor not on camera. And at this stage of the campaign, people were not receptive to the governor direct to camera, which was interesting. We had done a lot of on camera ads four years ago. But voters in this environment did not respond warmly; they felt that it was too political.

Voters told us they wanted data and specifics. But we also did not want to drop the human equation. So we created a series of longer web ads that were focused on individuals who had really suffered in the Obama economy. We found a way to show that Mitt Romney was in touch with voters who were not like him.

Web advertisement: "Iowa"

DEBORAH RAGLAND: Every week it's harder at the grocery store. You stay the same, everything goes up so you're falling behind every month.

VOICEOVER: Millions of Americans are struggling under the Obama economy. Here are a few of their stories.

TROY KNAPP: At Webster City, Frigidaire was there for a hundred, you know a hundred years or whatever and they just up and said hey, we're done here, you know?

JASON CLAUSEN: When the economy went bad a month after my divorce, I lost my job, I lost my house.

RAGLAND: Everybody's looking for ways to cut costs I guess.

VOICEOVER: This is Deborah Ragland, of Webster City, Iowa.

RAGLAND: I've been looking for a job for two years. Haven't found any. My unemployment benefits did run out and we're just trying to get by.

CLAUSEN: There's two things in this world I care about. It's going to work and paying my child support.

VOICEOVER: This is Jason Clausen of Mason City, Iowa.

CLAUSEN: I kept working. It's the last remaining Frank Lloyd Wright-designed hotel in the world. I had to rebuild all the staircases in there, and I got to the last stair and I took out my Sharpie and I wrote J. Clausen, and I wrote father of Eva Grace Clausen.

KNAPP: You grow up around here you know everyone. Everyone looks out for you.

VOICEOVER: This is Troy Knapp of Alton, Iowa.

KNAPP: My dad doesn't like me getting unemployment. He hates it. Because he grew up in that mentality you don't get unemployment. You don't live off the government. You do everything, you pay for everything your own way. My neighbor across the street's the same way. I end up going over and helping Damon in Iowa Falls, he's a good friend of mine. He does moving and storage, and then I help him dig graves on the side. But I've probably dug a couple hundred graves.

CLAUSEN: The *Des Moines Register* reporter was there. In passing, I gave him the story about that step, how my daughter's name was under there. That was the front page of the *Des Moines Register*. To this day, my daughter and I, when she's feeling down, we go to that step. I call it our step.

RAGLAND: It's hard to know where to put your trust. It's going to get tougher I think.

KNAPP: That's the problem. A lot of people around here when Barack, ya know, was running and all that. Everyone believed, everyone had hope. They all thought "man, this guy's gonna get something done.'

KNAPP: When he is in office now it just seems like nothing's getting done. It seems like it's all talk. You can say whatever you want. But it's not about saying what everyone wants to hear, it's about doing it.

VOICEOVER: Hope and change has not been kind to millions of Americans, but they still believe in this great country, and deserve a leader who believes in them: Mitt Romney.

RAGLAND: So we're just going to sit tight and see how things go, and see if the next president turns it around.

We did a whole series of these. Different regions. Different stories. And it's always difficult to get them out there but we tried on the web to get these out to people. It was always the challenge. We didn't have the web presence that the Obama campaign had.

Let me address what I think is one of the great underreported and misunderstood aspects of this campaign: dollars spent on television. We spent about half of what the Obama campaign did on television. The confusion comes from the amount spent by pro-Romney super Pacs. But what we discovered—to our surprise and our obvious disappointment—is that those ads just didn't move numbers much. I don't think it was the quality of the ads, many of which were superb. But I tend to think it was the inability to coordinate with the campaign. They ran these ads and there was never a coordinated approach or message and they just didn't sink in with voters.

Eighty percent of the pro-Obama ads were paid for by the Obama campaign and that gave them a huge advantage. They could buy more ads, since they got a lower rate for the ads than the super Pacs paid. But most importantly, they obviously could coordinate. Starting in May, they just swamped us on television.

Until the convention—and few people understood this—the only ad dollars we could spend were primary dollars gathered at under $2,500 limits. That is a huge disadvantage. The Obama campaign outspent us during the summer in key states by margins of three or four to one. We spent every cent we could on television and even borrowed an additional $20 million just to try to stay alive. But it gave them the ability to attack us on multiple fronts. I don't think this is something that most journalists and observers understand. They say, "You let Obama define you." Which is sort of like saying to the guys at the Alamo, "You let Santa Anna outnumber you." It wasn't an active choice.

Our numbers showed that the positives that the Obama campaign were running didn't move the number a lot. There are a lot of times you have to run positives to get permission to run negatives. But when they started running negatives, it did work. And we needed to respond to it. They had so much money and were attacking on so many fronts, it was impossible to respond to every charge. So we made hard decisions and tried to respond to the most critical.

TV advertisement: "Shame on You"

ANNOUNCER: Barack Obama's attacks against Mitt Romney. They're just not true. The *Washington Post* says on just about every level this ad is misleading, unfair and untrue. But that's

Barack Obama. He also attacked Hillary Clinton with vicious lies.

HILLARY CLINTON: He continues to spend millions of dollars perpetuating falsehoods.

ANNOUNCER: Mitt Romney has a plan to get America working. Barack Obama: Worst job record since the Depression.

HILLARY CLINTON: So shame on you Barack Obama.

Part of what we needed to do was go on the offense to get the Obama campaign to respond to stuff so that they would take off some of their attacks against us and be forced to respond. We did this with the attack on welfare.

TV advertisement: "Rise and Fall of Welfare Reform"

BILL CLINTON: A new bill restores America's basic bargain of providing opportunity and demanding in return responsibility. This bill will help people to go to work so they can stop drawing a welfare check and start drawing a pay check.

CARL LEVIN: Why should an able-bodied person receiving welfare benefits not be required to work?

JOHN KERRY: I believe it's an important change. Yes people ought to work, hardworking American citizens should not be required to carry people.

JOE BIDEN: I introduced a concept of work fair in 1986; I remembered being pilloried by my colleagues on the Democratic side at the time for suggesting that there be mandatory work requirement for anyone receiving welfare.

BARACK OBAMA: I was not a huge supporter of the federal plan that was signed in 1996.

ANNOUNCER 1: I would not probably have supported the federal bill that was passed.

ANNOUNCER 2: The Obama administration quietly offered to issue waivers to the work requirements in the law.

The Obama campaign had to respond to the welfare stuff. We also took advantage of the President's statements about "didn't build it."

TV advertisement: "These Hands"

BARACK OBAMA: If you've been successful you didn't get there on your own . . . If you got a business that—you didn't build that somebody else made that happen.

JACK GILCHRIST: My father's hands didn't build this company? My hands didn't build this company? Through hard work and a little bit of luck we built this business. Why are you demonizing us for it? It's time we had somebody who believes in us. Someone who believes that achievement should be rewarded not punished. We need somebody who believes in America.

MITT ROMNEY: I'm Mitt Romney and I approved this message.

It's fair to say in the summer we were trying to stay alive because we were being heavily outspent. We were fighting as best we could to stay on the offense and not completely go on defense. It worked to a certain degree. We realized that our goal had to be getting to the debate alive. That was what we could hope. Interestingly as we continued to test different ways to present messages, we found that after the convention, people responded much more favorably to Governor Romney on camera, probably because he was one of two people who were going to be president and they know new a lot more about him. They looked at him differently. He had grown as a candidate. There's just something about this process that changes people. We were able to use him on camera. Let me show an example:

TV advertisement: "Ohio Jobs"

MITT ROMNEY: The questions Ohio families are asking is who can bring back the jobs. Under President Obama we've lost over half a million manufacturing jobs and China has passed us in manufacturing. I'll stand up to China. I have a detailed plan to create 12 million new jobs including producing our own energy in the ground in Ohio. I'm Mitt Romney and I approved this message because Ohio families can't afford four more years like the last four years.

And in the debates

MITT ROMNEY: Let me repeat what I said.

JIM LEHRER (Offscreen): Alright.

MITT ROMNEY: I'm not in favor of a five trillion dollar tax cut. That's not my plan.

My plan is not to put in place any tax cut that will add to the deficit. That's point one.

So you may keep referring to it as a five trillion dollar tax cut, but that's not my plan.

BARACK OBAMA: OK.

MITT ROMNEY: Number two, let's look at history. My plan is not like anything . . .

TV advertisement: "The Choice 2"

[GRAPHIC] MITT ROMNEY: on President Obama's record

MITT ROMNEY: His policies haven't worked. Median income's down 4,300 dollars a family.

And 23 million Americans out of work. He said that he'd cut in half the deficit.

[GRAPHIC]: Under President Obama: Medicare and Social Security at risk

MITT ROMNEY: He just hasn't been able to put in place reforms for Medicare and Social Security to preserve them. That's what this election is about.

It's about who can get the middle class in this country a bright and prosperous future, and assure our kids the kind of hope and optimism they deserve.

I'm Mitt Romney and I approved this message.

TV advertisement: "Too Many Americans Are Struggling"

MITT ROMNEY: Too many Americans are struggling to find work in today's economy. Too many of those who are working are living paycheck to paycheck, trying to make falling incomes meet rising prices for food and gas. More Americans are living in poverty than when President Obama took office, and 15 million more are on foodstamps. President Obama and I both care about poor and middle-class families. The difference is: my policies will make things better for them. We shouldn't measure compassion by how many people are on welfare.

We should measure compassion by how many people are able to get off welfare, and get a good-paying job. My plan will create 12 million new jobs over the next four years, helping lift families out of poverty and strengthening the middle class.

I'm Mitt Romney, and I approved this message because we can't afford another four years like the last four years.

We ran that continuously after the 47 percent came out and did a 30-second version as well.

TV advertisement: "Together"

MITT ROMNEY: There are two very different paths the country can take. One is a path represented by the President, which at the end of four years would mean we'd have 20 trillion dollars in debt.

I'll get people back to work with twelve million new jobs. I'm gonna make sure that we get people off of foodstamps, not by cutting the program, but by getting them good jobs. I'll work with you. I'll lead you in an open and honest way.

And to make sure that we all together maintain America as the hope of the Earth.

I'm Mitt Romney, and I approved this message.

One of the constant streams of attacks that the Obama campaign ran against us was aimed at women. In the fall when we had more money, we addressed it with a number of ads. Here's one.

TV advertisement: "Welcome Daughter"

ANNOUNCER: Dear daughter, welcome to America.
Your share of Obama's debt is over 50,000 dollars, and it grows every day.

[GRAPHIC]: . . . $50,000 for each person. U.S. Department of Treasury.
Obama's policies are making it harder on women. The poverty rate for women? The highest in 17 years.

[GRAPHIC] . . . highest level in 17 years. U.S. Census Bureau 09.12.2012.
More women are unemployed under President Obama: more than five and a half million women can't find work.

[GRAPHIC]: . . . over 5.5 million women unemployed. Bureau of Labor Statistics 09.10.2012.
That's what Obama's policies have done for women. Welcome daughter.

MITT ROMNEY: I'm Mitt Romney and I approved this message.

I want to close with one other thing. There have been some articles about our buying. We set up our buying in-house. We didn't pay any commissions. We just paid salaries. It worked very well for us. It gave us complete control. There was total transparency. There were buyers hired to do it. There was a pretty tough CFO type who was in charge. Now as you can imagine, since there's a world out there that depends on commissions on advertising there were people who didn't like it when people did this. And there was an effort to discredit it.

Buying television's incredibly complex and an incredibly difficult process to understand. It's the only process I know where the FCC requires sellers to file sworn affidavits showing what they've actually sold. When you look at the reconciliation process, rebates, and what we actually paid for spots versus what the Obama campaign paid for spots, we felt that we got an excellent bang for our buck. We brought in the CFO types in the Romney campaign. They're not people who like to waste money. The whole idea was to save commissions. We probably saved $8 to $14 million in commissions. They did an excellent job for us. I have no dog in this fight. They weren't working for me. They were working for the campaign.

I wanted to say that on the record because I really hate to see a lot of misperception out there. And there was some sort of oppo [oppositional] research, for lack of a better word, dropped on this buying operation by those that didn't like the fact that we weren't going to outside firms. But they did a really good job for us and worked really hard. It was the right model for us.

JIM MARGOLIS:

We were surprised that there wasn't a definitional hit on the president earlier. Not necessarily from you, but in that period that was during your primary and during the spring that [the super PACS] would take that opportunity while you were in the midst of winning the nomination to do some of the definition on us to the extent that that was possible. Were you surprised or did you—

STUART STEVENS:

Everything about super PACS surprises me. I hate it. The only thing I can liken it to is putting out a daily newspaper and your lead is going to be sent over by somebody else with your story with your lead picture. And you have no idea what it is. They're just going to drop it in. It could be on the new Mars lunar landing or it could be on a murder. You have no idea. It's the most confounding horrible situation. Everybody thinks that people really do things with nods and winks. We weren't nodders and winkers.

JIM MARGOLIS:

If it's any consolation, we felt the power of that $500 million or $400 million—

STUART STEVENS:

Oh, it's out there. It's just—

JIM MARGOLIS:

I mean, we—

STUART STEVENS:

It's a very inefficient way to spend money. The whole idea that you can't coordinate things makes it inefficient.

JIM MARGOLIS:

Right.

STUART STEVENS:

I think that the law has to get in a better place. I think one of the burdens the Obama campaign bears is walking away from federal funding, which was one of the great post-Watergate reforms. I don't know how we're gonna get this genie back in the bottle. I don't have any good answers. But I think the idea that both sides had to raise all this money is bad for democracy.

I think that where we are with super PACS is bad for democracy. If you think about campaign funding for five minutes, it seems easy. If you think about it for ten, it seems impossible because there are so many conflicting First Amendment issues.

JIM MARGOLIS:

I certainly share the frustration on the super—

STUART STEVENS:

One of the major problems that we found is that you were able to introduce new information about Mitt Romney. There's very little new information you can introduce about the president on an area that we were willing to go to. It—that is an advantage that you had. There were certain advantages that we had. People knew about the economy. That's why you had to bet on the economy to do that.

JIM MARGOLIS:

Let me ask another one. As David indicated earlier today, we felt toward the end, some of the messaging, some of the spots you showed at the end touched emotionally with women in a way that maybe was a little different than what we had seen in some of the earlier advertising. The spots you showed with real life, real people were quite powerful and quite emotional.

At times there was this very hard edge. And at other times, sort of the softer "gold watch" approach. "He did a great job. Now, let's give him the gold watch and go to someone new. We thought you might've had an opportunity to say, "He is a good guy. He shares a lot of the same values that you have. But you know what?" And you did some of this. "It's not working. And so, we need a new person on the field." And I felt that when you were doing that, that had some traction.

STUART STEVENS:

Well, some of the super PACs did very good jobs.

JIM MARGOLIS:

They did some of that. How did you guys feel about that?

STUART STEVENS:

We always needed to do three things at once. This was always our reality. We always needed to tell people more about Mitt Romney. We always needed to tell people more about what Mitt Romney was going to do. And we always needed to help define the president and the race. I'm not a press basher at all. In the other part of my life, I write. So it would be sort of self-loathing. Not that I'm averse to self-loathing. (LAUGHTER) But I don't think it would be inaccurate to say [that there was] a more friendly press environment on the other side. So, it's more difficult for us to communicate messages. We always had to make very, very tough choices.

And I think Neil and his whole polling team were absolutely brilliant at forcing us to do what we needed to do to survive. What we were asking ourselves was not what would be nice to do. Not what would be good to do. But if we did not do this, we would be dead. That's the way we were looking at this. Every day, we had this meeting, a couple of brilliant guys who were working for [Neil] would do all the analytics on what was running.

There was a tremendous fog of war, particularly the way you guys were running all those tracks and all the super PAC [content]. We aggregated all the messages, [and did] not just look at them as spots. It was something I always wanted in campaigns. And it worked very well. So we had a very clear picture of what was happening. So it wasn't as if anything snuck up on us.

We were surprised by different turns and this. But the choices we made were deliberate choices with the full knowledge that by doing this, you're not doing this. A lot of these choices are very hard choices. I had just done the Senate race in Ohio for Portman where we had more money. That was more fun. (LAUGHTER) There were easier choices.

KATHLEEN HALL JAMIESON:

Jim, my scholarly colleagues will never forgive me if I don't ask you to explain the slide with all the boxes that you teased us with. Is there a way to put it back and give us a quick explanation?

STUART STEVENS:

The slide that you had that tracked was almost exactly like the slide that we had tracking your stuff every day.

JIM MARGOLIS:

Right. I just want to say for the record, it may have felt like you were getting outspent in some of those days three or four to one. And that may have been the case in some of those markets, us versus you.

STUART STEVENS:

More in the summer.

JIM MARGOLIS:

But we were feeling like we needed to pay attention to and respond to that super PAC piece. And that really did shift in terms of the equalization. We've got to be a little careful here because this isn't a magic solution. This is one additional tool that helps at focusing the advertising.

Media Buy – Rentrak

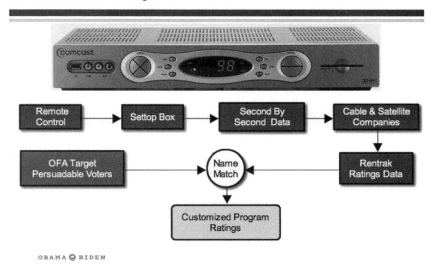

OBAMA ● BIDEN

Using Dish, satellite, and Direct TV, the box—the box, which is your set top box, measures everything you are doing second to second on your television, whether you're staying on an ad, whether you're changing channels, when you change, how long you're there, and so on.

What we were able to do with an incredible analytics operation that exists inside OFA (OBAMA for America) that supplied information and data throughout the campaign, across all the different elements of the campaign, was take this data as people use that remote control. It is measured by the set top box second by second. It sees what you're doing. That data is collected by these satellite companies, Direct TV. It goes to Rentrak, which is a commercial company that would be thrilled that today I've said their name (LAUGHTER) and is collected. Now we can see that Kathleen, at her house—I can't tell that it's Kathleen, but we know [have additional information] when we combine it with the OFA data from door knocks, phone calls, voter registration rolls, some consumer information, all the things that tell us about that person at that house.

We combine that data with what they're watching through a third party. So we don't actually know specifically it's Kathleen. But we know that there's an undecided voter there, a persuadable voter. We have all of these demographic inputs and all of that rich data from the campaign.

When we merge it together, we now say, "Aha. This group of people who look like this, watches this programming, is a persuadable target or turnout target." Some people's [viewing habits] surprise us. They're looking at "TV Land." We never had bought "TV Land" before. But there was a certain group, just by way of example, that were watching programming that was out of the norm and different from what we usually buy. We found them even though they were on cable channels with relatively low ratings, and so on.

But we started to be able to look in a much more precise way. What did it do for us? One more tool. You have the Nielsen data. You have what the buyers know or [what] are the likely hot shows coming up in September. You know who's in rerun. You know when the Olympics are coming. What you can't quite do with that box is know how the Olympics will rate.

But it is a rich additional piece of a puzzle that allows you to target advertising to smaller groups of people much more specifically. I would say [this] is probably 10 percent to 15 percent more efficiency, not 50. But if you're spending $450 million and talking to people a little bit more directly, you had a good day.

STUART STEVENS:

Did you use social media aggregate metrics to monitor how your spots were reaching these? Or to look at your dialogues?

JIM MARGOLIS:

Yeah—

STUART STEVENS:

And if so, what if you don't mind—

JIM MARGOLIS:

There were a whole series of places that we went to get feedback and information. We had, for example, online, Joel, you should really speak to some of this. We had an online—what did we call that?

JOEL BENENSON:

We had an online community.

JIM MARGOLIS:

Community.

JOEL BENENSON:

We would rotate them in and out and we'd keep them in for certain number of times. David Binder did this stuff. He does all of our qualitative. And we could both use it to drop in a few qualitative questions or show a spot or show a clip of a debate or something.

STUART STEVENS:

We were using it to show an aggregate of the Twitter, Facebook, the chatter.

JOEL BENENSON:

We would get aggregates but not in deep detail. Maybe you were getting deep detail. We would get aggregate numbers on YouTube views, all the macro level numbers—But not at a granular level. We had—

STUART STEVENS:

But—

JOEL BENENSON:

—other research we were using.

STUART STEVENS:

How were you testing spots?

JIM MARGOLIS:

Lots of different ways. Always online. And we—

STUART STEVENS:

And how did you find that worked for you?

JIM MARGOLIS:

I think you would get different opinions. I think what you want to do is have as many measures as possible. So having an online community, having online ad testing. We did focus groups. We did dials periodically. But

I would say most of the time, we were doing focus groups every night. We were doing live focus groups, online ad testing always on everything. And then community—

STUART STEVENS:

Negatives and positives online?

JIM MARGOLIS:

Yeah.

JOEL BENENSON:

We tested—

JIM MARGOLIS:

Everything was tested.

JOEL BENENSON:

Remember, when you're going online, by the way, you're not getting a representative sample. You're only talking to swing voters. So—

STUART STEVENS:

We did online.

JIM MARGOLIS:

We also did triads with some frequency.[1]

STUART STEVENS:

And what did you find was the most useful?

JIM MARGOLIS:

This is where sometimes there are disagreements on probably your side too. I—

STUART STEVENS:

I thought it also.

JIM MARGOLIS:

(LAUGHTER) Because we had multiple sources of information, it was that combination that you would look at it and you'd say, "Okay, what are we hearing in the verbatims? What's coming out of that triad?" I'm not going to believe three people sitting in a room who just dinged my ad that was a great ad. But I'll take that point. You know, I see what they're saying. And then, you'd say online, "Hmmm." Probably lookin' at that the most seriously. What are the actual numbers? How much did we move in vote? What happened to attributes? Biggest sample. And then being able at some broader level to do the larger focus groups and so on would be helpful.

JOEL BENENSON:

Let me just jump in quickly. To Stuart's question. You're not looking for something that's most useful. You're looking for the confluence of information you get that tells you about what's really going on beneath the surface with people on that particular issue in that particular dynamic. And how is your ad connecting with them or not connecting with them? So if you think of it as a normal quantitative exercise or qualitative exercise, you could say, "Ah, none of it's perfect. None of it's useful." But you're trying to aggregate it with all the brain power we had.

JIM MARGOLIS:

Did you test everything?

NEIL NEWHOUSE:

We tested a ton of stuff. A ton of stuff we tested, obviously, never saw the light of day. We tested online. We did a ton of focus groups. Because of the way our campaign was structured, we ended up testing stuff right before it went on the air. You'd test it and next day it'd be on the air. We had to move ahead.

We were doing focus groups every Monday night and every Sunday and Wednesday night of the last 10 weeks of the campaign. You tested ads. You tested messages. You find out what's on voters' minds. We ran outta swing voters, basically, in Columbus.

Jim Margolis:

Same problem.

Kathleen Hall Jamieson:

And did you use Rentrak?

Neil Newhouse:

No, we did not.

Kathleen Hall Jamieson:

Anything comparable to Rentrak?

Neil Newhouse:

No, nothing.

Stuart Stevens:

With the amount of money that we had to spend, what we were buying was pretty obvious. We used a lot of tools for our buying. But we didn't get to the [point of asking] what about "TV Land"? We were still in news adjacency world. We were still in the obvious stuff for the most part.

We were still at building blocks of sort of what you would buy. We used a lot of analyticals for that. But the honest to God truth is that, had you sat down to the buy without those analytics, you would have bought pretty much, I bet, 90 percent of the same stuff.

Jim Margolis:

Absolutely right. 90 percent is sort of the right number. It's the 10 percent that you're trying to improve around the edges. And I would also say that the later you go when you're up with 3,000, 4,000, 5,000 points within a—

Stuart Stevens:

See, we never were. We just never got there. That's exactly it.

Notes

1. There are several types of focus groups that are commonly conducted (http://thoughtleadership.sismarketresearch.com/the-market-research-journal /2012/11/7/what-is-a-focus-group.html):

1. Diad: Focus Group with two respondents
2. Triad: Focus Group with three respondents
3. Mini Focus Group: Focus group with approximately 4–5 respondents
4. Standard focus group: Focus group with 8 respondents
5. Gang Test or Survey: Focus group or test with more than 12 respondents

Chapter 7
Polling

Neil Newhouse

Neil Newhouse, *partner and co-founder of Public Opinion Strategies, has twice been named "Pollster of the Year" by the American Association of Political Consultants. Prior to serving as the lead pollster for Romney for President, Newhouse was the pollster for the successful U.S. Senate campaigns of Scott Brown (Mass.) and Rand Paul (Ky.) as well as a dozen members of Congress. He has worked in public opinion research for more than 25 years, directing the research for thousands of individual projects. During the 2008 election cycle, Newhouse was the Republican partner for the* NBC News/Wall Street Journal *polls. He has won praise from both sides of the political aisle, having worked on dozens of successful gubernatorial, Senate, and House campaigns, is frequently cited in a range of major national publications, and has appeared as a talking head on the nightly news regarding politics and campaigns.*

I'm going to walk you through how we saw the data throughout the campaign and then go through the exit poll data just a little bit. First let me walk through the assumptions we made in the polling.

Number one, we thought this was going to be a wrong track election [with the] economy being the main issue. Obviously, the economy remained the issue, but wow, I could say this a number of times during this presentation. If you had told me ahead of time that we were looking at a 46 percent right direction election I would have been shocked. I would have said, "[If that's the case] we're gonna be in big trouble." Second, the assumption that we made was that during the historic election of President Obama in 2008, the Obama campaign did a phenomenal job of getting out the vote, of identifying African Americans who were likely to vote. You hit census data numbers. It was a remarkable effort.

We thought that 2012 would be different in some respects. Number one, younger voter participation wouldn't be as high because the enthusiasm wasn't there. We thought [the] African American vote would hold steady, in terms of percent composition electorate. We thought [the] Hispanic vote would increase.

Neil Newhouse

What happened was younger voters increased their vote share. The best example, Joel, has got to be Colorado, where 20 percent of the voters were between ages eighteen and twenty-nine. And in the last election, 2008, [that percent] was 12. That's extraordinary, if those exit poll numbers are right.

In Ohio, African American turnout went from 11 percent to 15 percent. There were 200,000 more African Americans who voted in Ohio in 2012 than in 2008. I find that extraordinary. If the exit polls are right, hats off to the Obama campaign for pulling that off. That's incredible.

And Hispanic turnout increased by three or four points in Florida and Nevada. It was not just the composition of the electorate the Obama campaign changed. It was a composite electorate in targeted states. The national numbers didn't mean a damn thing. It was what happened in individual states.

Third is more voters disapproved of the job that President Obama [had done] than approved him. The negative intensity far outweighed

ASSUMPTION #1

ASSUMPTION WE MADE:

This was a "wrong track" election, with the economy being the main issue.

WHAT HAPPENED:

It was a wrong track election, but not to the extent we needed.

BELIEVE IN AMERICA

ASSUMPTION #2

ASSUMPTION WE MADE:

The Obama campaign changed the composition of the electorate in 2008 in the historic election of Barack Obama. But, 2012 would be different: Young voter participation would decline, the African American vote would hold steady, and the Hispanic vote would increase a point.

WHAT HAPPENED:

Younger voters increased their vote share, African American turnout not only held at previous levels, but in Ohio increased four points AND Hispanic turnout increased by three to four points in Florida and Nevada.

BELIEVE IN AMERICA

ASSUMPTION #3

ASSUMPTION WE MADE:

More voters disapproved of President Obama than approved of approved of him, with negative intensity far surpassing positive.

WHAT HAPPENED:

Exit polls showed that a majority of Election Day voters (54%) approved of the job Barack Obama was doing.

 ROMNEY   BELIEVE IN AMERICA

the positive intensity. All you've got to do is go back to the 2010 election and look at the approval rating of the president, the extraordinary high disapproval and strong disapproval numbers of the president, to understand where that intensity came from.

Then you go through the updating of this election. Throughout the last month or so of the campaign, the president's job approval rating ranged from 48 to 50 to maybe 51 percent. What was the president's job approval rating in the exit polls on Election Day? 54 percent. 54 percent job approval? We saw that at exit polls on election night. We looked at each other and figured, "Well, either they've really screwed up the exit polls or we're in deep trouble." As it turns out, obviously, we're in deep trouble.

Fourth, we ask a question in all of our surveys, "How interested are you in the upcoming election?" A scale from one to ten. [The answer] gives you an idea of the campaign interests, gives you an idea of the intensity of voters. Voters who rate their interest at ten [are] much more likely to vote. Work we'd done in past voter research that indicated that even people who [answered] "one" would still vote. We had done a study in California where 40 percent of voters who rated their interest on a one to ten scale, at one, which is the very lowest number, actually voted. So we knew it wasn't an ideal predictor of who's going to vote.

ASSUMPTION #4

ASSUMPTION WE MADE:

Just as Democratic enthusiasm and interest in the 2008 campaign contributed to an Election Day tilt toward the Democrats, we would get a similar tilt toward the GOP, making the partisan composition of the electorate far more even than in 2008.

WHAT HAPPENED:

The "enthusiasm gap" that we saw in our polling did not translate into a more level playing field for the GOP as the Obama campaign turned out low propensity/low interest voters.

 ROMNEY   BELIEVE IN AMERICA

But it gave you an idea of the intensity of the vote. Every measure in this election showed that we had an edge in terms of intensity, in terms of campaign interest, just as the Obama campaign had in 2008. Yet what happened on Election Day is the turnout effort simply washed away whatever intensity advantages we had. You look at people who have more interest in the campaign. Didn't make a damn bit of difference, because the Obama campaign was turning out their low propensity voters. We didn't screen them out of our surveys, but they just didn't show up in the highest level of campaign interest. So those are a number of the assumptions we made.

People have talked about where we were after the primaries. After the primaries, Mitt's image, his favorable, unfavorable image in our swing states was dead even at 43-43. That's not the ideal position to be in after having essentially won the Republican nomination.

Second, there's a question we asked on information flow. "Has what you've seen, read or heard about Mitt Romney or his campaign for president given you a more favorable or less favorable impression of him?" It's the leading indicator of image, leading indicator of the ballot.

In order to have your ballot numbers going up, you probably ought to have a positive information flow. We were sitting at the end of the Republican primaries in May at minus 14 on this measure. In other

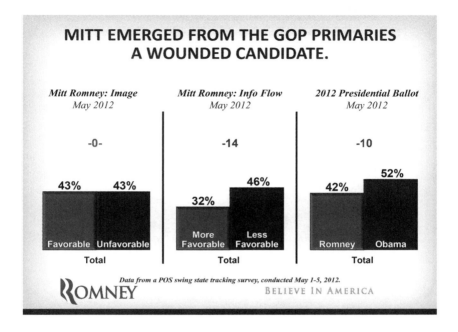

MITT EMERGED FROM THE GOP PRIMARIES A WOUNDED CANDIDATE.

| *Mitt Romney: Image* May 2012 | *Mitt Romney: Info Flow* May 2012 | *2012 Presidential Ballot* May 2012 |

-0-   -14   -10

| 43% Favorable | 43% Unfavorable | 32% More Favorable | 46% Less Favorable | 42% Romney | 52% Obama |

Total   Total   Total

Data from a POS swing state tracking survey, conducted May 1-5, 2012.

ROMNEY   BELIEVE IN AMERICA

words, we're not gaining support. In the ballot test, Obama's sitting at 52 to 42 in these target states. We're down by ten points. This is when the Obama campaign is actually getting ready to go on the air, attacking us.

We're already minus ten. Our image is dead even. Our info flow is minus double digits and now we want to try to get across a positive message. And Obama unfairly attacks us. Supposed to be funny. Sorry— okay. (LAUGHTER) You look at the image and information flow differences between Obama and Mitt.

Obama's sitting at 56-42, fave-unfave. And our info flow, 38-41. His image flow at 38-41. He's minus three. We're minus 14. When you ask voters, "Do you approve or disprove of the job Obama's doing?" He's sitting at 45, 47, 48 percent. But his favorability, his likeability was 72 percent. 72 percent of voters like Obama. 26 dislike. 54 dislike his policies. Jim, exactly the point you raised earlier, which is, "I like him. He's a nice guy, but I disagree with his policies. It's time for a change."

That's what we were trying to get across. Throughout our focus groups, everything else we're doing in the campaign, we had to pull people back on the language we used. All of our fundraisers, our key supporters, want us to go out and beat the living snot out of President Obama and they want to be negative because they felt that way. They

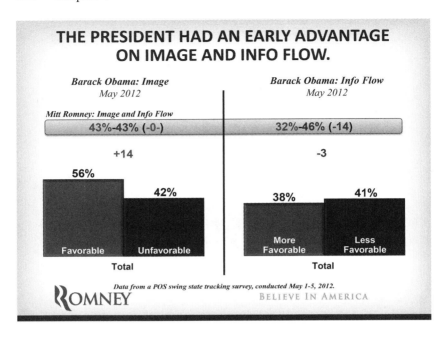

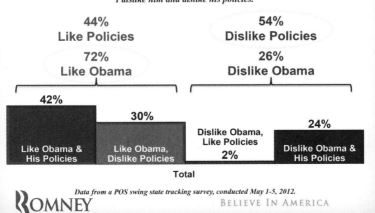

wanted to call the guy a liar. It's like, "Guys. The key voters we're after in the election are not the people you're talking to. The key voters we're after are people who voted for Obama in 2008, for God's sake. You can't tell them they were stupid. You can't tell them what a stupid mistake they made four years ago." [You can't say], "Wake up," and slap 'em across the head. [You could say], "Hey, listen. You tried. We hoped for change, but it didn't turn out that way." And so you had to reason with them in a little bit different language. We tried to push the campaign that direction. This is a key chart that shows that.

The president also had a huge advantage among independent voters, a group that Mitt ended up winning, but the ballot test among independent voters was down by 11 points in May. So the ideal time for us to go on the air with a positive ad, telling what voters are going to do right? Also ideal time for the Obama campaign to say, "You know what? We got this guy down. Let's put our foot on his shoulder and keep him down," which is what you guys did.

So by mid-summer, state of the race. Obama campaign's been on the air beating us. So our image, obviously, in July, 14 to 16. Our image has gone down three points. We're not just dead even. We're inverted, inverted at 47-44-47. Our information flow is 31 more favorable and 52 less favorable.

We have gotten worse since the end of the Republican primaries. We're down by 21 points in terms of information flow, not an ideal place for us to be. Yet, the other thing is the ballot test. We actually went up a couple points, margin of error stuff, so we argued publicly, "It's not making any difference. They're spending all these millions of dollars and they haven't moved the ballot test." That was true. What they had moved, though, was information flow and image.

They made it tougher for us to improve later on because they had some of this negative image of Mitt ingrained in voters. All that was true in terms of the ballot test, but underneath the ballot test we knew the numbers had moved. We knew that race was shifting. By late July we were still winning on which candidate can do a better job of turning the economy around.

We were lagging on enacting policies [that would] help me and my family and address the concerns of middle class Americans. The point we were trying to push from research and from all the focus groups, [and] other work we're doing is voters felt Mitt was better on the economy and they gave him that. But in the focus groups they said, "Yeah, he can turn the economy around. He'll be good for the economy, but I'm worried about what he's going to do for me."

There was a sense of, "What about my economy?" And so we tried to personalize it. That's why we talked about wages. That's why we talked

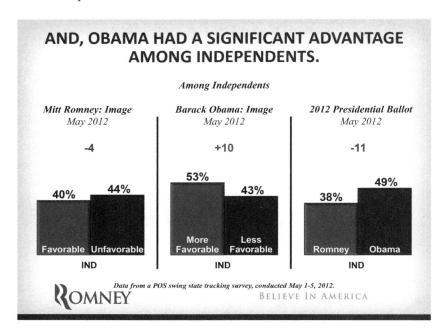

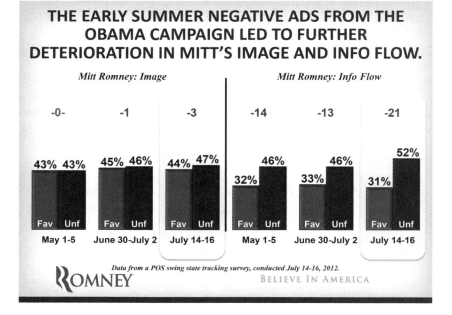

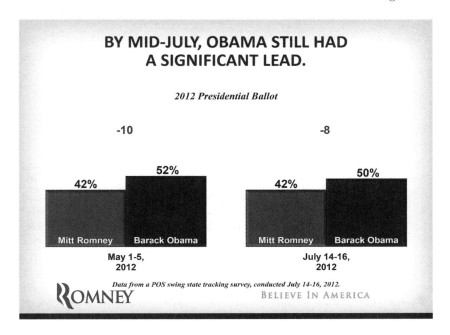

BY MID-JULY, OBAMA STILL HAD A SIGNIFICANT LEAD.

2012 Presidential Ballot

-10   -8

52%   50%
42%   42%

Mitt Romney   Barack Obama   Mitt Romney   Barack Obama
May 1-5,   July 14-16,
2012   2012

Data from a POS swing state tracking survey, conducted July 14-16, 2012.

ROMNEY   BELIEVE IN AMERICA

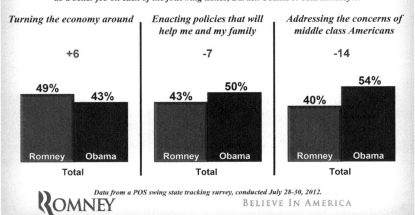

BY LATE JULY, MITT WAS WINNING ON THE ECONOMY, BUT LOSING THE EMPATHY VOTE TO OBAMA.

Regardless of which candidate you may be supporting in the race for President, who do you believe will do a better job on each of the following issues, Barack Obama or Mitt Romney...

Turning the economy around | *Enacting policies that will help me and my family* | *Addressing the concerns of middle class Americans*

+6   -7   -14

49%   54%
        43%   43%   50%   40%

Romney   Obama   Romney   Obama   Romney   Obama
Total   Total   Total

Data from a POS swing state tracking survey, conducted July 28-30, 2012.

ROMNEY   BELIEVE IN AMERICA

about some of the more personal aspects of the economy. People thought he could fix the economy, but by doing so he's gonna fix it for those who are higher up, for the rich. We needed to make sure that people understood it was for average folks.

So pre-convention, our image has finally edged back up to plus two in one survey, 48, 46. Obama's image, plus seven, 53, 46. We've moved back up a little bit. The reason we moved back up is we hit on welfare reform.

We had a good couple weeks going into the convention with welfare reform, with Medicare and [with] Paul Ryan. So our image moved up. Our info flow was now minus nine. We picked back up on info flow. Obama's was minus 11. We're now minus two points going to the convention. Not bad. We felt pretty good about where we were. Then we went through the Republican and Democratic conventions. One of the most significant things that happened in this campaign happened after the Democratic convention, and that is the mood of the country [changed]. "Do you think the country's headed in the right direction? Is it pretty seriously off on the wrong track?" is the Dow Jones Industrial Average of politics. When voters think things are going well, they reelect incumbents. When they think things are going poorly, they kick them out of office. This is an extraordinarily difficult measure to move. It takes the economy moving.

The numbers have not crossed, right direction, wrong track, for nine years. This is the longest period of sustained pessimism the country's ever gone through. In the 2008 election, 17 percent of Americans say the country's headed in the right direction. 2010 election, it was 20 percent. We went into this election a year ago at around 20 percent right direction and then going into the convention it was 34, 35 percent. After the convention, 42 percent of Americans believe the country's headed in the right direction. We looked at these numbers. And it's like, "Oh my God."

It was a combination of Democrats coming home, of the Bill Clinton speech, of Barack Obama's speech, of a sense that Obama and Clinton instilled in Americans that sense that, "Hey, we really are headed in the right direction; we're on the right track. You just got to stay with us a little bit longer. Stay the course and things will get better."

That shift from 34 right direction to 42 caught us completely off guard because you can't move those numbers. Yet they moved them. That's an extraordinary shift. It wasn't just right direction wrong track. Obama's approval went from minus one to plus three. His reelect over a new person after the primary went from minus one to plus seven. A majority of voters saying now that they want to reelect him.

And the image bump we got before the convention, it's gone. It's gone completely. We're now back at one to one, 48-48. And Obama's at plus 10, 54, 44. This is the point and time where I think I was quoted as

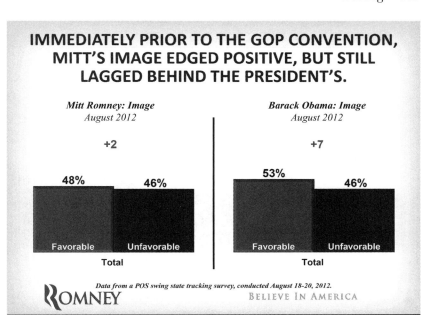

IMMEDIATELY PRIOR TO THE GOP CONVENTION, MITT'S IMAGE EDGED POSITIVE, BUT STILL LAGGED BEHIND THE PRESIDENT'S.

Mitt Romney: Image
August 2012

+2

48%   46%

Favorable   Unfavorable

Total

Barack Obama: Image
August 2012

+7

53%   46%

Favorable   Unfavorable

Total

Data from a POS swing state tracking survey, conducted August 18-20, 2012.

ROMNEY   BELIEVE IN AMERICA

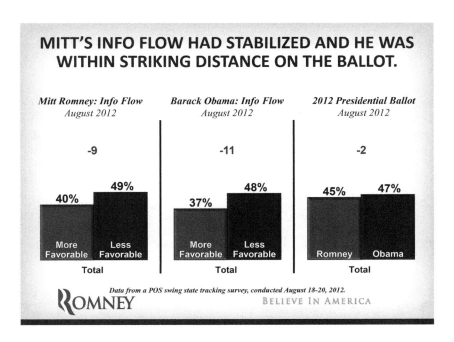

MITT'S INFO FLOW HAD STABILIZED AND HE WAS WITHIN STRIKING DISTANCE ON THE BALLOT.

Mitt Romney: Info Flow
August 2012

-9

40%   49%

More
Favorable   Less
Favorable

Total

Barack Obama: Info Flow
August 2012

-11

37%   48%

More
Favorable   Less
Favorable

Total

2012 Presidential Ballot
August 2012

-2

45%   47%

Romney   Obama

Total

Data from a POS swing state tracking survey, conducted August 18-20, 2012.

ROMNEY   BELIEVE IN AMERICA

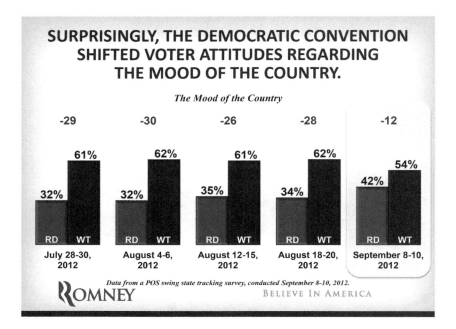

SURPRISINGLY, THE DEMOCRATIC CONVENTION SHIFTED VOTER ATTITUDES REGARDING THE MOOD OF THE COUNTRY.

The Mood of the Country

	-29	-30	-26	-28	-12
RD	32%	32%	35%	34%	42%
WT	61%	62%	61%	62%	54%
	July 28-30, 2012	August 4-6, 2012	August 12-15, 2012	August 18-20, 2012	September 8-10, 2012

Data from a POS swing state tracking survey, conducted September 8-10, 2012.

ROMNEY   BELIEVE IN AMERICA

saying, "Oh, it's a sugar high. It's nothing more than just a sugar high." And I'm thinking, "Oh, please, God. Please be just a sugar high," because these numbers were tough stuff.

Look at the information flow on the right-hand side on Barack Obama. He'd gone from minus 11, minus 12 to the week after the convention, plus two. A 14-point shift in information flow. We have verbatims on all of our surveys. We got tired of reading these damn verbatims, week after week, about how positive that damn convention was and [about] President Clinton's speech. I'd write my emails every morning. "Well, you know, again, convention still comes up," because there's nothing else taking its place.

So that's in the middle of September, where we stood. And Obama's vote support was up to 49 to 44. We're down by five points, September, eight to ten after Labor Day.

And we all knew after Labor Day it's tough moving numbers. You move numbers maybe through advertising, through earned media, and the debates. And beyond that, it's really tough moving numbers after Labor Day. And on the issues, turn the economy around.

We're now up by just one point. Our strength, we're up by one point and we've fallen further behind on those empathy issues. This is not a high point for the campaign, obviously. Then we have the state of the

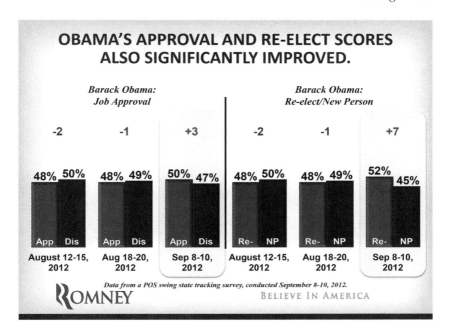

OBAMA'S APPROVAL AND RE-ELECT SCORES ALSO SIGNIFICANTLY IMPROVED.

Barack Obama: Job Approval

Barack Obama: Re-elect/New Person

| -2 | -1 | +3 | -2 | -1 | +7 |

Data from a POS swing state tracking survey, conducted September 8-10, 2012.

ROMNEY   BELIEVE IN AMERICA

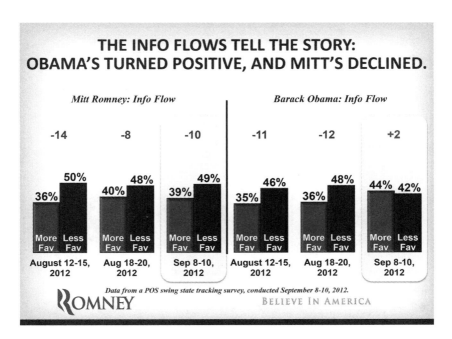

THE INFO FLOWS TELL THE STORY: OBAMA'S TURNED POSITIVE, AND MITT'S DECLINED.

Mitt Romney: Info Flow

Barack Obama: Info Flow

| -14 | -8 | -10 | -11 | -12 | +2 |

Data from a POS swing state tracking survey, conducted September 8-10, 2012.

ROMNEY   BELIEVE IN AMERICA

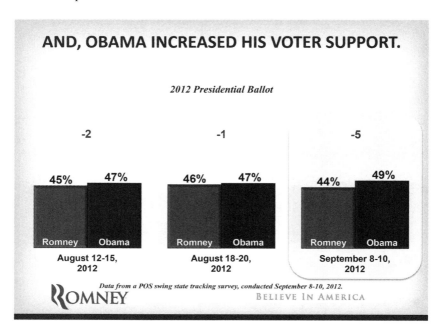

AND, OBAMA INCREASED HIS VOTER SUPPORT.

2012 Presidential Ballot

-2

45% Romney   47% Obama

August 12-15, 2012

-1

46% Romney   47% Obama

August 18-20, 2012

-5

44% Romney   49% Obama

September 8-10, 2012

Data from a POS swing state tracking survey, conducted September 8-10, 2012.

ROMNEY   BELIEVE IN AMERICA

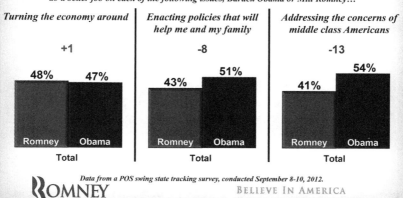

ON THE ISSUES, OBAMA PULLED EVEN WITH MITT ON THE ECONOMY FOR THE FIRST TIME, AND THE PRESIDENT WIDENED HIS LEAD ON EMPATHY.

Regardless of which candidate you may be supporting in the race for President, who do you believe will do a better job on each of the following issues, Barack Obama or Mitt Romney...

Turning the economy around

+1

48% Romney   47% Obama

Total

Enacting policies that will help me and my family

-8

43% Romney   51% Obama

Total

Addressing the concerns of middle class Americans

-13

41% Romney   54% Obama

Total

Data from a POS swing state tracking survey, conducted September 8-10, 2012.

ROMNEY   BELIEVE IN AMERICA

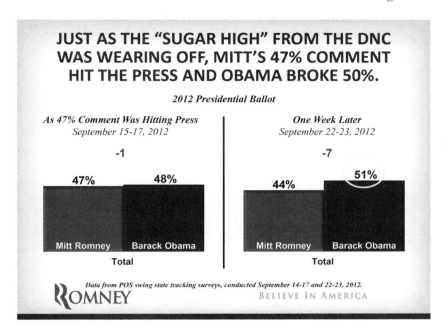

JUST AS THE "SUGAR HIGH" FROM THE DNC WAS WEARING OFF, MITT'S 47% COMMENT HIT THE PRESS AND OBAMA BROKE 50%.

2012 Presidential Ballot

As 47% Comment Was Hitting Press
September 15-17, 2012

-1

47%   48%

Mitt Romney   Barack Obama
Total

One Week Later
September 22-23, 2012

-7

44%   51%

Mitt Romney   Barack Obama
Total

Data from POS swing state tracking surveys, conducted September 14-17 and 22-23, 2012.

ROMNEY   BELIEVE IN AMERICA

race late September. The 47 percent number came out on a Monday night or whatever it was.

We were in the field. And we had come back a little bit. Our ballot test was 47-48. We're down by one point. One week later, we were down by seven. We actually pulled our tracking during this week because we knew what we were going to find. How we're going to respond to the issue. Why throw good money after bad right, because you know what? We don't need another five depressing emails from me to the campaign, saying, "Guys, we're falling further behind."

We're at 44-51, September 22, 23. Look at Mitt's information flow, minus 21 points. Obama's at plus one, 41, 40. We needed a real game changer. We needed something to turn this around. We're not only dead even on fixing the economy. We're now down by two points.

So this is a tough time. This is when we brainstormed and tried to figure out, "Okay, guys. We got to get out of this. It's not a quick fix to move away from the 47 percent. But we've got to push our way through it." And we did push our way through it. Came into the first debate having recovered a little bit. The 47 percent was certainly still out there in the water, but we'd moved through it a little bit.

So going into the first debate, our image was plus one and Obama's image was plus two. Coming out of that debate, this was like night and

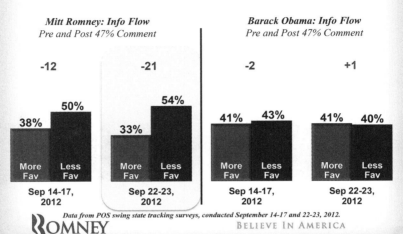

MITT'S INFO FLOW DROPPED TO LEVELS NOT SEEN SINCE THE SUMMER'S NEGATIVE AD BLITZ.

Mitt Romney: Info Flow
Pre and Post 47% Comment

Barack Obama: Info Flow
Pre and Post 47% Comment

-12   -21   -2   +1

50%
38%

54%
33%

41% 43%

41% 40%

More Fav / Less Fav
Sep 14-17, 2012

More Fav / Less Fav
Sep 22-23, 2012

More Fav / Less Fav
Sep 14-17, 2012

More Fav / Less Fav
Sep 22-23, 2012

Data from POS swing state tracking surveys, conducted September 14-17 and 22-23, 2012.

ROMNEY   BELIEVE IN AMERICA

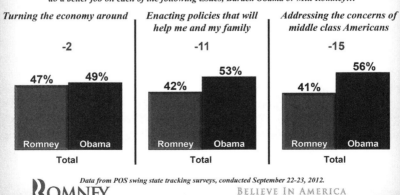

OBAMA WON ON THE ECONOMY FOR THE FIRST TIME AND EXPANDED HIS LEAD ON EMPATHY TO A NEW HIGH.

Regardless of which candidate you may be supporting in the race for President, who do you believe will do a better job on each of the following issues, Barack Obama or Mitt Romney...

Turning the economy around

Enacting policies that will help me and my family

Addressing the concerns of middle class Americans

-2   -11   -15

47% 49%

42% 53%

41% 56%

Romney / Obama
Total

Romney / Obama
Total

Romney / Obama
Total

Data from POS swing state tracking surveys, conducted September 22-23, 2012.

ROMNEY   BELIEVE IN AMERICA

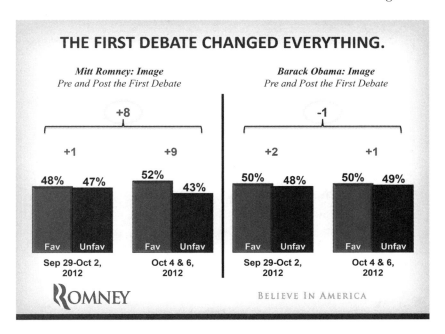

THE FIRST DEBATE CHANGED EVERYTHING.

Mitt Romney: Image
Pre and Post the First Debate

Barack Obama: Image
Pre and Post the First Debate

+8

-1

+1   +9   +2   +1

48% 47%   52%   43%   50% 48%   50% 49%

Fav   Unfav   Fav   Unfav   Fav   Unfav   Fav   Unfav

Sep 29-Oct 2,
2012

Oct 4 & 6,
2012

Sep 29-Oct 2,
2012

Oct 4 & 6,
2012

ROMNEY   BELIEVE IN AMERICA

day. Our image went to 52-43. And Obama's image went to 50, basically staying exactly the same. My kind of offhand comment about this is that this is the first time these voters actually got a chance to see Mitt Romney for who he is. During the whole 90 minutes of that first debate, I don't recall him outsourcing a single job, laying off a single worker, sending any jobs to China, closing down any businesses. Voters sensed in Mitt Romney somebody they had not really been introduced to before. It was a new Mitt Romney and after that point and time, what we saw in our data was Mitt's vote was comprised mostly of, especially in that September period of time, voters who really are anti-Obama. There wasn't a lot of pro-Mitt.

After that first debate, we got much more pro-Mitt. We had a sense of, "I'm really for this guy," rather than just against the other guy. That came through in our fundraising. It came through in our volunteers and everything we did. These numbers reminded me of what happened in the South Carolina primary when we had two debates the last week of the South Carolina primary. I think it was Monday and Thursday night. Newt Gingrich took on the moderators. The first debate started at nine o'clock, so we finished our polling before nine o'clock. We went into the first debate literally ten points up. We were back in the field on Tuesday night. We were now six points down. I don't know how you do that. It's an extraordinary change over a very short period

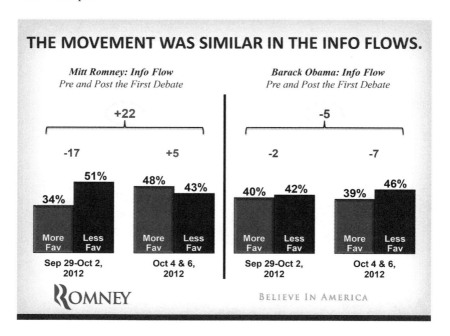

THE MOVEMENT WAS SIMILAR IN THE INFO FLOWS.

Mitt Romney: Info Flow
Pre and Post the First Debate

Barack Obama: Info Flow
Pre and Post the First Debate

of time. And it's the same kind of thing we saw here. Overnight, the numbers changed.

Mitt's information flow, look at the dates here. September 29th to October 2nd, we're minus 17. October four, six, we're at plus five, a 22 point shift. And it's not like Obama's numbers changed that much. It wasn't about Obama. It was more about Mitt Romney. Then in our data, he took a lead in the ballot, 48-47.

It's a one-point margin. It's the swing states, not individual state stuff. So we thought we'd picked up some decent ground here. Getting ahead, I think the hurricane did a number of things in this race that are probably underestimated. It stalled our campaign message for a good five or six days. We were not messageless but just simply had to put a hold on our campaign. That was number one. Secondly, it focused Americans' attention away from the political campaign and on the disaster [that] was happening in the Northeast.

And third, as I said at Harvard the other day, I think it did for President Obama what the [first] debate had done for us, to a lesser extent. It put him back in the role of being president and reminded voters of what he was like as president, reminded voters what they liked about him. They felt better about him after seeing how he handled it, how he went to the states. It put him in the position of authority. Voters were

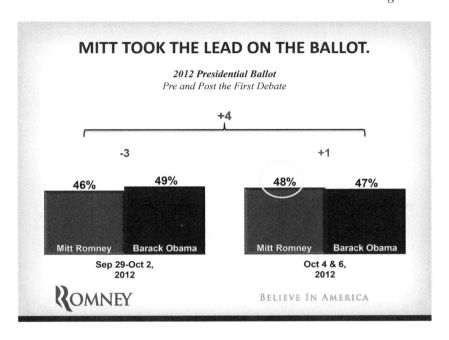

MITT TOOK THE LEAD ON THE BALLOT.

2012 Presidential Ballot
Pre and Post the First Debate

+4

-3

+1

46%

49%

48%

47%

Mitt Romney | Barack Obama

Mitt Romney | Barack Obama

Sep 29-Oct 2,
2012

Oct 4 & 6,
2012

ROMNEY

BELIEVE IN AMERICA

HURRICANE SANDY WAS A SIGNIFICANT FACTOR TILTING LATE-DECIDING VOTERS TOWARD OBAMA.

In your vote for president, how would you rate the importance of Obama's hurricane response? Total and by Ballot	Total	Romney	Obama
The most important factor	15%	26%	73%
An important factor	27%	33%	65%
A minor factor	22%	46%	51%
Not a factor	31%	70%	28%

Data from the 2012 national Exit Poll among 26,565 respondents, conducted November 6, 2012.

ROMNEY

BELIEVE IN AMERICA

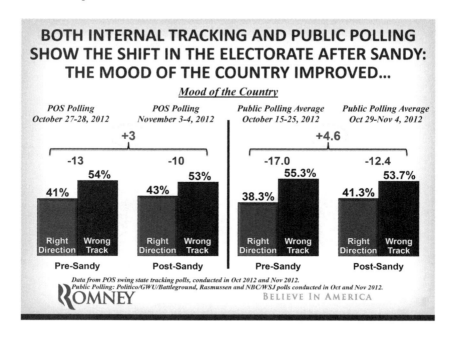

BOTH INTERNAL TRACKING AND PUBLIC POLLING SHOW THE SHIFT IN THE ELECTORATE AFTER SANDY: THE MOOD OF THE COUNTRY IMPROVED...

Mood of the Country

| *POS Polling* *October 27-28, 2012* | *POS Polling* *November 3-4, 2012* | *Public Polling Average* *October 15-25, 2012* | *Public Polling Average* *Oct 29-Nov 4, 2012* |

+3   +4.6

-13   -10   -17.0   -12.4

54%   53%   55.3%   53.7%

41%   43%   38.3%   41.3%

| Right Direction | Wrong Track | Right Direction | Wrong Track | Right Direction | Wrong Track | Right Direction | Wrong Track |

Pre-Sandy   Post-Sandy   Pre-Sandy   Post-Sandy

Data from POS swing state tracking polls, conducted in Oct 2012 and Nov 2012.
Public Polling: Politico/GWU/Battleground, Rasmussen and NBC/WSJ polls conducted in Oct and Nov 2012.

ROMNEY   BELIEVE IN AMERICA

reminded of why they liked him. I think [that] had a significant impact in the race. As Joel'll tell you, I take some of these public polls with a grain of salt, as we all did in this campaign. I think I'd probably take some of the exit poll data with a grain of salt, but taking voters at what they said, 15 percent of voters said that Obama's response to the hurricane was the single most important factor in how they're going to vote. I have a hard time believing that it's 15 percent, but 17 percent of those voters made up their minds who they're going to vote for in the last few days of the campaign. That works out to two and a half percent. It's a significant number.

Now look at the public data and our own data. The mood of the country increased three points pre-hurricane, post-hurricane on our data; in the public data increased four and a half points. It improved because people saw other Americans rallying behind the effort to help the victims of Hurricane Sandy. So that's number one. It improved the mood of the country.

Second is Obama's approval rating. Our numbers stayed the same. Public numbers went up two points. It hit 50 percent.

Third, the exit poll says 67 percent approve the job the president was doing on handling the hurricane. 16 percent disapprove. Voters approved of the job he was doing there.

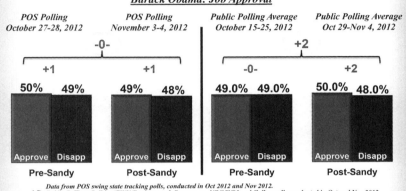

OBAMA'S APPROVAL WAS UNCHANGED IN OUR TRACKING BUT SLIGHTLY IMPROVED IN PUBLIC POLLING.

Barack Obama: Job Approval

| *POS Polling*
October 27-28, 2012 | *POS Polling*
November 3-4, 2012 | *Public Polling Average*
October 15-25, 2012 | *Public Polling Average*
Oct 29-Nov 4, 2012 |

-0-   +2

+1   +1   -0-   +2

50% 49% 49% 48% 49.0% 49.0% 50.0% 48.0%

Approve Disapp | Approve Disapp | Approve Disapp | Approve Disapp

Pre-Sandy   Post-Sandy   Pre-Sandy   Post-Sandy

Data from POS swing state tracking polls, conducted in Oct 2012 and Nov 2012.
Public Polling: Politico/GWU/Battleground, Rasmussen, NBC/WSJ and Gallup polls conducted in Oct and Nov 2012.

ROMNEY   BELIEVE IN AMERICA

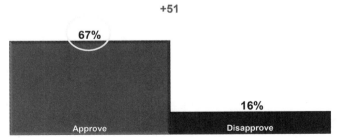

FULLY 67% OF VOTERS APPROVED OF OBAMA'S HANDLING OF HURRICANE SANDY.

In general, do you approve or disapprove of the way Barack Obama is handling the aftermath of Hurricane Sandy?

+51

67%

16%

Approve   Disapprove

Total

Data from a national NBC/WSJ survey among 1,000 likely voters, conducted November 1-3, 2012.

ROMNEY   BELIEVE IN AMERICA

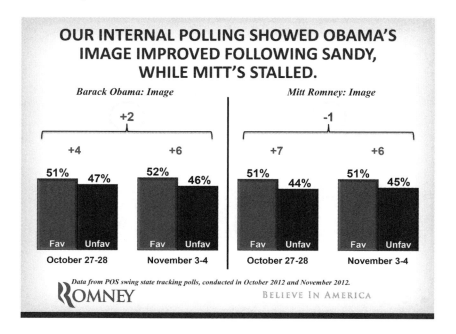

OUR INTERNAL POLLING SHOWED OBAMA'S IMAGE IMPROVED FOLLOWING SANDY, WHILE MITT'S STALLED.

Data from POS swing state tracking polls, conducted in October 2012 and November 2012.

His image went up two points during this period. Our image dropped a point. It's just minor changes, but he had a little bit of wind at his back. His information flow went from minus five to minus one to plus four. Ours lost a point.

Finally, I ask a question to try to get at the momentum question. "Do you think Barack Obama's campaign is gaining ground? Are they losing ground or staying about the same?" Going into the hurricane, gaining ground 23, losing ground 35. Coming out of the hurricane, 29, 26.

You look at these numbers and say, "This last week has really been difficult for us and this reinforces there is something else going on here." You look at the individual states. Obama's information flow in each of the target states increased by at least one in every single state, which is indicative of [the fact that] the Obama campaign closed extraordinarily well.

We didn't close as well. I argued pretty strongly three weeks out that we weren't five or six points down in Ohio or ten days out. We weren't five or six points down in Ohio. I thought we were more dead even. If we were five or six points down and we went through this stuff during the last ten days of the campaign, we couldn't have ended up minus three points in the state. I argued that we actually probably lost ground over the last few days of the campaign and ended up, where we were

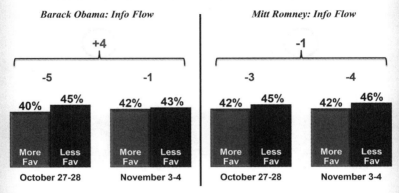

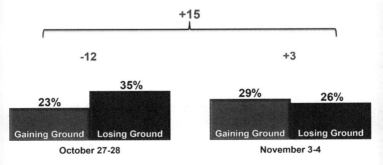

SANDY HELPED OBAMA'S INFO FLOW IN THE TARGET STATES.

Barack Obama: Info Flow	Oct 27-29	Oct 30-31	Nov 1	Change From 10/27-29
CO	39-44	40-41	45-44	+6
FL	41-46	40-44	44-46	+3
IA	38-46	42-45	40-40	+8
NH	39-46	40-45	43-43	+7
OH	39-44	41-44	40-44	+1
VA	40-43	N/A	39-41	+1
WI	39-43	37-40	45-45	+4
Swing States	38-47	41-45	42-42	+9

ROMNEY   BELIEVE IN AMERICA

once tied, minus three or so. So Obama had some wind at his back. When you look at the ballot test, pre-Sandy, post-Sandy in our internal data Obama had a net two in the external stuff, the public stuff, plus 1.4. It's a significant difference.

Would it have made a difference on Election Day? Absolutely. Would it have made a difference in the results on Election Day? No. [The outcome] would have been [known] later in the night and forced you guys [to drink] more coffee or more alcohol, but it probably wouldn't have made a difference. I think we could have won Virginia, potentially Ohio, Florida, but we were then stuck. New Hampshire was out of reach and Colorado's out of reach and Iowa never came into play, at least at the very end. So we would have been stuck. But it would have been a closer night.

Digging into a couple of things that would happen on Election Day, the change in the mood of the country over the past year has been extraordinary. 20 percent right direction, 70 percent, 74 percent wrong track a year out from Election Day ended up on Election Day being 46, 52, and the Real Clear Politics average of voters prior to Election Day was 41-54. This is how the Obama campaign changed the composition of the electorate. This is what they did. The average of all the public polls had 41 right direction. We ended up 46 right direction on Election Day.

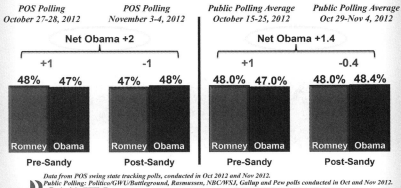

THE PRESIDENT'S MOMENTUM SHOWED IN THE BALLOT: OBAMA'S BALLOT SUPPORT IMPROVED, WHILE MITT'S REMAINED ABOUT THE SAME.

2012 Presidential Ballot

| POS Polling October 27-28, 2012 | POS Polling November 3-4, 2012 | Public Polling Average October 15-25, 2012 | Public Polling Average Oct 29-Nov 4, 2012 |

Net Obama +2   Net Obama +1.4

| +1 | -1 | +1 | -0.4 |

| 48% 47% | 47% 48% | 48.0% 47.0% | 48.0% 48.4% |

| Romney Obama | Romney Obama | Romney Obama | Romney Obama |
| Pre-Sandy | Post-Sandy | Pre-Sandy | Post-Sandy |

Data from POS swing state tracking polls, conducted in Oct 2012 and Nov 2012.
Public Polling: Politico/GWU/Battleground, Rasmussen, NBC/WSJ, Gallup and Pew polls conducted in Oct and Nov 2012.

ROMNEY   BELIEVE IN AMERICA

VOTERS WERE PRETTY EVENLY DIVIDED AS TO THE DIRECTION OF THE COUNTRY — A FAR CRY FROM A YEAR AGO.

The Mood of the Country

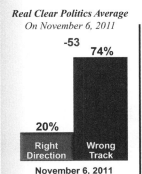
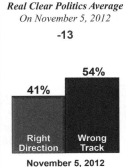
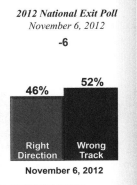

| Real Clear Politics Average On November 6, 2011 | Real Clear Politics Average On November 5, 2012 | 2012 National Exit Poll November 6, 2012 |

-53   -13   -6

74%   54%   52%
20%   41%   46%

| Right Direction Wrong Track | Right Direction Wrong Track | Right Direction Wrong Track |
| November 6, 2011 | November 5, 2012 | November 6, 2012 |

Data from the RCP average of polls and from the 2012 national Exit Poll among 26,565 respondents, conducted November 6, 2012.

ROMNEY   BELIEVE IN AMERICA

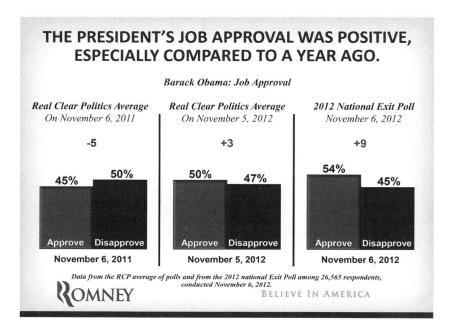

THE PRESIDENT'S JOB APPROVAL WAS POSITIVE, ESPECIALLY COMPARED TO A YEAR AGO.

Barack Obama: Job Approval

Real Clear Politics Average
On November 6, 2011

-5

45%   50%

Approve   Disapprove

November 6, 2011

Real Clear Politics Average
On November 5, 2012

+3

50%   47%

Approve   Disapprove

November 5, 2012

2012 National Exit Poll
November 6, 2012

+9

54%   45%

Approve   Disapprove

November 6, 2012

Data from the RCP average of polls and from the 2012 national Exit Poll among 26,565 respondents, conducted November 6, 2012.

ROMNEY   BELIEVE IN AMERICA

Obama's job approval, 45 percent a year ago. The average of voters on Election Day, Real Clear Politics at 50. And yet the voters on Election Day, 54. Not a single survey done prior to Election Day showed the President's job approval above 51 percent. Not a single survey. Yet he ended up with 54.

This was the point that Jim and others made. Voters didn't believe the economy was in good shape. They thought it was in bad shape. But who did they blame? They blame George W. When you guys talk about, "Hey, we inherited a mess," that's exactly what the voters would tell us in focus groups. He inherited all this. We keep saying, "Yes, but he failed to make things better." That was a key line for us. If we talked about Obama's failed presidency, voters would react negatively.

When we said Obama's policies have failed to make things better, we'd get a better response from people.

We won white voters by 20 points, but in this changing political environment we didn't get anywhere near where George W. came with Hispanic voters in 2004.

Ohio. When Republicans win independents by 10 points in Ohio and win Republicans by a wider margin than you lose Democrats, you usually win the state. That's usually the way you win. And yet with a 7-point Democratic advantage in the state, we again came up short.

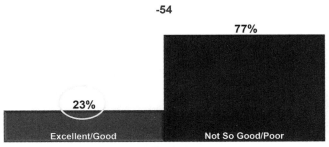

FEW BELIEVED THE NATION'S ECONOMY WAS IN GOOD SHAPE.

Do you think the condition of the nation's economy is: Excellent, Good, Not so good or Poor?

-54

77%

23%

Excellent/Good

Not So Good/Poor

Total

Data from the 2012 national Exit Poll among 26,565 respondents, conducted November 6, 2012.

ROMNEY   BELIEVE IN AMERICA

YET, VOTERS TENDED TO BLAME W. MORE THAN OBAMA.

Who is more to blame for current economic problems: Barack Obama or George W. Bush?

-15

53%

38%

Barack Obama

George W. Bush

Total

Data from the 2012 national Exit Poll among 26,565 respondents, conducted November 6, 2012.

ROMNEY   BELIEVE IN AMERICA

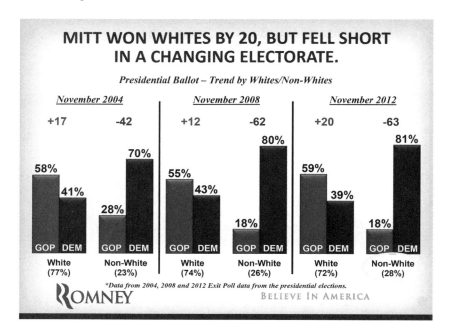

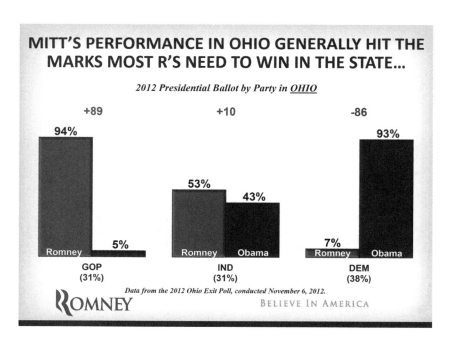

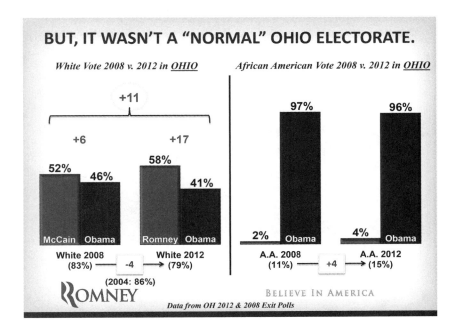

It wasn't the normal electorate.

Let me go to the difference between 2010 and 2008. 2010, the electorate in Ohio on Election Day was dead even, Republican versus Democrat, 36-36. In 2012, the Democrats had a seven-point advantage. We thought it would be a two or three.

JOEL BENENSON:

Why did you look at 2010, where if you look at 2008, the Democrat advantage is plus eight, and on Election Day in 2012 it's plus seven? Why were you factoring 2010 in to a presidential year?

NEIL NEWHOUSE:

We weren't factoring it in. But we thought—

JOEL BENENSON:

The Democratic spread is right where it was in the last presidential election in Ohio.

THE 2012 ELECTORATE IN OHIO CLOSELY RESEMBLED 2008 IN TERMS OF AGE AND PARTISANSHIP.

Ohio Voters	2008	2012	2010
18-29	17%	17%	12%
30-44	27%	24%	23%
45-64	39%	41%	48%
65+	17%	18%	17%
Republican	31%	31%	36%
Independent	30%	31%	28%
Democrat	39%	38%	36%

Data from exit surveys conducted in Ohio in 2008, 2010, and 2012.

ROMNEY   BELIEVE IN AMERICA

NEIL NEWHOUSE:

In 2004, it was five points our direction.

JOEL BENENSON:

That's eight years ago.

NEIL NEWHOUSE

Yeah, I know. But we thought you guys had the most extraordinary year in 2008. Elected an African American president. Our base was lethargic. We stayed at home. Democrats are energized. Republicans weren't. Looking at the disparity between [2008] energy and enthusiasm and campaign interest [and that in 2012], the same kind of margins that we saw for Obama in 2008 we're looking at on our edge for 2012. But it obviously washed out.

But here's a question, Joel. 229,000 fewer white voters came to the polls in 2012 than 2008. And yet white voter population in the state didn't decline. 209,000 more African Americans voted in the state. That's an incredible achievement.

FURTHER, THE RAW NUMBER OF WHITE VOTERS IN THE STATE FELL BY MORE THAN 300,000.

OHIO

➤ **329,081 fewer whites voted in 2012 than in 2008.**

➤ **209,205 more African Americans voted in 2012 than in 2008.**

➤ **Mitt lost the state by 166,214.**

 BELIEVE IN AMERICA

COMPLICATING OUR OHIO EFFORTS, WE LOST LATE DECIDERS BY 20 POINTS.

Ballot by Decision Timing – OHIO

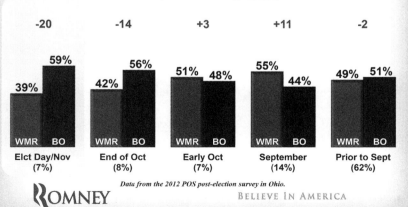

| -20 | -14 | +3 | +11 | -2 |

Data from the 2012 POS post-election survey in Ohio.

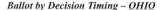 BELIEVE IN AMERICA

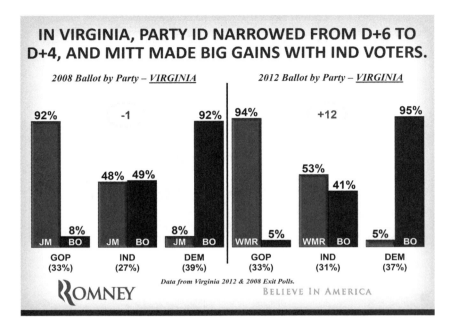

IN VIRGINIA, PARTY ID NARROWED FROM D+6 TO D+4, AND MITT MADE BIG GAINS WITH IND VOTERS.

2008 Ballot by Party – VIRGINIA   *2012 Ballot by Party – VIRGINIA*

Data from Virginia 2012 & 2008 Exit Polls.

ROMNEY   BELIEVE IN AMERICA

We lost late deciders in the state by 20 points. Campaigns that lose late deciders don't generally win elections. Same story in Florida, but let me go to Virginia. At least according to exit polls, it wasn't the difference in African Americans or minorities. It was the difference in white women.

That's an issue that came through in the data. White female vote, white male vote, Mitt got six points higher.

We won white men by 30 points in 2012, an increase over 2008, but we were unable to move our numbers among white women, simply because [of] the impact the Obama campaign had on us, especially in the Richmond market and also in the D.C. market advertising among white women.

In nine target states, there were 527,000 fewer white voters who voted, but 780,000 fewer white men voted and 281,000 more white women. So we had a falloff among white men, an increase among white women. We traded voters we were winning by 22 points with voters we're winning by 6 points. That's not a very good tradeoff for us.

Finally, Hispanic voters.

With Florida Hispanics, we started at 31 percent of the vote and we end up at 39 percent of the vote. We had a very difficult time moving Hispanic voters. That was an extraordinarily challenging effort for us. And the same

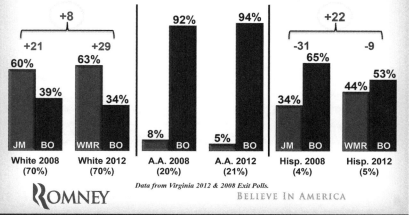

OBAMA DID NOT SHIFT THE DEMOGRAPHIC MAKE-UP OF VA LIKE OTHER STATES, AND MITT IMPROVED AMONG WHITES AND HISPANICS.

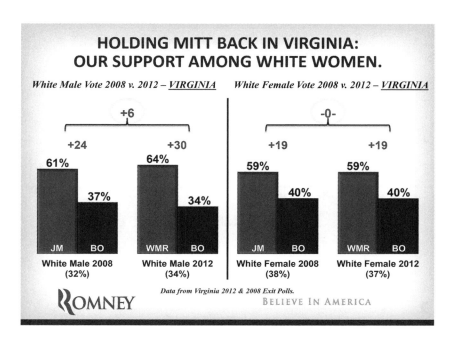

HOLDING MITT BACK IN VIRGINIA: OUR SUPPORT AMONG WHITE WOMEN.

IN THE NINE TARGET STATES, 527,000 FEWER WHITE VOTERS CAST BALLOTS THAN IN 2008. BUT, THE FALL-OFF WAS ACTUALLY AMONG WHITE MEN.

White Voters in the <u>Nine Target States</u>

'08 White	'12 White	Difference	'12 Average Ballot Romney-Obama (D/S)
23,735,161	**23,207,551**	**(527,610)**	**56%-43% (+13)**
'08 White Men	'12 White Men	Difference	'12 Average Ballot Romney-Obama (D/S)
11,588,913	**10,808,307**	**(780,606)**	**60%-38% (+22)**
'08 White Women	'12 White Women	Difference	'12 Average Ballot Romney-Obama (D/S)
12,161,685	**12,442,694**	**281,010**	**52%-47% (+6)**

BELIEVE IN AMERICA

WHILE HISPANICS WERE A KEY TARGET, WE NEVER REALLY MOVED THE NEEDLE ALL THAT MUCH WITH HISPANIC VOTERS.

Florida Hispanic Ballot Trend: Romney/Obama

	6/12	9-10	9-17	9-24	10-1	10-8	10-15	10-24	10-29	Exits
	54%	57%	57%	58%	56%	52%	48%	53%	47%	60%
	31%	29%	31%	32%	32%	35%	39%	38%	41%	39%

Nevada Hispanic Ballot Trend: Romney/Obama

	6/12	9-17	9-24	10-1	10-8	10-15	10-24	10-29	Exits
	69%	67%	68%	72%	67%	69%	65%	66%	71%
	19%	21%	20%	22%	22%	21%	27%	25%	24%

Data from POS tracking surveys in Florida and Nevada.

BELIEVE IN AMERICA

MITT'S CHALLENGES

> ➤ **Primary Wounds**
> ➤ **Obama Campaign Early Summer Attacks**
> ➤ **The 47%**
> ➤ **Hurricane Sandy**
> ➤ **The Auto Bailout Issue**
> ➤ **Bain**
> ➤ **"Out of touch with the middle class"**
> ➤ **Women's Issues**
> ➤ **Demographic Challenges:**
>   - Young voters
>   - Hispanic
>   - Women
>   - African American

  BELIEVE IN AMERICA

thing in Nevada. In Nevada, we just moved them from 19 percent to 24 percent. By the time we got around to our Hispanic advertising when we had money, which was around the convention, the Obama campaign had already basically positioned us negatively among Hispanics. And what was interesting among Hispanics is it wasn't just the immigration issue. It was the health care issue. It was Obamacare. We thought the gatekeeper issue among Hispanics would be immigration, but for us it turned out to be the sense that Mitt wasn't in touch with them, didn't care about their issues, their values, their concerns and the fact that he wanted to repeal Obamacare. Correct me if I'm wrong, the only time you guys mentioned Obamacare as a positive in your advertising was among Hispanics. Probably right, right?

JIM MARGOLIS:

That's about right. Trying to think whether we—

JOEL BENENSON:

But he certainly used the word Obamacare all the time.

NEIL NEWHOUSE:

So finally, the challenges we faced were primary wounds, the early attacks, the 47 percent, the hurricane, the auto bailout issue, Bain, out of touch with middle class, women's issues, and then the demographic challenges. Younger voters, Hispanics, women, African Americans. Bottom line is, the Obama campaign, as much as we didn't believe you when you said what you were going to change the composition of the electorate you did it again. And you did it not just across the board but in the key target states. Raising the number of African Americans in Ohio from 11 percent to 15 percent. At the same time, I think your advertising probably depressed some of our white vote in the state.

Very effective campaign. We thought we were in this ball game after that first debate. We needed a great first debate and got it. Mitt performed. When push came to shove, when the chips were down, Governor Romney really did come through. He had a great performance. We were unable to really sustain that all the way through and then that last ten days of the campaign with the hurricane we fell short. So hats off to the Obama people. And I'm interested in what Joel has to say next.

MALE VOICE #1:

What I want to hear is how Joel arranged the hurricane.

Joel Benenson:

Joel Benenson is the only Democratic pollster in history to have helped win three U.S. presidential campaigns. He has been the chief pollster and a senior strategist for President Barack Obama since the beginning of his 2008 campaign, and worked on President Bill Clinton's 1996 race. As the President and CEO of Benenson Strategy Group, which he founded in 2000, Benenson has served as a strategic advisor and consultant to heads of state, members of Congress and other national political leaders, Fortune 100 CEOs, and major advocacy and charitable institutions. Working in partnership with Project New West and a broad coalition, Benenson's research framed the winning messaging strategy that overwhelmingly defeated the Personhood Amendment in Mississippi, one of the most conservative states in the nation. He has worked with leading advocacy organizations including AARP, SEIU, and Clean Energy Works as well as some of America's largest businesses.

I want to go back to 2011 and try and outline for you how we shaped a lot of the strategic things and tested them and got to that point in our

Joel Benenson

polling that a lot of these folks talked about today. I want to make one point about the Obama team here. All of us are saying the same thing today. We didn't have a single discussion about what any of us were going to present.

I also want to touch on a few things before I get into the underlying data that formed our strategic thinking about this campaign. We really try to challenge conventional thinking. We're constantly challenging our assumptions with the data. We try to find new ways to ask questions because sometimes the conventional questions can be misleading. Before I summarize some of those examples and get into the data, I've got to say a couple of things about Neil Newhouse, who is my friend and colleague. I have had the good fortune in the last two elections to run against the two best Republican pollsters in America, Bill McInturff, his partner, and Neil Newhouse.

On the Obama team, we had an enormous group that did our analytics work. We had 50 guys in what they called a cave. They had a strobe light. They were pretty funky and all young. They all looked like they were right out of Silicon Valley. We had state pollsters who were experts in their states, people like Paul Harstad polling in Colorado and Iowa, people like Diane Feldman in Ohio. They did individual tracking in those states. Some messaging, analytics guys did modeling and I did this battleground universe that started out as 14 swing states.

I do want to make a couple of points quickly. And I'm going to make an offer. I don't want to put Neil on the spot, but if Kathleen wants us to come back here someday and do a poll-to-poll comparison of the history of the race, I'd be willing to do it because I find some of his numbers fascinating. I can tell you from our perspective, and Stephanie and Jim are going to nod their heads when I say we never had a 10-point lead. We would never win this race by 10 points in my polling. The highest we got was 7 and that was only after the 47 percent in September for three days and then it was down to 6 and then down to 5 before the first debate. In our battleground universe, our race from the end of August before the conventions to Election Day was either 50-46 or 49-46, except for that brief period after the 47 percent tape, when we got up at one point to 51-44.

I do not believe Sandy had any effect at all on this race. Neil made a point that I actually violently agree with. Most people in the election had made up their minds. Actually, if you look at where people were by September first, if you believe the exit poll, and I think Neil and I both agree on taking it with a grain of salt. But 70 percent of the people [in the exit poll] said they had made up their mind by September first. We had a 7-point lead among them. That converts to a 4.9 lead in the overall electorate. Mitt Romney would have had to have won the remaining 30 percent by 17 points to make up that 4.9. Neil said it. It's a massive undertaking in two months. Almost impossible.

One of the things to think about [is] the right track, wrong track number. Neil says it's the Dow Jones of presidential elections. When we looked at our data, and I think Neil's data says the same thing, if you go back and look at November 2011, one of the things we had to figure out was how do we win a campaign? We knew it was winnable from the beginning, when the right track, wrong track number's 32 and we're leading in the horserace. I know Mitt Romney was less known at the time, but all throughout that, even in early November, right track, wrong track was still in the 30s in some of these polls. Neil showed how it moved up a little more in the public polls in the fall. But we were still winning. The information flow was interesting because we asked that kind of question. I don't know if we asked it differently. You know, pollsters do.

From the Outset, We Knew We Had to Make Up Ground with Targets We Had Identified

		% Obama 2008	% Obama 2011†	Change 2008-11
Targets	Urb/Suburb Coll Edu Men (17%)	48%*	42%	-6
	Low Income Whites (<$40K) (18%)	50%*	36%	-14
	White Independent Women (15%)	49%	37%	-12
	18-34 Yrs (25%)	64%*	49%	-15
Obama Base	Union HH (20%)	60%	53%	-7
	Hispanics (8%)	65%	59%	-6
	Liberals (19%)	88%	82%	-6
	African Americans (11%)	95%	89%	-6

BSG
*2008 vote share estimated
from exit polls
† Horserace vs. Romney

BSG Poll, 8/31/11

We always had Obama having a little better information flow than Neil showed and Romney always having a little worse. In fact the only time we saw Romney get above water on the information flow was after the first debate.

So we started out back in August of 2011 knowing we had to make up a lot of ground. If you look at the data up here, we had some key targets. There were a couple of other things that we knew. We knew all of those numbers that people talk about, the 7.2 unemployment, the right track, wrong track.

We knew that we were going to have to win in that kind of environment. We couldn't anticipate an economic boom over the next 12 months. So we started out looking at where we were with some core groups in our electorate from 2008. We circled three groups in August [with whom] we felt we had lost significant ground from Election Day 2008, a group we call low-income whites, people who are white, making less than 40,000; white, independent women, where we were down 12 points; and young voters eighteen to thirty-four. There is some overlap among those groups. There's no question. There are some young college grads who are in that white low-income group. They're not hitting their earning potential yet. Those double-digit declines told us that we had significant ground to make up with our targets.

All the way through, as everybody said, we assumed that Mitt Romney was going to be the Republican nominee. In fact through 15 or 16 months of polling, I think there was only one week where I ever put anybody else in a horserace with President Obama. I think it was [former House Speaker Newt] Gingrich one time, probably right before Florida, just to see how he did. We never altered our assumption about that.

One of the things we knew is that if we were going to be running against this environment, we'd have to look at the historical context of all these numbers. As Axe said, Ronald Reagan was the president who won with 7.2 percent unemployment. He broke a barrier. No president had been reelected with unemployment higher than 5.6 percent before Ronald Reagan. So you knew you could look at all these metrics and say it doesn't matter. You could beat that. Reagan beat it. (LAUGHTER) Neil's partner [Bill McInturff] swears by the Michigan Consumer Sentiment Index. Nobody's been reelected with it above 78 percent, but when you looked at it historically, no president in history had a consumer sentiment as low as it was for Barack Obama on the day he got elected when it was 55 percent.

So as we got up into the mid-'60s to 70 percent, still 8 points below that threshold for the consumer confidence index, we had had the biggest percentage increase from [the date we were elected]. We knew that structurally where we started from might have mattered. What we were going to have to do in this campaign, as Jim pointed out, was not just make this a choice but make it a forward-looking choice about economic values in vision.

They were fundamentally saying through most of the campaign, from my point of view, that Barack Obama had failed. He'd made this recovery worse. They were describing him as a failure. So we wanted to make sure that we defined values pretty simply for ourselves. We looked for the fault lines. What were the things that people really identified strongly with us that mattered in their lives? And what were the things about the Republicans [they don't identify with]? In August of '11 we're also determined to make Mitt Romney wear the jacket of the Republican Party and its most extreme policies. So our values, what you got through us, was progress through middle-class security in terms of jobs, home refinancing, retirements, same set of rules, hard work pays, and responsibility is rewarded. We knew that people in the wake of the economic crisis had lost the sense of fairness in the American economy. They believed the deck was stacked against average working Americans and that bothered them. All they wanted was to get back what they put in. "If I've worked hard for a company for 20 years and were a loyal, good, high-performing employee, give me more than a nine cent an hour raise. You're profitable. I'm not asking for much, just give me enough

Identify Fault Lines: Make This Election a Choice Built on a Contrast of Economic Vision and Values

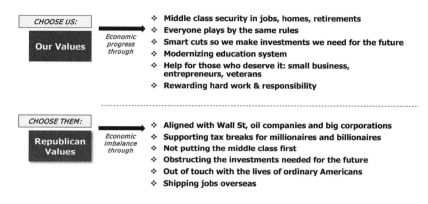

CHOOSE US:

Our Values — *Economic progress through*

- ❖ Middle class security in jobs, homes, retirements
- ❖ Everyone plays by the same rules
- ❖ Smart cuts so we make investments we need for the future
- ❖ Modernizing education system
- ❖ Help for those who deserve it: small business, entrepreneurs, veterans
- ❖ Rewarding hard work & responsibility

CHOOSE THEM:

Republican Values — *Economic imbalance through*

- ❖ Aligned with Wall St, oil companies and big corporations
- ❖ Supporting tax breaks for millionaires and billionaires
- ❖ Not putting the middle class first
- ❖ Obstructing the investments needed for the future
- ❖ Out of touch with the lives of ordinary Americans
- ❖ Shipping jobs overseas

to keep up with my bills." Those values were very important. On the economic proposal side, that meant helping people who really deserved it, small businesses who are keeping their companies alive, veterans who are coming back from war.

Before Romney ever started, he was aligned with a Republican Party that basically wanted to let Wall Street write its own rules again; Wall Street, who people still believed was at the epicenter of the financial crisis. The American people actually believed Wall Street manipulators were the second ranked culprit when gas prices went up. Oil speculators from Wall Street manipulators were right after oil companies. People had a very dim view of Wall Street. The more you tied yourself to them, the more you were misaligning yourself with the voters. There was nothing in the Republican policies that was really speaking to the middle class. And they had really, in fact, become the party that was committed to obstructing the kinds of investments that people believed we needed for our future.

We tried to identify these fault lines, which we did through a lot of research. We tested these things not just in isolation but in terms of their relationship to the economy, and also knew where people associated negative things with the Republican Party and where the president was associated very positively. This is an important one. It gets back to the

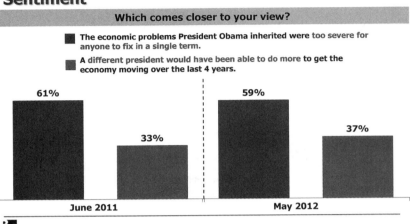

Voters Always Had Layered View of Econ Crisis: GOP Attacks on POTUS Didn't Align with Voters' Sentiment

Which comes closer to your view?

■ The economic problems President Obama inherited were too severe for anyone to fix in a single term.

■ A different president would have been able to do more to get the economy moving over the last 4 years.

61%   33%   59%   37%

June 2011   May 2012

right track, wrong track question. One of the things that we had to dig deeper at was why were we winning if these numbers were so bad? Why were we still a few points ahead of Romney? Even right from the beginning, we had a slim lead. That was number one.

David Binder and his focus groups were masterful. You'd go through 20 to 30 minutes of focus groups. And we're only talking to swing voters, by the way. We're talking, as Neil said, only to the swing voters that mattered. We knew if we kept enough of our people who voted for us, 53 percent in 2008, we're going to win. Our target was to get to 51 percent. We weren't looking to replicate a 53 percent win; we wanted to get to 51 percent. What we did is dig more deeply into economic attitudes because if people are so disappointed, if they feel that they had all this hope for Obama and the economy's not back and you can't say there's progress yet—why are they still even considering him? Why was he in their consideration set?

Binder did a lot of qualitative work about this. When we tested some of these ideas out, qualitatively, we found out that people believed this was an extraordinary crisis. It was unlike anything that they had seen in their lifetime. That meant we never wanted to just use the word recession. Why would you? If you make it a recession, it's just an ordinary thing. So [focus groups] helped inform our language about how to

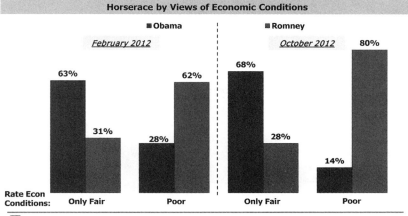

POTUS Won the Votes of Those Who Characterized Economy as "Only Fair"

Despite low rating of econ, these voters were overwhelming on POTUS's side

Horserace by Views of Economic Conditions

■ Obama   ■ Romney

February 2012   *October 2012*

In general, how would you rate the condition of the national economy today? Is it. In your opinion, are economic conditions in the country...?

shape the context a little bit. The other thing that we heard in focus groups and then we tested quantitatively was whether they thought any president, anybody else, could have fixed it. And so we threw it in quantitatively to see what happened.

You can see we looked at this question in June 2011. And by 61 to 31, people were saying that the economic problems were too severe for any president to fix and only about a third of the people thought a different president could have made it better. A year later, those numbers are barely changed. There was something these voters understood about the context of what the country had just gone through that was more powerful than what most of the conventional metrics would tell us.

We found a way to reframe this crisis. If you're the president, you're going to sound whiny if you say, "Boy, this is some mess I inherited." If you're the president, you can't say "nobody could have fixed this." The only person who could have said that did, in September of 2012, and his name was Bill Clinton. And he said it explicitly.[1] But we have language that the president was using that kind of pulled the same triggers: "The crisis wasn't created overnight and it wouldn't be solved overnight. Wouldn't be solved overnight." That wasn't asking them for patience. It was tapping into something that we knew from the data, something that they fundamentally believed.

Again, going back to traditional economic metrics. We asked an economic approval rating question on the economy, excellent, good, only fair, or poor. You put the word "only" in front of fair to put it into the negative column because fair is a word that's more balanced. I can tell you that during the course of this campaign, although I stopped asking it in October, we were never above 15 percent combined saying excellent or good. So you're looking at 80 percent of the people, 78 percent of the people saying the economy's only fair or poor. They would divide almost evenly. We had to figure out what was going on here.

In early 2012, we looked at the horserace among people who said "only fair," a negative rating of the economy. We were winning them by almost two to one. This told us that when you talk about the economy, you can't talk about it in traditional terms. They're not thinking of it as a normal economic downturn, as a normal recession. The issues that are nagging at them about the economy go back to some of those values I talked about, not just the unemployment rate, not just jobs, not just business creation and manufacturing, but their lives. Their lives had been impacted. They were judging the recovery very close to home. Did they see fewer for rent signs up in small businesses in the neighborhood? Were there more help wanted signs up in the storefronts? Were more for sale signs on houses coming down quickly?

We plotted the poll numbers after the job numbers came out the first Friday of every month. Somebody asked earlier did we sit on the edge of our seats every Friday. Those job numbers never impacted our polling data. Very surprising. In fact, we didn't see the bump you showed in early September, coming out of the Democratic Convention. I'm wondering if your data was picking up anything there because the job numbers in September were actually not good that first Friday. That was a weak month where we started to worry about the fall. So you look at these numbers on this slide and say, don't just use regular metrics to figure out what's really nagging at swing voters on the economy.

That's one of the things that kept driving us back to values and vision and this idea of middle class security, and how do you build an economy that works for average people? So we knew [that] voters always understood the context. We test attitudinal statements on an "agree-disagree" scale all the time.

Our job is not to help tell the president what to say. It's [to] help him make the most persuasive argument for his case. Jim showed the section from the speech in Kansas. Sometimes we [test] three different phrases he says at different times and find the one that seems to have the most impact. That's the way you use polling most effectively. 91 percent of

Voters Always Understood the "Context"; Were Hungry For Balance and Investments

Complexity and Context	The deep recession and record debt weren't created overnight and won't be solved overnight.	91% agree

Balance	"We can't just cut our way to prosperity. We need to cut waste from government and live within our means, but we also need to make the investments that will make a difference for ordinary Americans today."	85% agree

Fairness	"What America needs is a balanced economic approach that asks everyone to pay their fair share and gives everyone a fair chance to succeed."	90% agree

BSG Polls 6/11

Americans agreed that this deep recession and record debt weren't created overnight and won't be resolved overnight. That's a pretty high number. These are swing voters in battleground states, [in that] 14 state universe. You don't get 90 percent agreeing on anything. You probably don't get that many people agreeing that the sky is blue.

Balance. They felt the deck was stacked against them, that things had gotten out of balance a bit. We detected a lot of suspicion about what I would call trickle-down economics in the Romney and the Reagan economic philosophy. The Democrats had tried to push back on that for 30 years, but really didn't do it. We would hear people talk about in focus groups. They would bring it up. "I don't think taxes really help people like us anyway, tax cuts for people at the top." They would remember: "Didn't we have a surplus when Bill Clinton left office? And didn't it get turned into a deficit under Bush?" That wasn't a piece of data that we took to mean they were blaming Bush at all. But it was really pretty significant to us that they had reprocessed a whole economic philosophy that the Republican Party had been promulgating for three decades. These swing voters weren't buying it anymore. They really found it was nebulous. They really didn't find that it was going to make their lives better. So we went back and looked at Governor Romney talking about, "We have to cut regulation. We've got to cut government. We've got to get it out of the way and unleash the private sector. Everything'll be lifted."

We knew cutting spending was one vulnerability for us. We looked at a simple statement that said, "We can't just cut our way to prosperity. We've got to cut waste, live within our means so we can make investments for our future." It's one of the core arguments we were making in terms of our economic argument. So we never just rested on who people thought was better for the economy. We wanted to know what they wanted from the economy and which things did they think would grow the American economy and have an impact on their lives.

Fairness and the idea of a balanced approach played out in terms of everybody having a fair share, everybody having a fair chance to succeed. The balanced approach also played out on the deficit and spending, which was our biggest vulnerability versus the Romney campaign. They used it a lot against us. But we felt pretty comfortable. We weren't leaning into the deficit, to be sure. But we felt very comfortable with our argument for a balanced approach included revenues. It asked the wealthy to pay a little more, cut spending that was wasteful, that we didn't need, but make investments in what we needed. This was a pretty good argument for us. We were comfortable fighting on that turf. The ethnography project in the spring of 2011 was pretty helpful with this.

In a nutshell, we invited 100 swing voters in three states to come online six times over a 16-day span. They were going to answer eight to ten questions a night. These questions were written the way a journalist—I'm a former journalist—would ask a series of follow-up questions. It was an entirely nonpolitical conversation that came out of a conversation I had with David Plouffe one day. I said, "You know, we're doing all these focus groups. We get at all these political issues all the time. We've never just spent a lot of time talking to people about their lives, their communities, their faith, their hopes and aspirations for their kids, their economic lives."

At the end of that 16-day period with 100 people, we had 14,000 pages of transcripts. Each person had spent on average an hour online a night on the site we were hosting, answering those eight to ten questions. We were able to analyze [not only] what each person said across every question, but what all 100 had said in answer to each question. Not one question about politics. We learned some of the things that were really driving people in terms of their reaction to this crisis was a sense that they wanted durability. We'd been through boom and bust cycles. We'd had the Internet bubble. We had the housing bubble. We had the mortgage bubble. They didn't want bubbles anymore. They wanted old-fashioned, long-term stability for American business and for American

Had Enough of Quick Fixes, Overpromising and Trickle Down Economics; Wanted Durability

% Agree with Statement (% Strongly Agree)	Total	Inds	Middle Class*
Durability: What America needs is a broad-based economy not a bubble economy	82 (47)	84 (50)	86 (46)
Investments: What America needs is to make the investments it will take to win the future	76 (47)	71 (40)	77 (55)
Middle Class Focus: What America needs is to build the economy from the middle out, not the top down	78 (39)	82 (38)	81 (33)

* Based on self-ID

working people. They were fearful of an education [system] they thought was going to fail their children. They wanted to make investments in things that they knew were going to be essential to that durable future: clean energy, renewable energy.

Coming into this, the Republican Party had the very oil-focused image of "drill, baby, drill." The Governor even said once in the debate. "You know the $4 billion subsidies for big oil? They don't matter. They don't need them."[2] Why didn't you get rid of them then? Why didn't you oppose them? I mean, if they don't need them, why are we giving $4 billion to oil companies that are costing you at the pump every time? I think the President talked about that in the debates.

They [the swing voters in the online ethnographic study] believed that we needed certain investments in high-tech manufacturing and they fiercely believed that we had to focus on America's middle class. In June of 2012 we had some economic theories and we had some vulnerabilities around the deficit. We were having a big tax argument, which Democrats have typically lost on, although we felt we had done well with it in 2008.

We asked, "How important were each of these in deciding your vote for president? Who'll take the steps needed to create an economy built to last?" That was a phrase we used often through the campaign. Built

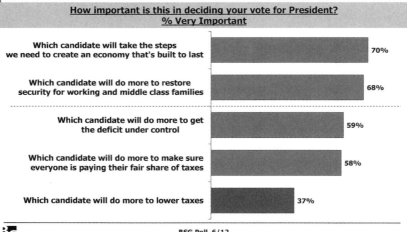

Voters Always Valued Economic Security, Durability Over Lower Taxes, Deficit Focus

How important is this in deciding your vote for President?
% Very Important

Which candidate will take the steps we need to create an economy that's built to last	70%
Which candidate will do more to restore security for working and middle class families	68%
Which candidate will do more to get the deficit under control	59%
Which candidate will do more to make sure everyone is paying their fair share of taxes	58%
Which candidate will do more to lower taxes	37%

BSG Poll, 6/12

Now I'm going to read you a series of different things someone might consider to decide who to vote for President. After each one, please tell me how important this is in deciding your vote for President in 2012.

to last connoted durability. It was the opposite of a bubble. 70 percent said it was very important to them. Not just important, very important.

"Which candidate would restore middle-class security?" 68 percent important, very important. "Who would do more to get the deficit under control?" People believed Mitt Romney would do a better job on the deficit, although by the time we get to the exit polls, I think we're almost even in the exit polls on that, 47 to 49, or something. But we knew that was always a weakness, but look at that. That's 10 points less intensity around getting the deficit under control. If you look at the two tax questions, who'll make sure everyone's paying their fair share" versus "which candidate will do more to lower taxes," there's a 21-point differential in intensity there. We knew we were on pretty good turf, fighting and inoculating on the deficit and the spending argument with the balanced approach. And we knew we were in good shape here, arguing on the taxes, if we continued to make it about values.

Jim and Stephanie talked about our basic core economic message at one point. This goes back to April. Mitt Romney's coming out of the primaries. This is a forced choice question which we asked sometimes. We just asked people which one did he agree with more. We pretty much gave Governor Romney his due here. This is what he was saying at that point. "To get our economy back on track is to get government out of

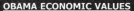

Our Economic Values Argument Trumped Romney's, Esp. among Important Targets

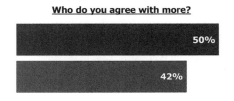

OBAMA ECONOMIC VALUES
The way to get our country back on track is to start building an economy <u>built to last</u> by <u>investing in manufacturing, small business and education</u> to create jobs our country needs and <u>train our children to succeed</u> in the new economy.

ROMNEY ECONOMIC VALUES
The way to get our country back on track is to <u>get government out of the way</u> and unleash the power of businesses and markets to <u>create jobs by lowering taxes and eliminating needless regulations</u> that tie employers' hands.

Who do you agree with more?

50%

42%

Also Resonated with

✓ **Low Income Whites:** 52% Obama / 39% Romney

✓ **White Independent Women:** 51% Obama / 38% Romney

✓ **Suburban Voters:** 52% Obama / 42% Romney

✓ **Youth (18-34):** 60% Obama / 32% Romney

BSG Poll, 4/12

Next, I'm going to read you two statements and get your view.

the way, unleash the power of businesses and markets to create jobs by lowering taxes and eliminating needless regulations that tie employers' hands."

We had a simple argument on the other side—that the way to get our economy back on track is to start building an economy built to last by investing in manufacturing, small business, and education to train our children to succeed in the new economy. We had a forward-looking message built on investments. He was about unleashing the private sector and getting government out of the way. You can see, by 50 to 42, people agreed more with our core argument.

It also resonated, if you can read the numbers on that little box on the right-hand side, [with] those low-income white voters I talked about. We had a 13-point advantage there. White independent women, a 13-point advantage. And our youth vote was pretty much where we needed it to be at 60 to 32. So we felt very comfortable having an economic argument with Governor Romney around our vision side of the equation.

I'm not going to spend much time on the tax debate. I don't know the last time you saw a poll [showing] anybody supporting lowering taxes for people over $250,000. The only people more likely to support a candidate who wanted to lower taxes on the top were Republicans. Republicans by 64 to 19 said they would be more willing to support a candidate

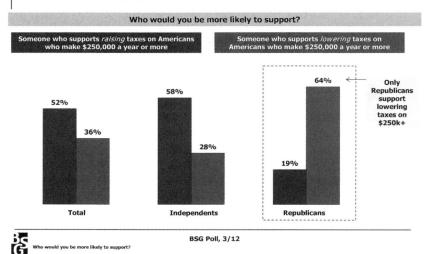

Democrats Won the Tax Debate – Again. President Made Same Case as 2008

Who would you be more likely to support?

Someone who supports *raising* taxes on Americans who make $250,000 a year or more

Someone who supports *lowering* taxes on Americans who make $250,000 a year or more

52%   36%   58%   28%   19%   64% ← Only Republicans support lowering taxes on $250k+

Total   Independents   Republicans

BSG Poll, 3/12

Who would you be more likely to support?

who would lower taxes for people making over 250,000. Look at independents. We don't define swing voters as independents, by the way. We have another combination of metrics that we use to create swing voters. I should have made this point at the beginning. We actually said, from the outset, we don't have to win independent voters to win the battleground states. We could lose them by about two or three points. Losing them by five probably [has] a little bit to do with the turnout.

We were committed to this idea of a forward-looking choice. I know these guys jumped all over the "you didn't build it" thing. We tried to put it in context, [to] show people they actually believe it. The Republicans were taking Obama's comments out of context. We didn't worry too much about "you build it."

We also had looked at the iconic question, [which] if you're running a referendum campaign is, "Are you better off than you were four years ago?" Governor O'Malley's [convention use] was not the first time that the Romney campaign or Governor Romney had actually used the question. It crept in. It wasn't a central theme. But we always knew if you asked were you better off, a plurality said "no." This was about as good as that number got for us. If we looked at it a few months earlier [than September] there were over 50 percent who said that they weren't better off. But then we also asked the question that said, "What's more important to your vote for president? Which candidate will make you better

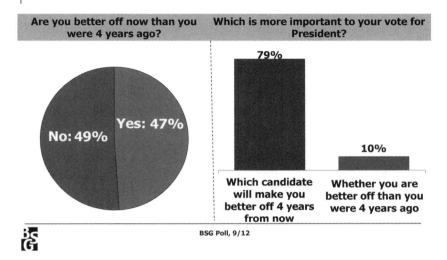

Resisting the Bait: *Forward* Looking Contrast Made "Better Off" Frame Irrelevant in 2012

Are you better off now than you were 4 years ago?

Yes: 47%
No: 49%

Which is more important to your vote for President?

79%

10%

Which candidate will make you better off 4 years from now

Whether you are better off than you were 4 years ago

BSG Poll, 9/12

off four years from now or whether you're better off than you were four years ago?" As you can see, by about eight to one they were very forward-looking and said "better off."

Jim showed you the ads about Governor Romney. I want to give you a quick insight into some of the polling data that we used to make sure we're on the right path and didn't go off-track with the messaging.

Voters never shared Mitt Romney's view of the economy. If you asked people [whether] the key to growing a strong economy in America is creating a healthy business climate or creating a strong middle class, they believed they were the job creators. By 57 to 34, they believed middle-class people spending money and buying products was really the way to create a strong middle class. Remember that Mitt Romney said at a campaign event, hey, businesses are hurting too here. I don't know if you remember that line. We tested whether people did think businesses were hurting too. They really didn't. They thought average people were hurting a whole lot more than businesses.

These things are all important. It is evident that when you look at some of these attributes, whether you understand the struggles of somebody like you, who's going to fight harder for families like yours, who's going to create an economy that's fairer for the middle class. These are not empathy attributes. These were core economic attributes to the

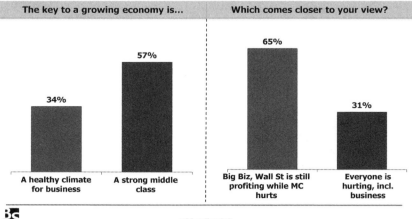

Voters Didn't Share Romney's View of Economy: See Middle Class, Not Business, as Key
Voters weren't connecting the success of business with their own prosperity

The key to a growing economy is...	Which comes closer to your view?

- A healthy climate for business — 34%
- A strong middle class — 57%
- Big Biz, Wall St is still profiting while MC hurts — 65%
- Everyone is hurting, incl. business — 31%

BSG Polls 1/12

American voters. I showed you before that Mitt Romney beat us on the economy. We've probed this in focus groups. It had to do with his "technical competence" on the economy. He never really made that strong connection with people's lives [or established] that he would make lives better. Our theory from the beginning was if we could stay close to even with him on the economy, we would win. If you look at the exit polls, on the metric that Kevin talked about, we won by about ten points on the economy. We were one point down in the exit poll. So we did play them to a draw on that attribute, even though it was not the central attribute to our campaign. The attribute central to our campaign was who would make an economy fairer for the middle class. That was the one we were always watching.

There was a lot of misperception around the Bain argument and his business record. We did a very complicated test. We took the business practices generically. We didn't link them to Mitt Romney. We wanted to find the things that people thought were simply wrong and that were harmful to people like them. So we had a forced choice question that said, "Do you think this is a normal necessary part of doing business? Or do you think it's one way to run a business, but it's simply wrong?" Then we would ask how harmful it was to you. So we had three metrics on the spectrum on each one of these things. I'm showing you four that came

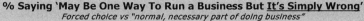

Voters Saw Certain Biz Practices as <u>Simply Wrong</u>, Not "Necessary" Part of Doing Business

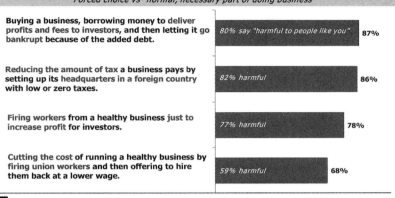

% Saying 'May Be One Way To Run a Business But <u>It's Simply Wrong</u>'
Forced choice vs "normal, necessary part of doing business"

Buying a business, borrowing money to deliver profits and fees to investors, and then letting it go bankrupt **because of the added debt.**
80% say "harmful to people like you" — **87%**

Reducing the amount of tax a business pays by setting up its headquarters in a foreign country with low or zero taxes.
82% harmful — **86%**

Firing workers **from a healthy business** just to increase profit **for investors.**
77% harmful — **78%**

Cutting the cost of running a healthy business by firing union workers and then offering to hire them back at a lower wage.
59% harmful — **68%**

BSG Poll, 1/12

out very high on both being harmful to people and simply wrong. We tested about 15 different things that could have been associated with how Governor Romney conducted business while he was at Bain. We picked out the ones that affected people in a way that said this is just crossing a line. This is going to hurt people like me.

They expected businesses to do things to remain profitable. We were very careful not to run against success, not to run against profits. The American economy depends on them. We did [have] an episode where surrogates went off the rails. But that was never our strategy.

We found that our strongest contrasts were rooted in economic values. If you look on the left, there's no data here, but this was culled from all the data we [had on] a link between Governor Romney's personal actions in business and his proposed policies. Stephanie referred to that. And these are the highlights of some of them. "Bankrupting businesses while you and your investors walk with millions." People thought that was outrageous. You hear the word bankruptcy. You think it's devastating. It's not a moneymaker. "Shipping jobs overseas to make a profit," which Bain had done. They were pioneers in outsourcing. Using tax shelters, I don't know if this came up in your focus groups, but we would spontaneously hear about the Swiss bank accounts in the Cayman Islands. There was a huge disconnect there. It wasn't just that he was

We Found Our Strongest Contrasts Were Rooted in Economic Values

Romney's Personal Actions and Policy Prescriptions Viewed as Benefitting Him and Those at the Top at Expense of Others

- **Bankrupted businesses but walked away with millions**

- **Ships jobs overseas to make a profit**

- **Uses tax shelters to avoid paying fair share – and encourages others to do the same**

Romney profits personally from actions Americans say are simply wrong

His policy ideas are based on the same values – top down economics

- **Shipped MA jobs overseas but gave corporations a tax break**

- **Will create a "boom and bust" cycle, adding to the deficit**

- **Gives huge cut taxes for millionaires, adding $600 billion to the deficit**

wealthy. They thought, "You're trying to scam somebody here. Why don't you just put your money in America?" Some of his policy ideas linked up to that.

We had a big debate in early 2012. David Axelrod was really the engine behind the Massachusetts record [attack]. Jim showed some of those ads. It was totally Axe's construct that we should say and test that Romney was promising the same thing in Massachusetts that he was promising now. I pushed against it and we tested it and I was wrong.

But the truth is, the governor had a very vulnerable record on Massachusetts. If he'd had a great record, you would have heard about it by the time you got to the general election. You didn't because there are simple facts. They came up with a complicated response on the 47th in job creation, which I never understood. We're taking an average over his whole term. [Mitt Romney] was governor for four years. Why shouldn't we take an average? [Massachusetts] had the highest per-capita debt when he left office. Believable facts. So if you're the deficit hawk and you've left the highest per capita debt in America, that's a problem. 47th in job creation, 48th in business creation. As Jim said, they lost manufacturing at twice the rate of the national average. You're the private sector guy. You're immediately undercutting a strength here. Giving tax breaks to 278 of the wealthiest families in Massachusetts while

Biz Record & Massachusetts Together Undercut the Central Premise of Romney's Campaign

> **Business record undermines Romney on values**
> **Massachusetts record undermines Romney on performance**

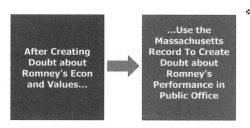

After Creating Doubt about Romney's Econ and Values... → ...Use the Massachusetts Record To Create Doubt about Romney's Performance in Public Office

❖ **Most effective Massachusetts vulnerabilities connect Bain record to how Romney governed -**
  ✓ Left highest per capita debt in nation
  ✓ 47th in jobs, 48th in biz creation
  ✓ Lost manufacturing jobs
  ✓ Gave tax breaks for 278 wealthiest while raising taxes and fees on the middle class
  ✓ Outsourced MA jobs

raising fees and taxes on average people and outsourcing were pretty potent indictments of a record of somebody who said he knew how to improve the economy.

[Governor Romney] always cited his unemployment rate [in Massachusetts]. The unemployment rate did go down under Mitt Romney. But the unemployment rate was below the national average when he took office in Massachusetts. It was higher [than the national average] when he left office. The reason it went down during that time is 200 and some thousand people left the state of Massachusetts, [which] had the second biggest migration of any state in America by the time he left office. The only other state that was higher was Louisiana in the aftermath of Katrina. We never talked about the population migration because we didn't want to bring New Orleans into it, but that was the reason he was able to get the unemployment rate [down]. People left the state.

So on the so-called empathy attributes, a 7-point scale, these are the fives through sevens. "We'll fight for people like you." We had a 9-point advantage in November. On "creating an economy that's fairer for the middle class," we had a 9-point advantage. You'll notice on "understanding how to get the economy moving again," we were down 6. We were very careful about calibrating our language on that, but it's very

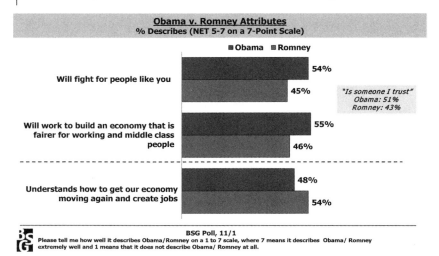

Fighting for Ordinary Americans Was Key Econ Attribute, Not Technical Understanding

Obama v. Romney Attributes
% Describes (NET 5-7 on a 7-Point Scale)

■ Obama   ■ Romney

Will fight for people like you
54%
45%

"Is someone I trust"
Obama: 51%
Romney: 43%

Will work to build an economy that is fairer for working and middle class people
55%
46%

Understands how to get our economy moving again and create jobs
48%
54%

BSG Poll, 11/1
Please tell me how well it describes Obama/Romney on a 1 to 7 scale, where 7 means it describes Obama/Romney extremely well and 1 means that it does not describe Obama/Romney at all.

clear that we were winning on those [items] driving people's economic attitudes. On the basic trust question, Obama was trusted by 51, 43.

I'm going to wrap up here with outcomes. I'm curious about how Neil's group did this. I told you we had these three buckets of data.

At the left [you see] the BSG battleground poll on Monday night, the last night we polled. We did a poll over Sunday and Monday, the last two nights, 800 interviews. When we apportioned out the undecided, we were at 51.1 to 47.7. If you take the battleground states from the exit polls, and I agree with Neil, you can't always count on them, they're pretty close to that 51, 47 in the battlegrounds.

What we were doing all the way along was taking the individual state polls from our state pollsters. We would aggregate them in proportion to our battleground universe. So if Florida was 20 percent of the battleground, we would take the horserace in the Florida poll from John Anzalone. That horserace would be worth 20 points. If Pennsylvania was 18 percent, that horserace was worth 18 percent. We had a bucket of four different state pollsters. When we aggregated those polls, there was about a four-point difference with our horserace. Our analytics team on the right who are also doing polls in the universe that we were polling in were at the same level, pretty much four points. This pattern wasn't just at Election Day. We were doing this check for about six months out.

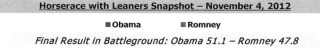

In Final Week of Campaign, All Three of Our Polling Platforms Showed Consistent Lead

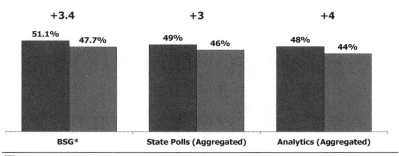

Horserace with Leaners Snapshot – November 4, 2012

■ Obama   ■ Romney

Final Result in Battleground: Obama 51.1 – Romney 47.8

	+3.4		**+3**		**+4**	
51.1%		47.7%	49%	46%	48%	44%
	BSG*		State Polls (Aggregated)		Analytics (Aggregated)	

*This number includes undecideds apportioned to candidates

These three buckets were never more than two points apart in the aggregate for the 14 states. That was a pretty remarkable pattern, [which] gave us a check on top of a check.

Lastly, I read something, I think by one of Neil's partners, about Romney winning independents. When you win independents, you usually win the election. As I said in the battlegrounds, we didn't think we needed to win [independents]. But we actually won the middle. Look at moderates, who are ideologically in the middle and are the plurality of the electorate, a bigger group than conservatives and liberals.

If you look at that top line in yellow and you compare George Bush's election in 2004, Bush lost moderates by nine points. You can win as a Republican without winning moderates, but Romney lost them by 15. His margin shrank by six. If you look at gender, the second line, Bush only lost all women by three points. Governor Romney lost them by 11. If you look at every group of women in every demographic, he underperformed with women versus men across the board.

Another thing is interesting and something that I think the Republican Party probably has to deal with going forward. White evangelicals were 26 percent of the electorate. Mitt Romney's margin among them is identical to Bush's in 2004. It's 78 to 21. But then you take the rest of the electorate, George Bush lost those folks by 13 points. Mitt Romney

Romney Lost Moderates Big; Also Underperfomed vs. Bush Among Men, Women & Non-Evangelicals

Exit Polls		Bush 2004		Romney 2012	
(2012 % of population)		*GB - JK*	*Margin*	*MR - BO*	*Margin*
Ideology	Moderate *(41%)*	45-54	-9	41-56	-15
	Liberal *(25%)*	13-85	-72	11-86	-75
	Conservative *(35%)*	84-15	+69	82-17	+65
Gender	Men *(47%)*	55-44	+11	52-45	+7
	Women *(53%)*	48-51	-3	44-55	-11
Evangelical	White Evang. *(26%)*	78-21	+57	78-21	+57
	All Others *(74%)*	43-56	-13	37-60	-23
Church Attendance	Weekly *(42%)*	61-39	+22	59-39	+20
	Occasionally *(40%)*	47-53	-6	43-55	-12
	Never *(17%)*	36-62	-26	34-62	-28

 Source: CNN

lost them by 23 points. So if this is the base of the Republican Party, and the rest of the universe is three-quarters of the electorate and they're losing ground with everybody else out there, then they're going to have to go through some of the reexamination that some folks are talking about already.

KATHLEEN HALL JAMIESON:

Could we ask both of you to comment on the effect of religion, if any?

JOEL BENENSON:

I think there's a generational divide in this country. The country's changing. On most issues, we see very different attitudes on people over 50 and under 50, but also under 40 and over 40. If you look at the big difference among people who go to church regularly, people who go occasionally, and people who don't attend, and go back to Bush's win, Romney lost ground among occasional churchgoers. They are people of faith. They're people who go to church. They just don't go every week. There's some big dynamic going on with faith. I think it's related to the overall change in the country.

NEIL NEWHOUSE:

I think it's more religiosity rather than religion. It's how often people go to church, rather than what religion they are.

KATHLEEN HALL JAMIESON:

So neither of you see evidence that Governor Romney's religion was a negative for him?

NEIL NEWHOUSE:

No, I don't think so.

KEVIN MADDEN:

In 2008, it was very raw experience on the religion issue. In many ways, then, it was the last bastion of acceptable bigotry, in the sense that I would get people say[ing] things that would be insulting if you were to preface it with any other religion or race. They would say it with no reservation whatsoever. In 2012, by and large, that did not appear at all. I was struck by it because I would get calls from reporters who would make snarky comments, whether it was something to do with the governor's religion or the LDS churches, the history of polygamy. They would do it openly. I don't think that they would do that about another religion. That had disappeared largely in 2012.

NEIL NEWHOUSE:

And you can't look at those 78-21 numbers, exactly the same numbers as [George W. Bush] got, and think that we had major problems with evangelicals or did better among Jewish voters. Mitt Romney actually got a higher percentage of Jewish vote than he did among Hispanics, which is not expected, I think.

KATHLEEN HALL JAMIESON:

So there's no evidence of people not showing up because of [Governor Romney's] religion?

NEIL NEWHOUSE:

I don't know how we'd show evidence of people not showing. I don't know how you show that.

Joel Benenson:

The only way you could extrapolate that, and I think Neil's point that we got our voters out is probably really the cause for this, is that the rural vote, compared to 2008, went down, while the African American vote, because there are a lot of African Americans still in rural parts of the country, the African American vote went up, although our models were not expecting a big increase. We stayed very conservative in our models. I mean the only thing you might be able to do is look back at that and say, "Was there some change?" But I don't, I think the driver—

Neil Newhouse:

I think it was more the middle-class hit. It was Bain. It was the other issues rather than religion. I don't think it—

Joel Benenson:

I agree with Neil.

Neil Newhouse:

We noticed, and this may be just something we imagined on our own, but we would look at the ads you were running by market and a couple of markets for some reason, Dothan, Alabama, comes up to me, did you use some of these as test markets? Did you use test markets in this campaign?

Joel Benenson:

Could that be a spillover from any other market? I don't know. Maybe it was a national cable thing. I don't know.

Neil Newhouse:

The pattern on the Democratic side is to run more ads, fewer running points behind a spot, but have the ads near each other in terms of message and thematic. We saw that a lot in your campaign. Nine different creatives in a market or eight different creatives in a market, none of which are hitting a thousand gross rating points. What's the theory behind that?

JIM MARGOLIS:

Most of them should have been hitting a thousand at some point, some of the '60s we did at lower levels. The other thing you may be missing is we also compute our national cable, which you wouldn't see in the local DMA ratings. Since we're buying some national cable, if that advertising [running] at 200 points national is the same message as what we are putting into that local market, we would add it in. Maybe we're at 600, 700 points in that local market and then adding in what we're getting from the national as well. Some things like the women's track would have low levels over extended periods of time, positive track, which we try to keep into the mix. We would often have [a track] at lower levels for more extended periods of time.

JOEL BENENSON:

One thing, were you here when Jim showed the ads, Neil?

NEIL NEWHOUSE:

Yes.

JOEL BENENSON:

Take the one on the 47 percent, for example. We had two ads we ran on the 47 percent. They may have overlapped, but they were reinforcing the same message.

JIM MARGOLIS:

That happens sometimes.

JOEL BENENSON:

The other one had people who were working. So they were both running at the same time.

Did you have three buckets of data like we had? Were you able to look state by state, take the analytics, the state pollsters and then yours?

NEIL NEWHOUSE:

Matter of fact we did. Our national was the same as yours. We had a nine-state national.

JOEL BENENSON:

From the beginning, you did nine.

NEIL NEWHOUSE:

We didn't do a national survey—

JOEL BENENSON:

We ended at nine.

NEIL NEWHOUSE:

We had nine. We had the individual, statewide stuff going. We had people who were experienced in each state, doing individual statewides. And we had our auto-dials. We had robo phone calls, which we called in the primary "poor man's tracking" because we were short on money in the primary. We were doing voter ID, layering cells on top of it, and then weighting the data and making sure it's representative. We were doing 3,000 to 5,000 interviews a night in the smaller states and 7,000 to 9,000 in the larger states. So we had a lot of data coming in. So we were looking in the same three buckets of information. Maybe not as sophisticated as your analytics, but what was interesting is there was real consistency in the auto-dial stuff. It rarely moved more than a point on any given night because of the raw number of interviews. We stopped on Sunday. I've had a bad experience polling on Monday night, before the election.

JOEL BENENSON:

I had a bad experience in a state called New Hampshire when I didn't poll on Monday and we ended up losing a race (LAUGHTER) everyone thought we were winning back in 2008. However, everybody on the Obama team has said, "No more New Hampshire jokes, right?" That was the rule.

MALE VOICE #1

Get out of jail free card now. (LAUGHTER)

NEIL NEWHOUSE:

Our last swing state nationally had us down by a point going into this. Ohio. Do you believe the 15 percent African American number?

JOEL BENENSON:

The number that I don't believe, actually, was the 12 percent in Colorado in 2008. I think that was probably higher—

NEIL NEWHOUSE:

Higher than?

JOEL BENENSON:

The youth vote in Colorado was probably higher than that. It's not as dramatic a jump as it's initially showing them. They're very careful about the state [exit poll] numbers right now. They tell you don't rely on them yet. We knew in May that we were behind on voter registration and, in particular, we were behind with young people in North Carolina. We ended up registering more voters in North Carolina than we thought we would, which was how we were even able to keep it close until the end. We were updating the list regularly. I mean, [Campaign Manager, Jim] Messina would tell you we were paying a fortune to update from secretary of states' offices every two weeks.

NEIL NEWHOUSE:

North Carolina's a great example. We kept thinking, "Okay, next week, we're going to pull [away]. And we could never get any separation. Just couldn't get any separation, at least not enough that our guys felt satisfied. So we would lower our gross rating points to your level. We'd try to mirror you, but we never felt comfortable enough in that state to pull it out.

JOEL BENENSON:

The other thing people ask me a lot was about [the two campaigns' different models] in terms of polling at the end being different maybe on the state by state basis? We never believed that the battleground electorate was really reshaped in 2008.In fact, if you do take the exit polls from 2004 and 2008, the percentage of people 18 to 29 who voted in the battlegrounds in our universe in 2004 was 18 percent. It was 18 percent in 2008. If nobody under the age of 30 had voted in 2008, the only states Obama would have lost that he won were Indiana and North Carolina. So we could have had an election in 2008 that was 30 and up. We stayed conservative. We looked for some growth in the youth, but at one point in September, we wanted to ratchet it down a bit. Did you ever look at models and run your stuff through a filter that was more like the 2008 electorate?

NEIL NEWHOUSE:

Absolutely. But the other thing is the press was talking about the national models. You and I weren't looking at national models. We're looking at 9-state, 12-, 14-state models. Those were significantly different. We went back and looked at all of our data that was weighted and unweighted. We'd looked religiously at unweighted data because that's how you miss something. When you start assuming you're going to weight this stuff every night and you're not looking at the unweighted stuff you make mistakes. Our unweighted data basically reflected the same kind of trends we were seeing. It wasn't minus seven or minus eight. It was more like minus two, three, or four points in terms of partisan affiliation.

JOEL BENENSON:

In your battleground universe, what you call your national, your nine state, in its entirety, what kind of Democrat, Republican spread did you have on ID?

NEIL NEWHOUSE:

Minus three.

JOEL BENENSON:

That's exactly where we were. We even started out with it tighter than that. Interesting.

Notes

1. Democratic National Convention, Charlotte, N.C., September 5, 2012: "Now, I like—I like—I like the argument for President Obama's re-election a lot better. Here it is. He inherited a deeply damaged economy. He put a floor under the crash. He began the long, hard road to recovery and laid the foundation for a modern, more well-balanced economy that will produce millions of good new jobs, vibrant new businesses and lots of new wealth for innovators. (CHEERS, APPLAUSE) Now, are we where we want to be today? No. . . . No president—no president, not me, not any of my predecessors, no one could have fully repaired all the damage that he found in just four years."

2. Presidential Debate, Denver, Colo., October 3, 2012:

> ROMNEY: Jim, let's—we've gone on a lot of topics there, and so it's going to take a minute to go from Medicaid to schools . . .
>
> LEHRER: Come back to . . .
>
> ROMNEY: . . . to oil, to tax breaks, then companies going overseas. So let's go through them one by one. First of all, the Department of Energy has said the tax break for oil companies is $2.8 billion a year. And it's actually an accounting treatment, as you know, that's been in place for a hundred years. Now . . .
>
> OBAMA: It's time to end it.
>
> ROMNEY: And in one year, you provided $90 billion in breaks to the green energy world.
>
> Now, I like green energy as well, but that's about 50 years worth of what oil and gas receives. And you say Exxon and Mobil. Actually, this $2.8 billion goes largely to small companies, to drilling operators and so forth.
>
> But, you know, if we get that tax rate from 35 percent down to 25 percent, why that $2.8 billion is on the table. Of course it's on the table. That's probably not going to survive [if] you get that rate down to 25 percent.

Index